The Many Faces of Martha of Bethany

Diane E. Peters

The Many Faces of Martha of Bethany

NOVALIS

© 2008 Novalis, Saint Paul University, Ottawa, Canada

Cover design: Audrey Wells
Layout: Audrey Wells, Francine Petitclerc
Cover image: © iStock
Business Offices:

Novalis Publishing Inc.
10 Lower Spadina Avenue, Suite 400
Toronto, Ontario, Canada
M5V 2Z2

Novalis Publishing Inc.
4475 Frontenac Street
Montréal, Québec, Canada
H2H 2S2

Phone: 1-800-387-7164
Fax: 1-800-204-4140
E-mail: books@novalis.ca
www.novalis.ca

Library and Archives Canada Cataloguing in Publication

Peters, Diane E. (Diane Elizabeth)
    The many faces of Martha of Bethany / Diane E. Peters.

Includes bibliographical references.
ISBN 978-2-89646-002-1

    1. Martha, Saint. 2. Martha, Saint–In literature. 3. Martha, Saint–Art.
4. Christian women saints–Biography. I. Title.

BS2480.M3P48 2008   225.9'2   C2008-902000-6

Printed in Canada.

We acknowledge the financial support of the Government of Canada through the
Book Publishing Industry Development Program (BPIDP) for our publishing activities.

5   4   3   2   1   12   11   10   09   08

Contents

List of Illustrations

Chapter 1

Late nineteenth-century stained glass window, Knox Presbyterian Church, Waterloo, Ontario
- Photograph by Diane Peters

Drawing of Martha's funeral based on bas-relief sculpture on the portal of the Church of St. Martha in Tarascon, France
- Source: E.-M. Faillon, *Les Monuments inédits sur l'apostalat de Sainte Marie-Madeleine en Provence* (Paris: Ateliers catholiques, 1848), tome 1, cols.1221-1222

Drawing of the reliquary of Martha in the Church of St. Martha in Tarascon
- Source: E.-M. Faillon, *Les Monuments inédits sur l'apostalat de Sainte Marie-Madeleine en Provence* (Paris: Ateliers catholiques, 1848), tome 1, cols. 1249-1250

Chapter 2

Contemporary stained glass window, Chapel at Bethany, Antigonish, Nova Scotia
- Used with permission of the Sisters of St. Martha, Antigonish

Urs Graf, *Meal at the House of Simon the Leper*, sixteenth-century woodcut from *Passio Christi*, Strasbourg, ca. 1507
- Source: Germaine Maillet, *Sainte Marthe* (Paris: Henri Laurens, 1932), p. 37

Woodcut illustration of Martha serving while Mary listens
- Source: Christian Jensen, *Um die Wende des Jahrhunderts (1900): Ein Denkmal zu Ehren des Names Jesus* (Beklum: Druck und Verlag des Sonntagsblatt für's Haus, 1900), p. 51

Chapter 3

Egg tempera plaque by Canadian artist Philip Aziz, created for the Sisters of St. Martha in Charlottetown, Prince Edward Island, 1954
- Used with permission of the Sisters of St. Martha, Charlottetown

Collegiate Church of St. Martha (rebuilt after destruction of original church in World War II)
- Photograph by Eleanor Scully, used with permission

Seventeenth-century engraving by Nicolas Auroux
- Source: Germaine Maillet, *Sainte Marthe* (Paris: Henri Laurens, 1932), p. 47

Chapter 4

Drawings of thirteenth-century seals of the city of Tarascon showing Martha and the tarasque
- Source: E.-M. Faillon, *Les Monuments inédits sur l'apostalat de Sainte Marie-Madeleine en Provence* (Paris: Ateliers catholiques, 1848), cols. 1215-1216

Chapter 5

Woodcut of Martha with the dragon (holding crucifix) from Jacobus de Voragine, *Legenda aurea* (Augustae Vindelicorum, Gintherus Zainer, ca. 1474)
- Source: Jacobus de Voragine, *Legenda aurea* (Augustae Vindelicorum: Gintherus Zainer, ca. 1475), Library of Congress, Washington, DC, Incun. X J 16, folio clxxxiii, verso

Milanese woodcut, fifteenth century
- Source: Germaine Maillet, *Sainte Marthe* (Paris: Henri Laurens, 1932), p. 45

Chapter 6

Coat of arms, Sisters of St. Martha, Antigonish, Nova Scotia
- Used with permission of the Sisters of St. Martha, Antigonish

Chapter 7

Drawing of Martha with the dragon (also with cross and pot of holy water) after the portal of the Church of St. Martha in Tarascon
- Source: E.-M. Faillon, *Les Monuments inédits sur l'apostalat de Sainte Marie-Madeleine en Provence* (Paris: Ateliers catholiques, 1848), cols. 1209-1210

Chapter 8

Contemporary icon, Bethany, Antigonish, Nova Scotia
- Used with permission of the Sisters of St. Martha, Antigonish

Contemporary statue, Bethany, Antigonish
- Used with permission of the Sisters of St. Martha, Antigonish

Model of float from the 2004 Tarasque celebrations, Tarascon, France
- Source: http://en.wikipedia.org/wiki/Tarasque

Martha of Bethany:
An Introduction

Now Jesus loved Martha and her sister and Lazarus.
(John 11:5)

In today's world, mention of the name "Martha" immediately brings to mind domestic diva Martha Stewart. While this Martha's reputation has been tarnished by reports of her questionable business dealings, detractors over the years have accused her of obsessive-compulsive behaviour in her pursuit of domestic perfection and of being over-zealous in her quest for "good things."

Ironically, such charges have been levelled for centuries against an earlier Martha—the biblical Martha of Bethany, sister of Mary and Lazarus. Theologian Elisabeth Moltmann-Wendel records a childhood reminiscence:

> When I think of "Martha" a picture from a children's Bible comes to mind. In it, Mary is sitting at Jesus' feet and listening to him, while in the background Martha is leaning against the kitchen door with an evil, mistrustful look on her face. As a child, I was always sorry for anyone called Martha .... There was something noble about 'Mary.' 'Martha' was rather common. Mary had an

aura of holiness, whereas Martha breathed cooking and the smell of the kitchen.[1]

Another commentator, Webb Garrison, notes:

Martha of Bethany vies with Mary Magdalene for the doubtful honor of being the most maligned of all the women among the circle of Jesus' intimates. Her name is seldom mentioned except in the same breath with that of her sister. Mary is always praised, while Martha is disparaged in tut-tut fashion. Martha fusses about the kitchen while Mary sits in rapture at the Master's feet. Martha is rather worldly; Mary is definitely spiritual. Martha puts the household chores above eternal values, while Mary demonstrates that it is more important to believe than to make sure the soup is served piping hot. It's that simple—according to practically all interpreters.[2]

The "Sunday school" portrait of Martha, derived from the account of Christ's visit to Bethany recorded in Luke 10:38-42, dominates the popular imagination. It overshadows even her confession of faith recorded in John 11:27, when she acknowledges Christ as the Son of God. However, any attempt to typecast Martha as a complaining busybody reflects an inadequate understanding of both her contribution to Christ's ministry and her influence on later Christian thought.

Who was Martha of Bethany?

While a number of works on female saints have appeared in recent years, little attention has been focussed on Martha, and her "full story" is still not widely known. This is regrettable, since she is a figure who provides a worthy inspiration and role model for modern women.

The "facts" that are known about her can be summarized fairly briefly.

Martha in the New Testament

Most people today know of Martha from New Testament references to her. The name "Martha" occurs three times in the canonical gospels and is used of only one person: the sister of Mary and Lazarus. Luke 10:38-42 records an incident in which Martha assumes the role of hostess to Jesus and his companions while her sister, Mary, listens to Jesus' teachings.

John 11:1 notes that Martha and her siblings lived in the village of Bethany. The family enjoyed a special relationship with Jesus: "Jesus loved Martha and her sister and Lazarus" (John 11:5). This chapter continues with an account of Jesus raising Lazarus from

the dead (John 11:11-44). Some time later, Jesus revisited his friends at Bethany. On this occasion, Martha once again serves the meal, while Mary anoints her Lord's feet with fragrant ointment and dries them with her hair (John 12:1-8). The anointing of Jesus is also described in Matthew 26:6-13 and Mark 14:3-9, but these gospels indicate that the event took place in the house of Simon the Leper. As a result, some commentators have suggested that Martha, the hostess, was Simon's wife or widow.

Both Luke and John portray Martha as practical, active, and outspoken. In Luke she takes charge of the mealtime preparations, and berates her sister in front of the guests for failing to help. In John's account of the raising of Lazarus, Martha goes out to meet Jesus as he approaches the village and chides him for not coming sooner. Her strong sense of practicality leads her to remind Jesus that, after four days in the grave, her brother's body will have begun to decay. Particularly noteworthy in John's account is Martha's confession of faith in Christ. While Mary remains at home, grief-stricken, Martha engages in a theological discussion with Jesus concerning the resurrection of the dead (John 11:21-27). This conversation reaches a climax when Martha asserts, "I believe that you are the Christ, the Son of God, he who is coming into the world" (John 11:27).

Martha in Literature of the Early Christian Period

Although no further mention is made of Martha in the New Testament accounts, her name appears in a number of the surviving gnostic and apocryphal texts from the first centuries of the Christian era: the *First Apocalypse of James*, the *Manichaean Psalm Book*, the *Pistis Sophia*, the *Gospel of Nicodemus*, the *Epistula Apostolorum*.[3] Such works provide interesting insights into the traditions of the early Christian church and Martha's place within them. However, the full extent of her influence is difficult to evaluate in light of current evidence.

For the most part, the writings of the earliest Church Fathers contain few references to Martha. Yet from the time of Origen in the mid-third century, Martha and her sister Mary played an increasingly prominent role in exegetical literature. Origen's homily on Luke 10:38-42[4] provides a model for later interpretations. For Origen, Martha symbolized action, and Mary, contemplation. Neither action nor contemplation could exist without the other. Origen also suggested that Martha could be seen as symbolic of the Synagogue and the Old Testament laws, while Mary represented the Christian Church and the new "spiritual law" (cf. Romans 7:14). Finally, Martha symbolized the Jews, who observed the precepts of the law, while Mary represented the Christians, who "set [their] minds on things that are above, not on things that are on earth" (Colossians 3:2).

Many of Origen's ideas were amplified in the works of later commentators, but his identification of Martha and Mary as types of the active and contemplative lives was particularly influential.

The Medieval Martha Cult

The origins and development of the cult of Martha in the Christian West are difficult to trace with certainty. As noted above, interest in Martha shown by the Church Fathers centred primarily on her symbolic role as the representative of the active life. A possible exception is a sermon attributed to the fourth-century bishop Ambrose of Milan, in which Martha is identified with the woman mentioned in Matthew 9:20, Mark 5:25 and Luke 8:43.[5] This identification, along with the attribution to Ambrose, is likely of later medieval derivation.

Brief notations in numerous medieval martyrologies suggest that from the late sixth century onwards, a feast day of St. Martha was celebrated on January 19, although few details as to the nature or extent of such celebrations are known. The earliest official reference to a feast on this date dedicated to Mary and Martha appears in a manuscript of the martyrology of Jerome, produced at Auxerre ca. 595. It is likely that the designation was attributable to a copyist's error—the result of confusion between the names of the early Persian martyrs Marius and his wife Martha and those of Mary (Maria) and Martha of Bethany.[6] Textual studies suggest that the Auxerre manuscript was widely copied.

As a result, what was probably an inadvertent mistake was at least partially responsible for the late medieval spread of the cults of Martha and Mary Magdalene, who had come to be identified with Mary of Bethany in the Christian West.[7] The confusion regarding Martha's feast day is further compounded by the fact that certain martyrologies and early calendars also suggest that the saint and her brother Lazarus were honoured on December 17. Opinion is divided on whether such references apply to anything more than local cults.

In the modern church calendar, Martha's feast day is celebrated on July 29, the date of her death according to two of the major surviving versions of her life, the *Vita Pseudo-Marcilia* and the *Vita Beatae Mariae Magdalenae*. The custom of commemorating Martha's death on this date likely arose sometime between the mid-twelfth and mid-thirteenth centuries. By the twelfth century, it was generally accepted that Lazarus and Mary Magdalene had travelled to Provence after the ascension of Christ. The inhabitants of Tarascon in Provence concluded that Martha probably accompanied her siblings, although no other town had laid claim to her relics. A search was undertaken in Tarascon, which already possessed a church dedicated to a Martha,[8] and in 1187, the body of "Martha of Bethany" was discovered. It was after this time that Martha's cult began to flourish.[9]

The Medieval Legends of Mary Magdalene

As the preceding discussion suggests, the legendary life of Martha is closely related to that of Mary Magdalene. When Martha is mentioned in the Scriptures, she always appears in the company of her sister, and the two are portrayed as contrasting figures. This in turn led to their roles in exegetical literature as representative of the active and the contemplative lives. The linking of the names of Martha and Mary in early medieval martyrologies led to the joint celebration of their feast day in the West, from the sixth century onwards, and in medieval hagiographical tradition the two continued to be closely connected.

The medieval stories surrounding Mary Magdalene are many and varied. A body of legend that was widely accepted in the East connected the saint with the city of Ephesus. In the mid-sixth century, Gregory of Tours wrote in his *De Gloria Martyrum* (1.30) that Mary Magdalene was buried there. Her tomb was reputedly next to the Cave of the Seven Sleepers.[10] By the seventh century she was honoured at Ephesus on July 22, the supposed date of her death.[11] Modestus, Patriarch of Jerusalem (630–634), recorded that she had gone to Ephesus to join the apostle John after the death of the Virgin.[12] Other traditions suggest that the Magdalene had accompanied John to Ephesus. These accounts of her arrival may have originated in the *Acts of John*, a second- or third-century apocryphal work that was widely copied in subsequent centuries, and of which only fragments survive today.[13] The Byzantine emperor Leo VI translated the supposed relics of Mary Magdalene from Ephesus to Constantinople in the late ninth century.

An alternate legend, which had relatively little influence, maintained that Mary Magdalene spent her final days in Palestine, where she remained after the ascension of Christ. After her death she was buried near Jerusalem. Her relics were later transferred to France. The earliest supporting documentation regarding this account of Mary Magdalene's later years is found in an eleventh-century document, the *Gesta episcoporum cameracensium*, written in support of claims by the Abbey of Vézelay that it possessed the Magdalene's true remains.[14]

The most influential Magdalene legends in the West in the later Middle Ages connected the saint with the south of France. According to one account, Mary Magdalene, Mary Jacobi, and Mary Salome became the companions of the apostle James, son of Zebedee, following Christ's ascension. Despite Paul's announcement in Romans 15:20-24 that he planned to visit regions "where Christ was not known"—including Spain—the tradition arose that James had previously evangelized Spain sometime between the ascension and his martyrdom at the hands of Herod (Acts 12:1-2), probably around 42 CE.[15] This legend was later expanded, probably in the twelfth century: after James's death, the three

Marys were said to have sailed to Gaul with Martha, Lazarus, and others, bringing with them the bones of the Holy Innocents[16] and the head of James. Mary Jacobi and Mary Salome disembarked at the site of what is now the town of Saintes-Marie-de-la-Mer in the Camargues region near the mouth of the Rhone, and their relics were "discovered" there in 1423.[17]

After the twelfth century, the "standard" Magdalene legend in the West was the Provençal version. According to this tradition, Mary Magdalene, Martha, Lazarus, Marcella, Maximinus and various other companions (depending on the particular variant of the legend) were put to sea in a rudderless boat. They eventually reached Marseille and began to evangelize the region. Among Mary Magdalene's converts was the prince of Marseille; through her intercession she obtained a son for him. Later, she miraculously saved the child and his mother after a storm at sea. Mary eventually withdrew to the wilderness of Sainte-Baume, where she lived a life of austerity and contemplation for 30 years. Each day her food was brought by angels descending from heaven. The latter half of this legend, focusing on the Magdalene's life as a hermit, likely arose as a result of the grafting into her "biography" elements from that of the fourth-century Mary of Egypt, one of the solitary Eastern ascetics who practised extreme forms of self-discipline as a means of gaining spiritual insight. From the late thirteenth century, the Dominican house at Saint-Maximin in Provence claimed to possess the saints' relics.[18]

A comparison of the legends concerning the activities of Mary and Martha in Provence reveals a number of similarities. Both are described as preachers or evangelists in southern France. Both perform miracles, including the raising of the dead. Both live austere lives. Both predict their own deaths, and both are buried under miraculous circumstances in which Bishop Maximinus of Aix plays an important role. Subsequent to their deaths, both saints continue to work miracles. Because of the close connections between Mary and Martha, some accounts of the lives of the two are "double lives" describing the histories of both. In other cases, especially in collections of saints' lives, common elements are discussed in the life of one saint and not in the other.

The Medieval Martha Legend

The details of the life of Martha are preserved in four major Latin documents, probably dating from the late twelfth and thirteenth centuries.[19] The earliest is likely that which has come down to us under the title *Vita Auct. Pseudo-Marcilia, Interprete Pseudo-Syntyche*.[20] It is attributed in the text to Martha's maidservant Marcilia (Marcella), who composed it in Hebrew; later it was said to have been translated into Latin by Syntyche (Sinticus or Syntex).[21] This life was probably used by both the author of the lengthy *Vita Beatae Mariae Magdalenae et Sororis Eius Sanctae Marthae*, a "double life" of Mary and Martha[22] that was likely compiled at Clairvaux by a follower of Bernard,[23] and by the French Dominican Vincent of Beauvais in the Martha chapters of his *Speculum Historiale*.[24] The most concise medieval account of Martha's life—and the most influential—was that included by Jacobus de Voragine in his *Legenda Aurea*. Of the four texts, three appear to be closely related: the *Vita Pseudo-Marcilia*, and the lives compiled by Vincent of Beauvais and Jacobus de Voragine. The *Vita Beatae Mariae Magdalenae* likely shared common sources but differs in a number of respects. Nevertheless, the basic outlines of the legend are similar.

The surviving versions of Martha's life all begin with an account of her family background. Martha and her siblings were said to have been of noble lineage. Their father is identified as the Syrian Theophilus in the *Vita Beatae Mariae Magdalenae*[25] and as Syrus in the other Latin sources; their mother, Eucharia, was a descendant of the royal house of Israel. From her the children inherited three towns: Magdala, Bethany, and a part of the city of Jerusalem. Martha is described as the epitome of virtue:

> she loved God greatly from her childhood, was highly skilled in Hebrew, and conformed to the precepts of the law. She was physically beautiful and of beautiful character, of considerable eloquence, and educated in the works appropriate to women. She was outstanding among all the pious noblewomen for her morals, her abundant charity and her great purity.[26]

To varying degrees, the Latin texts go on to recount Martha's activities as recorded in the New Testament. Both Vincent of Beauvais and the pseudo-Marcilia author refer to the traditional association of Martha and Mary as prototypes of the active and contemplative lives. Pseudo-Marcilia also makes the assertion, unusual in exegetical literature, that Martha can be seen as a prototype of the Christian Church.[27] Next, all texts describe with differing amounts of detail the dispersion of the apostles after Christ's ascension. The emphasis is on the journey of Martha to Provence with her sister Mary Magdalene and other companions, their arrival at Marseille, and their work of conversion among the people of the region surrounding Aix.

Central to all versions of Martha's life is the account of her battle with the dragon of Tarascon. This huge beast, half animal and half fish, had long terrorized the countryside, devouring passers-by and overturning ships. It is described as a descendant of the mighty Leviathan, mentioned in the book of Job (40:23, 41:1), and of an animal known as the bonasus. Because the natives had been unable to control it, they called upon Martha for help. She encountered the dragon in the forest, confronted it with a cross and holy water, and subdued it. Subsequently, it was slain by the people. The name of the place was later changed to Tirasconus or Tarascon, because the dragon was known as "Tirascurus."

Following her victory over the beast, Martha lived in austerity at Tarascon, where she was joined by a group of disciples who formed a religious community around her. Martha performed many miracles, including raising to life a young man who had drowned, and changing water into wine at a banquet held to celebrate the dedication of her home as a basilica.

Martha was warned of her death a year in advance, and from that time onwards she suffered from fevers. On the eighth day before her death, she had a vision of angelic choirs bearing the soul of her sister, Mary Magdalene, to heaven. Knowing then that her own death was imminent, she encouraged and instructed her companions. In the middle of the night before the day of her death, those keeping watch fell into a deep sleep. A sudden violent gust of wind extinguished the lamps and a crowd of evil spirits gathered around Martha. The watchers awoke and rushed out to find a flame to rekindle the lamps. During their absence, Mary Magdalene appeared and relit the candles and lamps with her own torch. Christ himself then entered into Martha's presence.

On the day of her death, Martha was carried outside and placed on a bed of ashes. She asked that the account of the Lord's Passion be read to her. She died as the words "Father, into your hand I commend my spirit" were pronounced. Her funeral was conducted by Christ and Bishop Fronto of Périgueux, who was miraculously transported to Tarascon when he fell asleep during a mass being celebrated at his own church.[28] This reference to the miraculous appearance of a saint at her funeral may have been grafted into the Martha legend as a result of confusion between Martha and the fourth-century Martin of Tours. The account of the latter's funeral, as recorded by Gregory of Tours in the first book of the *Miracles of St. Martin*, is very similar to that of Martha, with Ambrose of Milan officiating rather than Fronto.[29]

After Martha's burial, numerous miracles took place at her tomb, including the healing of Clovis, king of the Franks. Again, the Martha/Clovis connection may have resulted from confusion

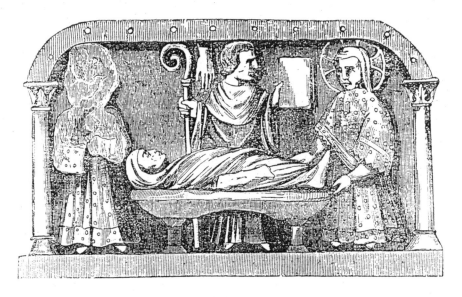

between Martha and Martin. The latter was adopted by the Merovingians as their patron saint following Clovis's conquest of Aquitaine in 507, and Gregory of Tours records in his *History of the Franks* that it was Martin to whom Clovis paid allegiance.[30]

The Rise and Fall of the Martha Cult

The cult of St. Martha was centred in southern France, although it was also highly popular in areas of northern Italy and southern Germany. Between the years 1200 and 1500, numerous Martha churches appeared, either newly built or renamed in her honour, and church institutions such as guilds, hospitals, and women's cloisters were founded in her name. Many of the newly emerging ecclesiastical orders vied to adopt her. She became a patron saint of various communities and brotherhoods—the Humiliati, the Franciscans, the Compagnia della Morte (which specialized in the care of those suffering from the plague). The Dominicans, in particular, looked to her as a source of inspiration: her biographers Vincent of Beauvais and Jacobus de Voragine were both Dominicans, as was Fra Angelico, who frequently depicted her in his paintings and often placed her in unusual settings, such as at prayer near Jesus in the garden of Gethsemane.[31] Elisabeth Moltmann-Wendel comments that "Martha was not the saint of a particular order, but for a great variety of groups became the image of revolution aimed at new responsible action in the world."[32]

Martha's cult flourished in the twelfth and thirteenth centuries, but its influence gradually declined. Undoubtedly the church itself played a role in the cult's downfall. Numerous heretical movements grew up in the area of France in which the Martha cult was centred.[33] In the late medieval period, one of the most infamous of these groups in Provence was the Albigensian sect, a branch of the Cathari. It was condemned by successive church councils from 1165 onwards, and Innocent III, pope from 1198 to 1216, launched a Crusade against it. In 1233 Gregory IX charged the Dominican Inquisition with its final elimination.

The Albigenses, like Martha, held to a moral doctrine of extreme austerity, and it is possible that some followers of Martha's cult were associated with or compared to this group. In his study of the Beguines, Ernest McDonnell points out that the members of these lay sisterhoods "took pleasure in reading scripture, saints' lives and patristic materials in the vernacular" and "did not hesitate to engage sometimes in preaching and the cure of souls"; moreover,

> beguine organization and daily discipline presented many additional features which characterized Albigensian and other anticlerical associations: the one year noviciate; admission ceremonies; justification of lay preaching; regular chapters with public chastisement; absolute secrecy for what transpired in them; prohibition on sleeping without a shirt;[34] [and] designation of the superiors of *beghinae clausae* as *magistrae* or *Marthae* ... Many zealots, both men and women, deluded by the absoluteness of austerity, therefore willingly adopted Catharist customs and organizations.[35]

The Beguine movement began in the diocese of Liège (Belgium) at the end of the twelfth century and spread through Flanders, France, and Germany in the thirteenth century. The main aims of the Beguine communities were philanthropic, especially the care of the sick and needy, but they also devoted time to religious contemplation. They had no common rule, mother house, or superior-general. Their activities met with increasing suspicion from the established Church. At the Council of Vienne in 1312, their teaching was condemned:

> Since these women promise no obedience to anyone and do not renounce their property or profess an approved Rule, they are certainly not "religious," although they wear a habit and are associated with such religious orders as they find congenial ... We have therefore decided and decreed with the approval of the Council that their way of life is to be permanently forbidden and altogether excluded from the Church of God.[36]

Surviving minutes of the Inquisition, dating from the later fourteenth century and taken from various sources, mention various "Marthas" and "Submarthas"—directors and under-directors of convents—who were suspected of being heretical.[37]

Church authorities were also undoubtedly distrustful of the Martha cult because it honoured a woman who occupied a powerful position. Martha was a heroine said to have saved the people of Tarascon; subsequently she became their confessor, spiritual leader, and protector.

The Martha cult prospered at a time when considerable ambivalence existed regarding "proper" female roles. Numerous books and articles have described the accomplishments of important women of the late Middle Ages. During this so-called age of chivalry and of courtly love, knightly troubadours sang the praises of their ladies in glowing tones; the thirteenth-century *Roman de la Rose* recommended that one should "Serve and honor all women. Spare no pain and effort in their service."[38] The Virgin Mary, the holy Mother of God, was elevated to new levels of honour and esteem. However, it has been suggested that "the chivalric manifestations of the romance"—as well as the burgeoning cult of the Virgin—

> are attempts to distance woman, to put her on a pedestal and thus put her out of the way. Moreover, the setting up of exemplary ethical ideals ... does not only work to relativize the female characters in the romance, but it is also, by negative implication, a means by which the poet, often didactic as well as entertaining in his intent, criticizes the society of his audience.[39]

It must also be kept in mind that at the same time as Woman was being "glorified," preachers continued to emphasize that it was Eve who had succumbed to the wiles of the serpent Satan and brought about the downfall of mankind. Women, despite the advances achieved by some, were still generally considered the "property" of their husbands; a thirteenth-century French law code, *Customs of Beauvais*, states that "In a number of cases men may be excused for the injuries they inflict on their wives, nor should the law intervene. Provided he neither kills nor maims her, it is legal for a man to beat his wife when she wrongs him."[40] Martha—a powerful, independent woman—could easily have been considered threatening by contemporary men and seen by them as an inappropriate female role model.

By the sixteenth century, the Church hierarchy had largely succeeded in its efforts to discredit Martha. Most theological discussion involving her had reverted to a focus on the Mary/Martha dichotomy expressed in the Luke 10:38-42. This is not to say that the more "heroic" Martha, renowned in legend, was totally forgotten. Martha continued to be honoured in Tarascon, where a number of the royal personages of France paid her homage. Documents from the city archives indicate that in 1470, Louis XI presented the town with a massive golden reliquary to contain her remains.[41]

In 1516, François I, King of France and count of Provence, stopped in Tarascon to venerate the tomb of Martha as he returned from Italy after his victory at Marignan. In 1564, Charles IX came to Tarascon with all his court, and in 1632, Queen Anne of Austria, wife of Louis XIII, made a pilgrimage to Martha's tomb. On at least two occasions—in 1650 and again in 1720—Martha was credited with protecting the inhabitants of the city in times of plague.[42] A number of the art works in the church of Martha at Tarascon date from the later seventeenth century, and commemorate her continuing power to heal. Right up to the present day, a festival honouring Martha's victory over the dragon, featuring a large mechanical reproduction of the beast, is observed annually in Tarascon on the last Sunday in June.[43]

In addition, at least two of the extant medieval versions of Martha's life circulated widely for several centuries. Vincent of Beauvàis's *Speculum Maius*, essentially complete by 1244, was a massive medieval encyclopedia dedicated to Louis IX of France. Of its three sections, the *Speculum Historiale*, which summarized the course of world history from creation to 1250, proved the most popular;[44] approximately 900 of its 3800 chapters are devoted to the lives of saints, including Martha and Mary Magdalene. A number of Latin manuscripts of the entire work survive; it was printed seven times between 1473 and 1624. The *Speculum Historiale* circulated separately and was translated into French, Catalan, and Dutch verse in the fourteenth century.[45] These vernacular versions also enjoyed great popularity.

The most influential collection of saints' lives in the later Middle Ages was that compiled by Jacobus de Voragine, a Dominican like Vincent. Originally entitled simply *Legenda Sanctorum*, or "Legend of the Saints," these concise summaries proved extremely popular. By the end of the thirteenth century, they were commonly known by the laudatory title of *Legenda Aurea*, or "Golden Legend." Over 700 manuscripts survive. The *Legenda Aurea* was also one of the earliest productions off the newly invented printing press. A list of fifteenth-century editions alone compiled by Robert Seybolt in 1946, includes 173 impressions: 97 in Latin and 76 translations.[46] While some of these works are considered spurious, 156 have been authenticated: the *Legenda Aurea* led the Bible in the number of editions issued in the fifteenth century.[47] These printed editions, especially those in vernacular languages, circulated widely, as stimuli to religious devotion. The collections of saints' lives in turn inspired other works of popular literature in which Martha was featured.

Knowledge of Martha's exploits was not only conveyed through literature. The majority of people in the Middle Ages were illiterate, so many of their ideas regarding theology and history were obtained not from reading but through art. Manuscripts and early editions of saints' lives were often illuminated or decorated with woodcut illustrations. Churches also contained paintings and sculptures that brought the lives and works of the saints before the eyes, and into the imaginations, of the general populace. Martha proved a popular subject in such works, especially in her role as dragon-tamer. Numerous extant artistic representations dating from the twelfth to the seventeenth century that portray her in various settings, derived from both the biblical and legendary records of her life.[48]

As the preceding survey suggests, Martha is not the one-dimensional character that she is often assumed to be by those who know of her only from biblical sources, especially Luke's account of a meal at Bethany. At various times in the past she served as an important role model for those active in the life and work of the Church, particularly for women, and she deserves to be better known today.

In the following chapters, the character of Martha will be explored from several perspectives. A chapter on Martha the servant surveys the exegetical literature on the Luke 10 passage and explores some related issues. A chapter on Martha as witness to the gospel discusses a number of themes: her declaration of faith as recorded in John, her identification as a "disciple" of Jesus and as a missionary, her role in apocryphal and gnostic literature, and her legendary activity as a preacher, evangelist, and spiritual leader in Gaul. Subsequent chapters examine Martha's role as a penitent and contemplative, her renown as a miracle-worker, her symbolic role as the Church, and her significance in the modern world.

2

Martha the Servant

The famous hostess ministered to the Lord and wished her sister
to minister in a like manner, for it seemed to her that the
whole world could not adequately serve so great a guest.
(*Legenda Aurea*, trans. D. Peters)

The best-known image of Martha is derived from the account of Jesus' visit to her home in Bethany near Jerusalem, as recorded in Luke 10:38-42:

Now as they went on their way, he entered into a certain village, where a woman named Martha welcomed him into her home. She had a sister named Mary, who sat at the Lord's feet and listened to what he was saying. But Martha was distracted by her many tasks; so she came to him and asked, "Lord, do you not care that my sister has left me to do all the work by myself? Tell her then to help me." But the Lord answered her, "Martha, Martha, you are worried and distracted by many things; there is need of only one thing. Mary has chosen the better part, which will not be taken away from her." (NRSV)

Since the early Christian era, this passage has been the subject of much analysis.

The literature falls into several categories. Some studies consider the episode within a broader context. The passage may be
treated as an extension of Jesus' response to the lawyer who asks
what he must do to in order to inherit eternal life (10:25-28).
He is told that he should love the Lord with all his heart, soul,
strength, and mind, and love his neighbour as himself. The parable
of the Good Samaritan (10:29-37), which immediately follows,
provides an example of love for neighbour, and the Martha-Mary

passage is considered an illustration of how one should demon-strate love for God.[49] Other authors have considered the passage as part of the broader Lukan travel narrative. This central section of the gospel (Luke 9:51–19:44) begins and ends with passages focusing on the theme of hospitality, particularly ways in which Jesus and his disciples were received. The Luke 10:38-42 per-icope is examined in the context of its contribution to the travel narrative's instruction about discipleship.[50] Still another approach is to discuss the three episodes described in Luke 10:25-42,[51] in relationship to the legal materials in Deuteronomy 1–26.[52]

On the other hand, many commentators consider the Martha-Mary story as complete in itself. Studies of this kind generally fall into one of two categories: textual analysis, which attempts to discover the "correct" reading of the text, and comparative an-alysis, which contrasts the responses of Mary and Martha to the visitor in their home.

Textual studies focus in particular on the second half of verse 42, recorded as "there is need of only one thing" in the New Revised Standard Version of the Bible quoted above. There are a number of possibilities supported by various early manuscripts of the text. These include the translations "one thing is needful," "one thing is necessary," "few things are needful, or only one," and the omission of the phrase entirely.[53] An extension of these types of studies are biblical commentaries that attempt to eluci-date the nature of the "one thing." For example, the textual com-mentary on this verse in *The New Oxford Annotated Bible* notes that "with delicate ambiguity Jesus rebuked Martha's choice of values; a simple meal (one dish) is sufficient for hospitality."[54] Other commentators take a less literal approach, defining the "one thing" that is required to attain salvation as attentiveness to the Lord's teachings.

Martha and Mary as Contrasting Figures

Of more importance for our present purposes are studies that compare and contrast the behaviours of Mary and Martha. As noted in the introduction, the image of Martha that a simple reading of the passage tends to evoke is not particularly positive, although, ironically, it is one with which many women find it easy to identify. The protagonists are reduced to caricatures— the "good" sister and the "bad" sister, the praiseworthy and the chastised.

The practice of contrasting a life of action and one of study and contemplation has a long history. B.G. Ockinga points out that it is found in the Rabbinic tradition; he refers in particular to the book of Ecclesiasticus, or the Wisdom of Jesus Ben Sirach, especially section 38.24–39.11, then goes on to compare the ideas expressed by Jesus Ben Sirach with those in the ancient Egyptian wisdom tradition.[55]

Negative views of Martha's activity appeared at an early date in the writings of the Church Fathers. In his sermon *On the Salvation of the Rich Man*, written at the end of the second century, Clement of Alexandria proclaimed:

> And he [the rich man] was capable of busying himself about many things; but one thing, the work of life, he was powerless, and disinclined, and unable to accomplish. Such also was what the Lord said to Martha, who was occupied with many things, and distracted and troubled with serving; while she blamed her sister, because, leaving serving, she set herself at His feet, devoting her time to learning: "Thou art troubled about many things, but Mary hath chosen the good part, which shall not be taken away from her." So also He bade him leave his busy life, and cleave to One and adhere to the grace of Him who offered everlasting life.[56]

The contrast between Mary-like and Martha-like behaviour proved an increasingly prominent theme in exegetical literature from the early third century onwards. As noted in the previous chapter, Origen's homily on Luke 10:38-42 provided a model for later interpreters.

Martha: the "Active Life"

Origen's ideas were especially well received in monastic circles. Representative of those who fell under their influence was John Cassian (ca. 365–435), who played an important role in bringing the ideals of Eastern monasticism to the West. Cassian spent ten or twelve years in Egypt and visited many of the anchorites; after the sack of Rome in 410 he fled to southern France. He expressed his views on the solitary life in his 24 *Conferences*, written between 420 and 430, which were reputed to be reports of discourses among Egyptian monks. In these works he stressed such qualities as freedom from earthly ties, solitude, and contemplation. Mary of Bethany was presented as an exemplum. Cassian noted, with respect to a monk's goal,

> To cling always to God and to the things of God—this must be our major effort, this must be the road that the heart follows unswervingly. Any diversion, however impressive, must be regarded as secondary, low-grade, and certainly dangerous. Martha and Mary provide a most beautiful scriptural paradigm of this outlook and of this mode of activity. In looking after the Lord and His disciples Martha did a very holy service. Mary, however, was intent on the spiritual teaching of Jesus and she stayed by His feet, which she kissed and anointed with the oil of her good faith. And she got more credit from the Lord because she had chosen the better part, one which could not be taken away from her ... The Lord locates the primary good not in activity, however praiseworthy, however abundantly fruitful, but in the truly simple and unified contemplation of Himself.[57]

Mary's attentiveness to the things of God is lauded. While Cassian's attitude towards Martha is sympathetic, she is viewed as less worthy than her sister.

Augustine referred to the Mary/Martha theme in at least twelve of his works. It is addressed at length in three: *Quaestiones in Evangelium in Luc* 2.20, Sermon 103, and Sermon 104. In these works Augustine emphasized the idea that Mary's response to Christ is preferable to that of Martha: she chose the one thing that was needful by focusing her attention on the One who brings all humanity into unity with himself. However, he points out that this did not imply Martha's activity should be held in disdain:

> How could she be rightly blamed, who was gladdened by so great a guest? If this be true, let men give over their ministrations to the needy; let them choose for themselves "the better part, which shall not be taken from them"; let them give themselves wholly to the word, let them long after the sweetness of doctrine; be occupied about the saving knowledge; let it be no care to them, what stranger is in the street, who there is that wants bread, or clothing, or to be visited, to be redeemed, to be buried; let works of mercy cease, earnest heed be given to knowledge only. If this be "the better part," why do not all do this, when we have the Lord Himself for our defender in this behalf? … And yet it is not so; but as the Lord spake so it is. So mark: "Thou art occupied about many things, when one thing is needful. Mary hath chosen the better part." Thou hast not chosen a bad part; but she a better … The Lord then did not blame Martha's work, but distinguished between their services.[58]

For Augustine, Martha symbolized the servant of the Word made flesh, while Mary symbolized the hearer of the eternal Word. From this analogy followed the identification of the two with the Church in the temporal world and the church in heaven. Martha's activity was considered representative of what transpired in present-day life, while Mary's foreshadowed that of the world to come:

> Ye see then, dearly Beloved, and, as I suppose, ye understand already, that in these two women, who were both well pleasing to the Lord, both objects of His love, both disciples; ye see … that in these two women the two lives are figured, the life present, and the life to come, the life of labour, and the life of quiet, the life of sorrow, and the life of blessedness, the life temporal, and the life eternal … What Martha was doing, that we are now; what Mary was doing, that we hope for. Let us do the first well, that we may have the second fully.[59]

Augustine used the example of Martha and Mary as an illustration in a number of other works not specifically concerned with the Luke 10 passage: Sermons 169, 179, 255, and 352, *De Trinitate* I.20, *De Bono Coniugali* 8.8, *Tractate in Ioannis* 15.18, *De Genesi ad Litteram* 4.14, and *Contra Duas Epistolas Pelagianorum* 3.22. In all cases, his major contention was that the form of service that Martha offered was necessary in this world, but would be superseded by a life of contemplation—anticipated by the actions of Mary—in the world to come. The "lives" represented by the sisters from Bethany, the active and the contemplative, represented different stages of Christian growth. In Sermon 255, he explains,

> In this time of our journeying we say "Alleluia" for solace on our way, and now the "Alleluia" is the song of the traveler for us; but we are advancing through a laborious path to a peaceful country where all our activities will be laid aside, and nothing will remain for us except the "Alleluia." Mary chose this most delightful part for herself: she remained at leisure; she continued to learn; she continued to praise. But Martha, her sister, was busy about many things. She was accomplishing what was, indeed, necessary, but not lasting; she was doing the work of the journey, but not that of her homeland; she was performing the task of the traveler, of one not yet in possession. In fact she, as hostess, had received the Lord and those who were with Him. Besides, the Lord had a body, and just as He deigned to assume a physical body for our sake, so He deigned to be hungry and thirsty. And, as a result of the fact that He deigned to be hungry and thirsty, He condescended to be fed by those whom He Himself enriched; He condescended to be received as a guest, not from need, but from favor. Therefore, Martha busied herself with what pertained to satisfying the needs of those who were hungry and thirsty; with solicitous activity she prepared what the Holy of Holies and His saints would eat and drink in her house. It was an important but transitory work. It will not always be necessary to eat and drink, will it? When we cleave to the most pure and perfect Goodness, there will be no reason for serving necessity.[60]

While this and other passages suggest that Augustine regarded the *vita contemplativa* as a reward given only in eternity, and as something separate from *vita activa*, the temporal struggle to earn it, numerous other passages suggest otherwise.[61] The contemplative life can begin on earth, although it will reach full completion only at the end of this world. It is the task of each individual to reconcile the demands of the active and the contemplative lives within himself or herself.

These two broad avenues of interpretation—viewing the sisters from Bethany as representative of either (a) alternative responses to God's Word, with Martha's role portrayed as the inferior one, or (b) progressive levels of spiritual development, with Martha's role considered inferior but necessary—dominated exegetical thought on the Mary-Martha passage during most of the later Middle Ages.[62] However, dissenting voices described Martha in more positive terms, and over time an increasing number of writers came to see the two "lives" as complementary.

This latter notion had been expressed as early as the fourth century. In his treatise on the gospel of Luke, Ambrose of Milan (ca. 339–397)—another writer who was important in the transmission of Origen's thought to the Christian West—distinguished between *intentio visionis* (the quality of seeing or focussing attention upon something) and *actio*, or action. He noted that the two did not occur simultaneously, but that they were intimately linked (I, 8). The one inevitably led to the other: if Martha had not first heard the Word, she would not have been spurred to service. Likewise, the contemplation of Mary later inspired her to act: John 12:3 describes how she washed Jesus' feet with her tears and dried them with her hair (I, 9). When considering the Luke 10:38-42 pericope specifically, Ambrose noted that Mary's attitude of contemplation was particularly commended by Christ, and that she thus served as an example for all believers (VII, 85). Nonetheless, Martha's service was not condemned. Citing I Corinthians 12, Ambrose put forth the image of the Church as one body with many members, where each member had need of the others. Wisdom resided in the head and activity in the hands, but all parts of the body were to be held in honour (VII, 86).

The interpretation of Gregory the Great (ca. 540–604) grew out of Augustine's. Gregory emphasized the notion that the allegory was applicable on a personal as well as a cosmic level: progress towards, and, to some extent, attainment of the goal of salvation were possible in this earthly life, and were not reserved for some future realm. The active life involved the exercise of the moral virtues: prudence, justice, fortitude, and temperance; the contemplative life was focused on the theological virtues: faith, hope, and charity.[63] Like Augustine, Gregory believed that the active life was necessary in this world, an essential counterpart to the contemplative life. However, he went on to suggest that it was possible to enter heaven by the pursuit of the active life alone:

> For the two lives, the active and the contemplative, when they be preserved in the soul, are accounted as two eyes in the face. Thus the right eye is the contemplative life, and the left the active life … When thou art not qualified for the contemplative life by a fitting degree of discretion, keep more safely to the active alone, and when thou failest in that which thou choosest as great, be content with that which thou heedest as very little, that if by the contemplative life thou art forced to fall from the knowledge of the truth, thou mayest by the active life alone be able to enter into the kingdom of heaven at least with one eye.[64]

Nevertheless, Gregory, like other commentators, saw the contemplative life as having greater merit than the active.

> Every one that is perfect is first joined to an active life in productiveness, and afterwards united to a contemplative life in rest. For that the life of contemplation is less indeed in time, but greater in value than the active, we are shown by the words of the Holy Gospel, wherein two women are described to have acted in different ways. For Mary sat at our Redeemer's feet…. but Martha eagerly prosecuted bodily services … Now Martha's concern is not reproved, but that of Mary is even commended. For the merits of the active are great, but of the contemplative, far better.[65]

The most desirable state was the union of the two lives. For this, Christ himself provided the model.

> He set forth in Himself patterns of both lives, that is, the active and the contemplative, united together. For the contemplative differs very much from the active. But our Redeemer by becoming Incarnate, while He gave a pattern of both, united both in Himself. For when He wrought miracles in the city, yet continued all night in prayer on the mountain, He gave His faithful ones an example not to neglect, through love of contemplation, the care of their neighbours; nor again to abandon contemplative pursuits through being too immoderately engaged in the care of their neighbours; but so to keep it together in the mind, in applying it to the two cases, that the love of their neighbour might not interfere with the love of God, nor again the love of God cast out, because it transcends, the love of their neighbour.[66]

Ideally, Christians striving for spiritual perfection would follow Christ's example, and the "two lives" would exist simultaneously within them.

Bernard of Clairvaux (1090–1153) expressed a somewhat similar sentiment, but put forward the Virgin Mary as the ideal. The feast of Mary's Assumption on August 15 had been celebrated as early as the ninth century, and by the eleventh, Luke 10:38-42 had been established as the Gospel lesson for the day.[67] Bernard's sermon for this feast day likened the village of Bethany to the world, and the sisters' house to Mary's womb. Both sisters dwelled there: Martha, the elder, had the privilege of receiving the Saviour on earth in her womb; Mary, the younger, prepared herself to receive the heavenly Christ. "Martha decorates the house; Mary fills it. The busyness (*negotium*) of Martha and the 'not idle leisure' (*non otiosum otium*) of Mary are both united in the Blessed Mother Mary. The 'best part' belongs to her, who is simultaneously a mother and a virgin."[68]

A particularly interesting image of the complementary and interdependent nature of the two "lives" is found in the *Rule for Hermitages* set forth by Francis of Assisi (ca. 1181–1226). He proposes that active "Martha-mothers" should care for their

"Mary-sons," allowing them to devote themselves fully to contemplation. However, neither role should be considered a permanent one:

> Those who wish to live religiously in hermitages should be three brothers or four at the most; two of these should be mothers and they may have two sons or at least one. The two who are mothers should follow the life of Martha, while the two sons should follow the life of Mary (cf. Lk 10:38-42) ... Those brothers who are the mothers should be eager to stay far from every person; and because of the obedience to their minister they should protect the sons from everyone, so that no one can talk with them. And the sons should not talk with any person except with their mothers and with the minister and his custodian when it pleases them to visit with the blessing of the Lord God. The sons, however, should sometimes assume the role of the mothers, as from time to time it may seem good to them to exchange [roles].[69]

A useful summary of the intimate relationship between contemplation and action is found in the *Summa Theologiae* of the Dominican friar Thomas Aquinas (ca. 1225–1274).[70] He notes that there are many arguments to support the position that the contemplative life is superior to the active, but that "in some circumstances and in some particular respect the active life has to be given preference because of the needs of this present life."[71] In addition, "the practice of the active life is beneficial for the contemplative life in that it calms our inner passions, which are the source of the images which interfere with contemplation."[72] In a later section of his treatise, dealing with religious orders, Aquinas argues strongly in favour of the kind of work "which flows from the fullness of contemplation, such as teaching and preaching ... this is better than mere contemplation. It is a greater thing to give light than simply to have light, and in the same way it is a greater thing to pass on to others what you have contemplated than just to contemplate." Those who engage in such activity have indeed chosen the "best part," followed in second place by those who engage in pure contemplation and finally by those who are merely "busy about external activities."[73]

Martha the Overzealous

The rival claims of "activity" and "passivity" as the most worthy way in which to express one's love of God presented great difficulty on the eve of the Reformation. Adherence to a life of austerity and a devotion to contemplation—long held to be "the better part"—were preached by a large number of the groups persecuted as heretics in the later Middle Ages. In addition, many theologians and preachers advocated both the value and the necessity of work in the service of the Lord. The result was a growing tendency to emphasize that Martha's "error" lay not in her activity as such, but in her over-activity.

The German Dominican and mystic Johannes Tauler (ca. 1300–1361) spoke often in praise of the active life. In his Sermon 47 he says,

> Everyone ought to do that work to which God has called Him, no matter how modest … There is no task so small, so insignificant or menial, that it is not proof of God's special grace … Why is it, then, there is so much grumbling, everyone complaining that his work stands in the way of his sanctification? It is God who gave him his work, and God never put a hindrance in our way … It is not the work that causes your trouble but the disordered way in which you go about it … If you remain content in your work it will be a proof, to you and to others, that you have been keeping your eye on God alone. When Our Lord reproved Martha, it was not because of her work—it was good and holy—but because she was overly concerned. We must perform good and useful work, in whatever way it comes to us; the care, however, should be left to God.[74]

He goes on to suggest that those listeners who neglect their God-given tasks in order to engage in contemplation are merely lazy.[75]

Many of the Protestant Reformers questioned the traditional stereotypes of Martha and Mary. Both Martin Luther and John Calvin were soundly convinced of the value of work, although they denounced the notion that worldly activity could be a means of justification.

Luther's assessment of Martha is quite harsh. Several passages in his writings state explicitly that he sees her as the epitome of "works justification." Here is one example:

Where the question is how to become a Christian and how to be delivered from sin, death and the devil, I must not discourse on the righteousness of the Law, on good works, on obedience to father and mother, on the giving of alms, or on entering a cloister, etc. Here it is of prime importance for me to listen to none but the Preacher. Thus we hear Christ the Lord telling Martha in the Gospel (Luke 10:42): "One thing is needful. Mary has chosen the good portion. You, Martha, are anxious about many things; you are busy. It is fine to work, to manage house and home, to be a burgomaster, to be a servant, to be a pastor. But this will not attain the goal. Mary has chosen and found the right thing to do. She is sitting at My feet and listening to what I am saying. This is proper; this is the right thing. This is the secret, just hear Me. This alone does it. Later on Mary will also do what you are doing now, solicitous Martha. That will all be attended to in good season." For this reason it is so important to distinguish between the righteousness of works and the righteousness of faith.[76]

Nevertheless, if one examines Luther's views on a woman's "proper" role, the less praiseworthy Martha more closely resembles his "ideal" female—the housewife who tends to the domestic needs of her family and guests. "Mary-like" behaviour was considered appropriate for men, but not for women.[77] Unfortunately, Luther's tendency to downplay women's capacity to comprehend and appreciate the subtleties of the Christian faith was widely held, both in his own time and in subsequent times.

Calvin also spoke out against the possibility of "works justification." Book Three of the *Institutes of the Christian Religion* (1559) examines "The Way in Which We Receive the Grace of Christ: What Benefits Come to Us from It, and What Effects Follow." Calvin proclaims that the righteous are justified by God alone. Faith is the instrument for receiving righteousness and "faith rests entirely upon God's mercy without the assistance of works."[78] Whole chapters are devoted to the topics "Boasting About the Merits of Works Destroys Our Praise of God for Having Bestowed Righteousness, as Well as Our Assurance of Salvation" and "Works Righteousness Is Wrongly Inferred from Reward." Nevertheless, good works are portrayed as "gifts from

God from which [the saints] recognize his goodness and ... signs of the calling by which they realize their election."[79]

Calvin makes no specific reference to the Mary and Martha story in the *Institutes*, but cites it in his *Harmony of the Gospels Matthew, Mark and Luke*. He suggests that it does not refer to the dichotomy between a life of action and one of contemplation:

> Now this passage has been wickedly perverted to commend what is called the contemplative life. But if we aim at bringing out the genuine sense, it will appear that Christ was far from intending that His disciples should devote themselves to idle and frigid speculations. It is an ancient error that those who flee worldly affairs and engage wholly in contemplation are leading an angelic life ... But we know that men were created to busy themselves with labour and that no sacrifice is more pleasing to God than when each one attends to his calling and studies to live well for the common good.[80]

Good works are the fruit of righteousness, the signs of God's calling. Martha's hospitality is reproached only because she "goes too far and is extravagant," whereas "Christ preferred frugality and moderate meals, so that the godly housewife should not be put to a lot of work." Secondly, "Martha left Him and was busy with unnecessary tasks and so made Christ's coming useless so far as she was concerned ... It was just as if someone received a prophet with honour but did not trouble to listen to him, but swamped his teaching by a great and superfluous preparation." And finally, "Martha thought she was in the right in all this bustling activity and so despised her sister for her godly desire to learn."[81] Calvin concludes that Christ's comment "Mary hath chosen the good part" does not imply that a comparison should be made between Mary and her sister, "as foolish and absurd expositors imagine. Christ is only saying that Mary has occupied herself in a holy and useful study."[82] The Christian is called to be receptive to God's presence, and worldly distractions should not be allowed to prevent him or her from achieving this end.

Similar ideas can be found in commentaries on the Luke pericope by numerous later writers. A sermon on Martha and Mary by the nineteenth-century Baptist preacher Charles Spurgeon (1834–1892) presents an analysis of the story that is very close to Calvin's. Spurgeon points out the need for balance in our spiritual life: "No man can be spiritually healthy who does not meditate and commune; no man, on the other hand, is as he should be unless he is active and diligent in holy service ... the difficulty is to maintain the two, and to keep each in its relative proportion to the other."[83] He expresses respect for Martha and that which she represents:

> I think it altogether wrong to treat Martha as some have done, as if she had no love for good things, and was nothing better than a mere worldling. It was not so. Martha was a most estimable and earnest woman, a true believer, and an ardent follower of Jesus, whose joy it was to entertain Jesus at the house of which she was the mistress.... Martha was serving Christ, and so was Mary; Martha meant to honour Christ, so did Mary; they both agreed in their design, they differed in their way of carrying it out ... Martha's service is not censured (only her being cumbered comes under the censure).[84]

He notes that he does not mean to do Martha an injustice by pointing out that the "Martha spirit"—which he sees as common in the church of his day—has shortcomings. It represents an attempt to "aim at making a fair show in the flesh," it "censure[s] those persons who are careful about Christ's word," it "derives satisfaction from mere activity," and it "expects to receive credit for doing more than is necessary." The Martha spirit "gets us away from the inner soul of service ... to the mere husks of service; we cease to do the work as to the Lord, we labour too much for the service sake; the main thing in our minds is the service, and not the Master; we are cumbered, and He is forgotten."[85] Spurgeon's listeners were urged to rediscover the "Mary spirit," which restores the focus on Christ and his teachings.

This exhortation to concentrate our attention on that which has true and lasting value is repeated in the works of twentieth-century theologian Paul Tillich (1886–1965), who described Mary and Martha as

symbols for two possible attitudes towards life, for two forces in man and in mankind as a whole, for two kinds of concern. Martha is concerned about many things, but all of them are finite, preliminary, transitory. Mary is concerned about one thing, which is infinite, ultimate, lasting. Martha's way is not contemptible. On the contrary it is the way which keeps the world running. It is the driving force which preserves and enriches life and culture. Without it Jesus could not have talked to Mary and Mary could not have listened to Jesus … There are innumerable concerns in our lives and in human life generally which demand attention, devotion, passion. But they do not demand *infinite* attention, *unconditional* devotion, *ultimate* passion. They are important, often very important for you and for me and for the whole of mankind. But they are not *ultimately* important. And therefore Jesus praises not Martha, but Mary. She has chosen the right thing, the one thing man needs, the only thing of ultimate concern for every man.[86]

In other words, we do well to follow in the steps of Martha—indeed, we have little choice but to do so. However, we must continuously monitor our priorities to ensure that, like Mary, our primary focus is on the things of God.

Martha the Unacceptable Woman

The majority of commentators on the Martha-Mary story in the last 30 years have been influenced at least to some degree by the women's movement. Of course, the history of advocacy on behalf of women's rights to study and learn can be traced back much farther. Early twentieth-century Canadian suffragette Nellie McClung (1873–1951) devoted a chapter of her book *In Times Like These*, written in 1915, to the question "Should women think?" She draws on the Mary-Martha story to support her arguments:

Martha has a long line of weary, backaching, footsore successors. Indeed there is a strain of Martha in all of us; we worry more over the stain in the carpet than a stain on the soul; we bestow more thought on the choice of hats than on the choice of friends; we tidy up bureau drawers, sometimes, when we should be tidying up the inner recesses of our mind and soul; we clean up the attic and burn up the rubbish which has accumulated there, every spring, whether it needs it or not. But when do we appoint a housecleaning day for the soul, when do we destroy all the worn-out prejudices and beliefs which belong to a day gone by?

Mary did take the better part, for she laid hold on the things which are spiritual. Mary had learned the great truth that it is not the house you live in or the food you eat, or the clothes you wear that make you rich, but it is the thoughts you think. Christ put it well when he said, 'Mary hath chosen the better part.'[87]

McClung goes on to outline the benefits to society that would result "if women could be made to think." These range from raising standards of sexual morality ("they would not wear immodest clothes, which suggest evil thoughts and awaken unlawful desires"), to protection of natural resources ("they would not wear aigrets and bird plumage which has caused the death of God's innocent and beautiful creatures"), and temperance ("they would not serve liquor to their guests, in the name of hospitality, and thus contribute to the degradation of mankind, and perhaps start some young man on the slippery way to ruin"). She concludes that "women make life hard for other women because they do not think."[88]

It is clear that McClung considers Mary and Martha not merely as "types," whose gender is immaterial, but as "female types." This pattern is also evident in more recent literature influenced by feminist thought. Commonly, Mary is put forward as a model of the "liberated" woman who dares to defy societal expectations regarding a woman's "proper" sphere of activity.

In some cases, these studies consider the story within a historical context, exploring the idea of Jesus' acceptance of women's rights to study and to learn. Ben Witherington III, for example, suggests that the Martha-Mary passage has a sound basis in historical fact (i.e., the situation in first-century Palestine, even though

Luke wrote and presented the narrative in his own language and style. Witherington explains,

> Though this story focuses on Martha and what she must learn about "the one thing necessary," Mary appears to know already, for she "was listening to his word." ... The use of the phrase "to sit at the feet of" is significant since evidence shows this is a technical formula meaning "to be a disciple of." If so, then Luke is intimating that Mary is a disciple and as such her behavior is to be emulated ... [In his reply to Martha] Jesus defends Mary's right to learn from Him and says this is the crucial thing for those who wish to serve Him. Jesus makes clear that for women as well as men, one's primary task is to be a proper disciple.[89]

Witherington does not belittle Martha's contributions; he comments further that "while Mary is taking on the not so traditional role of disciple, Martha is engaged in what some would call 'woman's work'—providing hospitality for her guest." Jesus' remarks in response to Martha's complaints "are neither an attempt to devalue Martha's efforts at hospitality, nor an attempt to attack a traditional woman's role ... Martha's service is not denigrated but it does not come first. One must reorientate one's lifestyle according to what Jesus says is the 'good portion.'"[90] Like Calvin, Witherington concludes that work, including work that is traditionally associated with women, is valuable as long as one's priorities are in order. In his later discussion of Jesus' women followers, Witherington notes that

> being Jesus' disciples did not lead these women to abandon their traditional roles in regard to preparing food, serving, etc. Rather it gave these roles new significance and importance, for now they could serve the Master and the family of faith. The transformation of these women involved not only assuming new discipleship roles, but also resuming their traditional roles for a new purpose.[91]

Despite the positive emphasis of such comments, various passages in his exegesis lead to the conclusion that Witherington views the traditional roles as the most appropriate for women.

Other commentators see the "liberating" message of the Martha-Mary story in a different light. It provides a beacon of hope to modern women. Not only should new opportunities be made available to them, but women should be encouraged to abandon the constraints of conventional, restrictive lifestyles. Gail Ransom presents the story as a modern parable of challenge. Her sermon in poetic form entitled "Chafing Dish, Apron Strings," views Martha in a way that is simultaneously sympathetic and damning:

My heart goes out to Martha. She and I are sisters,
cut from the same fabric.
Anxious to serve.
Anxious about many things.
Attempting to show hospitality and warmth through what
we do rather than who we are.

… Martha and I have much company.
Perhaps you.
Are you anxious about many things?
Attempting to dish out according to cultural requirements?
Serving systems which promise great favors for your obedience
—high paying jobs, social status, a sense of belonging?

We Marthas can easily fool ourselves into thinking that we are serving society, progress, the common good—or, yes, even ourselves—through our frantic, fractured, distracted efforts. … Better to pile up the packages, the cookie jars, the coffee mugs, the rock and roll, the TV set, the shopping malls, the Hallmark cards, the birthday gifts, the three-piece suits, the six-course meals—than face each other as merely human, fully present, ready to be touched, changed, moved by the presence of another, by the presence of an incarnate God.

But Mary did it. What a brave woman she was! Perhaps she knew her need so intensely that she could not do otherwise, only listen and learn, listen and learn, listen and learn as a parched sojourner thirsty for the Way.

... We are called to do likewise, to leave our kitchens and chafing dishes, to unwrap our apron strings and sit at the feet of Jesus, God-with-us, to listen and learn, listen and learn.[92]

Somewhat similar is Constance Parvey's description of Mary, who assumes "the posture of a disciple" when she sits at the feet of Jesus. She notes that Jesus' response awarded her this status and protected her from Martha's demand that she return to "a woman's place."[93] J.A. Fitzmyer's commentary on Luke sets up an apposition between Martha "the perfect hostess" and Mary "the perfect disciple."[94]

The new stereotypes of Mary the Liberated Woman and Martha the Traditional/Domesticated Woman provide an interesting reflection of women's changing roles in the late twentieth century. Unfortunately, these kinds of interpretation often seem to imply, intentionally or otherwise, that women's traditional roles and activities are unacceptable and outmoded, despite the fact that many women take offence at such generalizations. As Frances Taylor Gench notes:

> The story of Martha and Mary evokes strong reactions, both positive and negative. Some hail it as one of the most liberating texts for women in the Gospels, in that it reflects an opening for women within the circle of Jesus' disciples and challenges traditional expectations about women's roles. Others, however, find it oppressive, in that it pits sisters against each other, establishes a good woman/bad woman dualism, and presents a seemingly ungrateful Lord as devaluing the hospitality that a hardworking woman proffers. Indeed, whenever women gather to discuss it, at least one usually expresses the following sentiment: "I have always hated this story!"[95]

Clearly, a different approach must be found if those who find it easy to identify with Martha are to receive some reassurances.

"Liberating" Martha

When Luke 10:38-42 is considered on its own, either apologetic excuses or a highly creative imagination is required if Martha is to emerge in a positive light. Some of the former have already been cited; isolated examples of the latter can also be found.

The most radical interpreter of the Martha-Mary story in the later Middle Ages was Meister Eckhart (ca. 1260–1327), a Dominican preacher and mystic. He refers to the passage in several of his sermons, but his Sermon 86 is particularly original in its thought. Eckhart rejects a strictly literal reading of the text. The traditional interpretation of the times is totally reversed. Eckhart proclaims outright that Martha, and the active life she represents, is the more worthy of emulation.

Eckhart sees Martha as the older and more mature of the two sisters. With respect to her request that Christ ask her sister to help her, he writes:

> Martha did not say this out of spite. Rather, she said it because of endearment... We might call it affection or playful chiding. Why? Note what follows. She realized that Mary had been overwhelmed by a desire for the complete fulfillment of her soul. Martha knew Mary better than Mary Martha, for Martha had lived long and well; and living gives the most valuable kind of knowledge ... Mary was so full of longing. She longed for she knew not what, and wanted she knew not what. We harbor the suspicion that dear Mary was sitting there more for her enjoyment than for spiritual profit. Therefore Martha said, "Lord, tell her to get up," because she feared that she would remain stuck in this pleasant feeling and would progress no further ... Martha was afraid that her sister would remain clinging to consolation and sweetness, and she wished her to become as she herself was. This is why Christ said, "She has chosen the best part," as if to say, "Cheer up, Martha; this will leave her. The most sublime thing that can happen to a creature shall happen to her: She shall become as happy as you."[96]

Eckhart concludes that Jesus' reply was not meant to chasten Martha but to assure her that her sister would someday reach her full potential—just as Martha herself had already done.[97] He reinforces this notion by explaining that Christ named Martha twice to indicate that she "possessed completely everything of [both] temporal and eternal value that a creature should have."[98]

Six centuries later, in 1899, a Methodist preacher, John D. Walsh, came to Martha's defence using an equally impressive argument. He notes that

> commentators and preachers ... have commonly exhibited Martha as a type of those persons who bestow too much attention upon temporal affairs, permitting the cares of the world to choke the growth of the implanted word of God, so that their lives become unfruitful. This error seems to us to be unjust to Martha, whom Jesus loved, and unfortunate for those who embrace it; for it causes them to lose a very practical lesson taught in Luke's story. We see very clearly, from the study of the real Martha and Mary, that a very high attainment in grace may be acquired by eminently practical persons, of whom Martha was surely a type.[99]

His rationale is unusual:

> it happens in many homes that one or more members of the family by reason of some physical or mental infirmity find themselves unable to do an equal share of labor. Such persons add somewhat to the ordinary burdens resting upon some other member of the family. Mary appears to have been one of this kind, and Lazarus may have been another. In such a home a woman of capacity for affairs finds that exercise which gives superb development to such abilities.[100]

Martha was this kind of woman. Walsh concludes,

> It is not necessary to condemn Martha in order to justify Mary; for, whatever merit there is in exalted service, either in housekeeping or in statecraft, there is one thing still more exalted, namely, love of God. This is the "one thing ... needful." Competent Marthas may exhibit their love by eminent works; emotional Marys may show their love without doing, or having ability to do, any works that the world appreciates or applauds. Great service is the privilege of the few; great love is the privilege of all men.[101]

Walsh, like Eckhart, presents Martha as the representative of all that is most praiseworthy in both the temporal and the eternal realms.

Elizabeth Schüssler Fiorenza, writing in the 1980s, returns to the historical roots of the Martha-Mary story and explores it within the context of the early Christian house church, the Lukan community. Like Eckhart and Walsh, she sees Martha as a positive role model, but her interpretation is situated in a feminist framework. She sees Martha as the leader a house church and considers the relationship between Martha as host and Jesus as guest one of independent equals, while that between Jesus and Mary is one of master and subordinate student. The Lukan Jesus' favouring of the "dependent" woman represents the evangelist's androcentric notions of what the role of women should be; the *silent* woman receives positive approval while the woman who argues for her own interests is silenced. It is also noted that "the text does not say that Martha is in the kitchen preparing and serving a meal but that she is preoccupied with *diakonia* and *diakonein*, terms that in Luke's time had already become technical terms for ecclesial leadership."[102] Thus the treatment of Martha as recorded by Luke "appeals to a revelatory word of the resurrected Lord in order to restrict women's ministry and authority. Its rhetorical interests are to silence women leaders of housechurches who like Martha might have protested, and at the same time to extol the silent and subordinate behavior of Mary."[103] The real "villain" in Schüssler Fiorenza's interpretation of the story is the storyteller: "it is not the Kyrios but the writer of Lk. 10:38-40 who promotes such patriarchal restrictions."[104] Schüssler Fiorenza concludes her analysis with two examples of a "hermeneutics of creative actualization"; these present "alternative" versions of the Mary and Martha story, "articulated in terms of women's contemporary experience ... feminist re-telling[s] ... that allow us to discard the message that divides, subordinates, and alienates one sister from another."[105] In these reconstructions both Martha and her sister are portrayed as leaders and disciples, women whose voices no longer need to be heard through the intermediary of male authority figures and who demand to be treated as equals by the men around them.[106]

Schüssler Fiorenza is only one of a number of modern commentators who have attempted to "rediscover," "resurrect," or "re-vision" Martha.[107] In doing so, most move beyond the Luke 10 passage. There is an extensive body of scholarly literature exploring Luke's attitude towards women and issues surrounding the notion of women and discipleship in the literary context of Luke-Acts. In other cases, the Martha-Mary pericope is considered in relationship to other texts that describe incidents in the lives of the saints from Bethany: in particular, the raising of Lazarus (John 11) or the subjugation of the dragon (from the medieval Martha legends). The additional aspects of Martha's character that emerge from these texts will be considered more fully later.

Martha the Servant as Role Model

Before concluding the survey of Martha's role as the hostess of Christ, it is useful to reflect briefly upon the merits of Christian service. The biblical passages that encourage a life of service are numerous:

He who is greatest among you shall be your servant; whoever exalts himself will be humbled, and whoever humbles himself will be exalted. (Matthew 23:11-12)

The King will say to those at his right hand, "Come, O blessed of the Father, inherit the kingdom prepared for you from the foundation of the world; for I was hungry and you gave me food, I was thirsty and you gave me drink, I was a stranger and you welcomed me, I was naked and you clothed me, I was sick and you visited me, I was in prison and you came to me." Then the righteous will answer him, "Lord, when did we see thee hungry and feed thee, or naked and clothe thee? And when did we see thee sick or in prison and visit thee?" And the King will answer them, "Truly, I say to you, as you did it to one of the least of these my brethren, you did it to me." (Matthew 25:34-40)

In many instances, Jesus places himself in the servant's role:

But whoever would be great among you must be your servant, and whoever would be first among you must be your slave; even as the Son of man came not to be served but to serve, and to give his life as a ransom for many. (Matthew 20:26-28)

Let the greatest among you become as the youngest, and the leader as one who serves. For which is the greater, one who sits at table, or one who serves? Is it not the one who sits at table? But I am among you as one who serves. (Luke 22:26-27)

Acts 6:1-6 describes how, following Christ's ascension, "seven men of good repute" were selected and ordained for the special ministry of serving the apostles and their followers.

The gospels contain a number of references to Jesus' presence in Bethany.[108] It is recorded that on two occasions Martha provided him with a meal.[109] While Martha's name is not mentioned specifically in any other accounts of Jesus' visits to the town, it is probable that he was a frequent visitor to her home. Of particular note is Luke's claim that Christ's final moments on earth were spent in Bethany (24:50). Undoubtedly, it was due at least in part to her hospitality that "Jesus loved Martha" (John 11:5).

In the more popular medieval literature surrounding her life, Martha's record of service is highly valued. Her hospitality is described in three of the four surviving Latin lives of this saint. In two, the *Vita Pseudo-Marcilia* and Vincent of Beauvais' *Speculum Historiale*, her hospitality is praised at length. In Vincent's words,

He who truly loves all, indeed He who truly is love, loved [Martha] so much that He turned aside to her home more than to any other, thus fulfilling the prophecy which says: "He is like a stranger in the land, and like a wayfarer who turns aside to tarry for a night."[110] O truly happy one, who deserves to have such a Guest, who serves the bread of angels! She welcomed this great Guest who is welcomed by angels and men, and is their shepherd. She fed him who feeds all creatures, this great King and Lord, who alone encloses all in the palm of His hand, whom many prophets and kings wish to see and do not see, to hear and do not hear. She welcomed and fed this Guest, a thing most gracious and worthy of praise. When the Lord was received into their home, each of the two sisters, Martha and Mary, chose to perform her own ministry, which pleased God greatly. Mary, sitting before the feet of the Lord, heard the words of his mouth, as if feasting on that which she preferred to eat. But Martha occupied herself greatly with the preparation of the feast. And because she received so distinguished a Guest in her home, she was eager to serve with the greatest of care: cleaning the house, setting the table, preparing the food. But it seemed to her that all the household was unable to give sufficient service to such a man, and that her sister should come to help her with the domestic chores. She wished that all her household would energetically prepare the feast. Therefore she stood before the Lord astonished, and complaining about this thing, she said: "Lord, do you not care that my sister leaves me to serve alone? Tell her to help me." But He, who is not a respecter of persons,[111] loved the different forms of service which were offered to Him: He received and praised the service of the one but did not condemn that of the other. The Saviour, as was customary, gratefully received the hospitality of St. Martha in a different way. How great a reward was set aside for her in the presence of God, for the liberal hospitality and cheerful spirit offered to the poor and needy: for He approved of the hospitality of this holy woman.[112]

In medieval artistic representations, Martha is frequently recognizable through such attributes as the soup ladle, broom and cooking pot,[113] all clearly derived from her image as presented in Scripture: that of the sister who assumes responsibility for serving guests (Luke 10:40; John 12:2).

Recent literature, especially that by feminist theologians, reveals much division with respect to the notion of service as Christian ministry. Some writers adopt the attitude that women should strive to be leaders rather than servants. For example, Elisabeth Moltmann-Wendel speaks of the liberated, dragon-conquering Martha of medieval legend, then comments that

> the Martha cloisters of modern times are unambiguously institutions with practical aims, above all, care of the sick. The Martha houses of nineteenth-century Protestantism were houses of deaconesses designed for service. Today Martha is the patroness of the cooks and housekeepers of the Catholic clergy, and an anti-emancipation movement in England bears her name. Martha has again been domesticated and ordered according to sex. After her short awakening in the Middle Ages, she has been integrated into the patriarchal church and society.[114]

Like the negative stereotype of Martha as the traditional woman discussed earlier, such thinking is far from being liberating for women. It intentionally belittles those who choose a lifestyle devoted to the care of others.

At the same time, other feminist writers have acknowledged that *diakonia* is central to understanding the mission and ministry of both Christ and the church as a whole.[115] One way of dealing with the issue of servanthood is to distinguish between *diakonia* (freely chosen service) and *douleia* (imposed service or slavery). Such "servanthood through choice" is not denigrating; it implies that society is not being allowed to dictate one's behaviour, and reflects a capacity to look outside of ourselves to see the needs of others.[116] Other interpreters extend this notion by redefining ministry; the theology of "freely chosen" service is combined with a changed understanding of the nature of the "power" implicit in ministry:

> Feminist liberation communities necessarily must dismantle clericalism, which is an understanding of leadership as rule that reduces others to subjects to be governed ... Such dismantling of clericalism is implied in the Gospel concept of ministry as *diaconia* or service. Diaconia is kenotic or self-emptying of power as domination. Ministry transforms power from power over to empowerment of others. The abdication of power as domination has nothing to do with servility ... Rather ministry means exercising power in a new way, as a means of liberation of one another. Service to others does not deplete the person who ministers, but rather causes her (or him) to become more liberated.[117]

According to such interpretations, the servant is seen as one who is truly free.

Elisabeth Moltmann-Wendel provides another, slightly different twist on the notion of servanthood. She writes that Jesus, in choosing to take upon himself the role of servant to others was, in fact, following the lead of women. In the social world of his day, serving at tables was seen as the work of those at the lowest end of the social scale; when Jesus announced that he had come "not to be served but to serve," he was representing a new order. "Serving is the characteristic behaviour in the new community; it is the renunciation of rule and hierarchical order: it shows 'the eschatological reversal of all power-relationships among men' ... Accordingly the women would have had an essential, formative share in Jesus' life-style and view of life."[118] The women who served were thus considered to be at the forefront of change. Interestingly, these insights of Moltmann-Wendel's are taken from a book published only three years after that cited earlier, where various "unliberated" Marthas are described and criticized.

While the notion of freely chosen servanthood is appealing, it has also been the subject of criticism. Elisabeth Schüssler Fiorenza maintains that "those singled out and socialized into subservience and a life of servanthood are not able to 'choose servanthood freely'" and that "the patriarchal church continues to exercise its ministry as 'power over' its people as long as it is structured into a hierarchy of power-dualisms: ordained/nonordained, clergy/laity, religious/secular, church/world."[119]

One of the most useful modern interpretations of the "message" of the Martha-Mary story is provided by Rosemary Radford Ruether. She points out that classical church tradition did not associate Mary and Martha with roles specific to women, but rather connected them with different aspects of Christian life, seen to include both men and women, and that this latter notion needs to be reaffirmed.

> The gospel of Jesus overcomes distinction of gender, race, and class. Women as well as men are included in study, and thereby also in the possibility of becoming teachers and preachers of the Christian message ... Does this mean that we devalue the work of women who cook and serve food by lifting up the right of women to study and teach? Perhaps we, like the classical Christian view, can now go beyond interpreting this text primarily in terms of women's roles, and see both as roles to which all Christians, both men and women, are called.

> All Christians are called to service. Central to Jesus' teachings is a transformation of values in which the hierarchy of aristocratic domination over servile labor is overcome. The very concept of the Messiah as one who comes to rule over others is transformed. Jesus comes not to be served but to serve. Service is no longer seen as the devalued work of women and slaves, but rather the "greatest of you shall be servants." That is to say, the men of the church who aspire to leadership should see such leadership as service, a language traditionally used for the work of women and slaves. This also means that service ceases to be devalued or "servile." It becomes the work of redemption, the work of bringing in God's kingdom on earth, doing God's will on earth, as it is in heaven. Women and slaves thereby are also liberated from servitude. They, alongside men of privileged classes, are disciples of rabbi Jesus, called to sit at his feet and preach his message.

... The Christian gospel calls us all, as those baptized into the new humanity in Christ, out of dominating rule and also out of devalued servitude. It calls us all into service for God's kingdom. But to understand the meaning of that call we must gather at the feet of Jesus and learn his teachings. This is indeed the first and better part, which should not be taken away from any of us, either because of gender stereotypes or because of busyness with the tasks of everyday life.[120]

Her comments confirm that it is indeed possible to take a balanced and integrative approach to a passage that has often been interpreted in ways that are harmful and divisive.

The Humanity of Martha

The major focus of this chapter has been the consideration of Martha as a symbol. As has been shown, traditional interpretations of the story told in Luke 10:38-42 have tended to view her and her sister as types, representative of varying concepts, and as raw material from which a message can be drawn. Rudolf Bultmann, for example, describes the passage as a "biographical apophthegm"—a brief anecdote or saying of Jesus' presented within the context of a historical situation.[121] Others have thrown into question whether the protagonists actually existed, or whether their names merely provided the pretext for the presentation of a lesson.

I would like to suggest that it can also be instructive to read the passage as a simple account of a real woman, Martha, who reacts to a specific situation in a certain way. She receives Jesus into her home for a meal, then finds herself left to attend to the preparations alone, while her sister, Mary, sits at the feet of their guest. Her annoyance builds as she works.

Two important elements are evident in the story. First, the manner in which Martha addresses Jesus indicates her particular closeness to him. She is comfortable in coming forward and expressing her concerns openly.

Second, her impetuous response to her sister's inactivity reflects a very human response to a frustrating situation. A number of passages in the Gospels describe similar situations. In some cases, these are justifiable: for example, Jesus' attack on the sellers and moneychangers in the Temple at Jerusalem[122] or Peter's lashing out when the soldiers come to arrest Jesus in Gethsemane.[123] In other cases—such as that of the Lukan Martha—frustration results when people or things do not live up to one's expectations. It is recorded by Mark that Jesus himself reacted in a manner somewhat similar to Martha when, tired and hungry, he approached the fig tree and "found nothing but leaves, for it was not the season for figs" (11:13). Undoubtedly he should have realized this—just as Martha probably would have realized that her sister was not wrong in wanting to listen to Jesus' preaching—but his reaction is immediate and damning: "May no one ever eat fruit from you again" (11:14). According to Mark, this event immediately preceded Jesus' angry outburst in the Temple. Yet the event described in a few brief verses is not the end of the story in the case of either Jesus or Martha. Mark notes that the next time the disciples passed by the fig tree, they saw that it had "withered away to its roots" (11:20), thus providing a figurative illustration of the power of God. Likewise, the image of Martha as an anxious housekeeper is not the final picture shown of her in the Gospels. In John she is presented as one who comes forward and makes a firm confession of faith (11:27).

This aspect of Martha's character—as one who acknowledges her belief in Jesus—will be examined more fully in the next chapter.

Martha the Witness

*"I believe that you are the Christ, the Son of God,
he who is coming into the world."*
(John 11:27)

There is no suggestion in the synoptic gospels (Matthew, Mark, and Luke) that Martha and Mary had a brother Lazarus, although the name does appear in Luke in the context of the parable of the rich man and Lazarus (16:19-31). The relationship between this story and John's account of the raising of Lazarus found in John 11 has been the subject of much speculation.

Some suggest that John's text is simply an elaboration of Luke's. According to this line of thought, John inserted the fictitious character of Lazarus into a historical setting to suit his own theological purposes. The underlying theme of the parable suggests folk material concerned with the reversal of fortune in the afterlife. Joachim Jeremias comments:

This is the Egyptian folk-tale of the journey of Si-Osiris and his father Setme Chamoïs to the underworld; it ends with the words: "He who has been good on earth will be blessed in the kingdom of the dead; and he who has been evil on earth will suffer in the kingdom of the dead." Alexandrian Jews brought this story to

Palestine, where it became very popular as the story of the poor scholar and the rich tax-collector Bar Ma'jan. That Jesus was familiar with the story is shown by his using it in the parable of the Great Supper [Matthew 22:1-10, Luke 14:15-24]. We have already told the beginning of the story—how the scholar's funeral was unattended, while the tax-collector was buried with great pomp. Now here is the end of it. One of the poor scholar's colleagues was allowed to see in a dream the fate of the two men in the next world: "A few days later that scholar saw his colleague in gardens of paradisal beauty, watered by flowing streams. He also saw Bar Ma'jan the tax-collector standing on the bank of a stream and trying to reach the water, but unable to do so."[124]

Luke expands this story to convey the message that even if one were to rise from the dead, the Jews would not believe. John then demonstrates the point by having Jesus raise "Lazarus"— whose name means, literally, "God helps."

An alternative view is that the parable was based on an actual historical event. Those who argue in support of this position note that the Lukan story is the only example of a parable in which a character is named.[125] It has even been proposed that Simon the Leper was the father of Martha, Mary, and Lazarus,[126] and that Lazarus died of leprosy. This theory would support the notion that the historical Lazarus served as a model for the Lukan parable, where his namesake sits at the gate of the rich man covered in sores (Luke 16:20) and an allusion is made to the possibility of his rising from the dead (16:31).[127]

An intermediary theory states that the Lazarus story in John is derived from an independent source that narrated the seven signs of Jesus, and that may or may not have had historical validity.[128] The existence of this document, known as the "miracle source," "signs source," or "semeia document," is widely accepted by modern scholars.[129]

Regardless of its origins, the account of the raising of Lazarus occurs at a pivotal point in John's Gospel, immediately preceding and, to some degree, precipitating the events of Passion week. It is described at some length in John 11:1-44. News of this resurrection serves to further incite the Jews against Jesus. He is no longer able to travel about openly. However, a few days after the miracle takes place, Jesus once again seeks refuge with his friends at Bethany, and enjoys a final meal with them on the evening before his triumphant entry into Jerusalem (12:1-11).

In John's text, Martha is shown to be involved in both events. She serves as hostess at the dinner, just as she did at the meal described in Luke 10:38-42. It appears that her sister Mary once again manages to avoid the kitchen duties. However, on this occasion there is no mention that Martha—whom some commentators have described as a chronic complainer—raises any objections. Of particular importance is Martha's role in chapter 11 immediately prior to the raising of her brother, where she steps aside from her domestic tasks and engages in theological discussion with Jesus (vv. 20-27):

> When Martha heard that Jesus was coming [to Bethany], she went and met him, while Mary sat in the house. Martha said to Jesus, "Lord, if you had been here, my brother would not have died. And even now I know that whatever you ask from God, God will give you." Jesus said to her, "Your brother will rise again." Martha said to him, "I know that he will rise again in the resurrection at the last day." Jesus said to her, "I am the resurrection and the life; he who believes in me, though he die, yet shall he live, and whoever lives and believes in me shall never die. Do you believe this?" She said to him, "Yes, Lord; I believe that you are the Christ, the Son of God, he who is coming into the world." (RSV)

This confession of faith occupies a key position in the narrative. However, it has not been until recent years that commentators have begun to explore its significance.

Martha as One to Whom Christ's Promise Is Revealed

For many centuries, commentators on John 11 tended to focus on the miracle that is described there. Martha's role, if noted at all, was generally mentioned only in passing: she provided the context for Jesus' proclamation of himself as "the resurrection and the life." In his *Tractate 49 on the Gospel of John*, Augustine explains,

> Jesus says to her, "Your brother will rise again." This was ambiguous. He did not say: I am now raising up your brother, but "Your brother will rise again." Martha says to him, "I know that he will rise again in the resurrection on the last day." About that resurrection I am sure, about this one I am uncertain. Jesus says to her, "I am the resurrection." You say: My brother will rise again on the last day. It is true! But through him through whom he will then rise again he can also rise now, because, he says, "I am the resurrection and the life." Hear, brothers, hear what he says … "And everyone who lives" in the flesh "and believes in me," even if he dies for a time because of the death of the flesh, "he shall not die forever" because of the life of the spirit and the immortality of the resurrection. This is what he said, "And everyone who lives and believes in me shall not die forever. Do you believe this?" She said to him, "Yes, Lord, I have believed that you are the Christ, the Son of God, who has come into the world." When I believed this, I believed that you are the resurrection, I believed that you are the life. I believed that he who believes in you, even if he dies, shall live, and he who lives and believes in you shall not die forever.[130]

A tendency to carry over into the discussion of John's text negative assessments of Martha based on Luke 10 is also evident. Origen, for example, begins his commentary on the Lazarus story by discussing the significance of Bethany as a "fitting home for Mary, who chose the good part, which was not taken away from her, and for Martha, who was cumbered for the reception of Jesus, and for their brother, who is called the friend of the Saviour."[131] Origen repeatedly alludes to the superiority of Mary, the contemplative sister, over the worldly Martha. Martha is portrayed as a person who cannot restrain from disbelief when she objects to Jesus' command to remove the stone, despite having been told by Jesus that he is the resurrection and the life; she is too taken up by earthly matters to understand higher truths even when informed directly (Book XXVIII.3, 5).

In his *Homily 62* on John 11:1-29, John Chrysostom (ca. 347–407) devotes more attention to Mary than to Martha. She was the one who anointed the Lord with ointment, and the one of whom Jesus said "Mary has chosen the best part."[132] Chrysostom seems at some loss to explain why it was Martha, rather than Mary, who first came out to meet Jesus, but finally concludes that it was because of Martha's need for extra reassurance:

> "How is it then," you will ask, "that Martha seems more fervent?" She was not more fervent, for it was not Mary who heard [His words about the resurrection] since Martha was the weaker. Indeed, though she had heard such sublime words, she said afterwards: "He is already decayed, for he is dead four days." Mary, on the contrary, though she had listened to no instruction, said nothing of the kind, but merely declared at once, with faith: "Master, if you hadst been here, my brother would not have died."[133]

Only an indirect allusion is made to Martha's similar declaration; it is noted only that "they" believed that Christ could have saved their brother from death, and furthermore that "they" also professed belief that God would give Christ whatever he asked of Him. In fact, this latter assertion was made by Martha alone, not Mary. Chrysostom's treatment of Martha's confession is also somewhat condescending:

> How did Martha know about the future resurrection? She had often heard Christ speaking of the resurrection; nevertheless she now had a great desire to see it take place. Yet, see how confused she still was. For after hearing: "I am the resurrection and the life," she did not say, in keeping with this: "Raise him up from the dead." On the contrary, what did she say? "I believe that thou art the Christ, the Son of God." What, then, did Christ reply to her? "Whoever believes in me, even if he die, shall live"—He was referring to the death of the body. "And whoever lives and believes in me shall never die"—referring to the death of the soul. "Therefore, since I am the resurrection do not be upset if Lazarus is already dead, but have faith. For actually this is not death."... She replied: "I believe that thou art the Christ, the Son

of God, who hast come into the world." It seems to me that the woman did not grasp the meaning of what was said. However, she did understand that it was something great, though she did not altogether understand it. That was why, when asked one thing, she replied another. Meanwhile, she gained enough profit so that she brought her grief to an end.[134]

The rest of the sermon is a tirade against women's tendency to "make a show of their mourning and lamentation."

In *Homily 63* on John 11.30-41, Chrysostom—like Origen in his commentary on John, Book XX—describes Mary's act of falling prostrate at the feet of Jesus as a further sign of her superiority over her sister:

> "Now she [Mary] fell at his feet." She was more fervent than her sister. She was not embarrassed because of the crowd, or by their suspicious attitude toward Him.... However she cast aside all human considerations, since her Master was present, and she was concerned about one thing only: showing honor to her Master.[135]

In *Homily 65* on John 11.49-12.8, Chrysostom describes Mary's anointing of Jesus, noting that

> Mary was not serving at table, for she was His disciple. In this case once again she was more deeply spiritual than Martha. For she was not lending her services as if called on to do so, nor did she minister to all the guests in common, but she paid honor to Him alone, and she approached Him, not as a man, but as God.[136]

Here Chrysostom's designation of Mary as a "disciple" is particularly significant. Unlike her sister, she is considered to be part of the select group of those especially close to Jesus.

Calvin's *Commentary on the Gospel of John* also draws upon the negative associations of Martha derived from Luke's gospel. He interprets Martha's initial greeting to Christ—"Lord, if you had been here, my brother would not have died"—as another complaint:

Her meaning may be expressed thus—"By thy presence thou mightst have delivered my brother from death, and even now thou canst do it, for God will not refuse thee any thing." By speaking in this manner, she gives way to her feelings, instead of restraining them under the rule of faith. I acknowledge that her words proceeded partly from faith, but I say that there were disorderly passions mixed with them, which hurried her beyond due bounds. For when she assures herself that her brother would not have died, if Christ had been present, what ground has she for this confidence? Certainly, it did not arise from any promise of Christ. The only conclusion therefore is, that she inconsiderately yields to her own wishes, instead of subjecting herself to Christ. When she ascribes to Christ power and supreme goodness, this proceeds from faith; but when she persuades herself of more than she has heard Christ declare, that has nothing to do with faith; for we must always hold the mutual agreement between the word and faith, that no man may rashly forge anything for himself, without the authority of the word of God. Besides, Martha attached too much importance to the bodily presence of Christ. The consequence is, that Martha's faith, though mixed up and interwoven with ill-regulated desires, and even not wholly free from superstition, could not shine with full brightness; so that we perceive but a few sparks of it in these words.[137]

Christ's reply to her—that her brother would rise again—prompts this comment:

The kindness of Christ is amazing, in forgiving those faults of Martha which we have mentioned, and in promising her, of his own accord, more than she had ventured plainly and directly to ask.[138]

She responds that she knows that her brother will indeed rise again, and Calvin notes:

We now see Martha's excessive timidity in extenuating the meaning of Christ's words. We have said that she went farther than she had a right to do, when she fabricated a hope for herself out of the feelings of her own mind. She now falls into an opposite fault; for when Christ stretches forth his hand, she stops short, as if she were alarmed.[139]

Her confession of faith in v. 27 does meet with some degree of approval:

> To prove that she believes what she had heard Christ say about himself, that *he is the resurrection and the life*, Martha replies, that *she believes that he is the Christ, and the Son of God*; and indeed this knowledge includes the sum of all blessings; for we ought always to remember for what purpose the Messiah was promised, and what duty the prophets ascribed to him. Now when Martha confesses that *it was he who was to come into the world*, she strengthens her faith by the predictions of the prophets. Hence it follows, that we ought to expect from him the full restoration of all things and perfect happiness; and, in short, that he was sent to erect and prepare the true and perfect state of the kingdom of God.[140]

Again, the emphasis is on the importance of Christ's promise rather than on Martha's declaration.

This is not to say that positive comments regarding Martha's witness cannot be found. Luther, for example, includes her in a list of those "whose eyes and hearts were opened by God... , [and who] relied on John's [i.e., John the Baptist's] testimony, and believed in the Lord Christ."[141] However, extended discussions of Martha's role in John 11–12 are a relatively recent phenomenon.

Martha's Significance in John's Gospel

Rudolf Bultmann, writing in the early 1960s, was one of the first to appreciate the depth of Martha's faith. He notes in his commentary on John's gospel that she makes not one but two important confessions in chapter 11:

> In the outburst of Martha vv.21f, expression is given to faith in Jesus' supernatural power. The first sentence—hardly thought of as a reproach, but rather as a painful regret—reveals the trust in the healer that Martha, no less than others, brings to him. It acts as a foil for the second sentence, wherein what is new

and proper to faith in Jesus comes to view: Martha knows that God will grant him any request. Of course, her statement is an indirect request to raise her brother; but it is significant that it is formulated not as a request but as a confession ... The saying therefore has transcended its situation and becomes an expression of faith in the ability of Jesus to help, indeed in Jesus as the Revealer to whom God gives everything.[142]

In his later comments on verse 32, Bultmann notes that Mary utters some of the same words as Martha, but the second statement is lacking; Mary thus represents the first step of faith, but her sister has advanced beyond this. She has not "attained Martha's certainty."[143]

With respect to verse 27, Bultmann suggests that Martha's answer to Christ "shows the genuine attitude of faith ... she can recognize that in Jesus the eschatological invasion of God into the world has come to pass. The names which her confession attributes to him are eschatological titles; and of these the third one is the most significant [and] most plainly affirms the inbreaking of the beyond into this life."[144] He also notes that it is "incomprehensible how many exegetes can say that Martha did not rightly understand Jesus;"[145] those who do suggest this generally refer to her objections to the opening of the tomb expressed in verses 39-40,[146] which, interestingly, Bultmann mentions without comment.

The impact of the women's movement has led to an increasing focus on the significance of women in the early church. In this respect, Raymond Brown's 1975 article "Roles of Women in the Fourth Gospel" is seminal.[147] Brown explores the historical context of the book of John and the late first century Johannine community. He notes that

there is not much information about church offices in the fourth Gospel and, a fortiori, about women in church offices. Perhaps the only text that may reflect directly on this is 12:2, where we are told that Martha served at table (*diakonein*). On the story-level of Jesus' ministry this might not seem significant; but the Evangelist is writing in the 90s, when the office of *diakonos* already existed in the post-Pauline churches (see the Pastorals) and when the task of waiting on tables was a specific function to which the community or its leaders appointed individuals by laying on hands (Acts 6:1-6). In the Johannine community a woman could be described as exercising a function which in other churches was the function of an "ordained" person.[148]

Brown goes on to discuss the way in which the gospel of John revises the traditions about Peter. He is not described as the first to view the risen Christ; rather, it is a woman, Mary Magdalene, to whom Jesus first appears. Brown then comments:

Giving to a woman a role traditionally associated with Peter may well be a deliberate emphasis on John's part, for substitution is also exemplified in the story of Lazarus, Mary, and Martha. The most famous incident in which Peter figures during the ministry of Jesus (and his other claim to primacy besides that of witnessing the first appearance of the risen Jesus) is the confession he made at Caesarea Philippi, especially in its Matthean form (16:16): "You are the Christ, the Son of the living God." Already the disciples had generally confessed Jesus as a "Son of God" (no definite article in Mt 14:33), but it is Peter's more solemn confession that wins Jesus' praise as a statement reflecting divine revelation. The closest parallel to that confession in the four Gospels is found in Jn 11:27: "You are the Christ, the Son of God;" and it appears on the lips of a woman, Martha, sister of Mary and Lazarus. (And it comes in the context of a major revelation of Jesus to Martha; it is to a woman that the mystery of Jesus as the resurrection and the life is revealed!) Thus, if other Christian communities thought of Peter as the one who made a supreme confession of Jesus as the Son of God... the Johannine community associated such memories with heroines like Martha.[149]

Brown also remarks on the significance of the fact that the writer of John's Gospel records Jesus' love for Martha and her siblings:

The importance of women in the Johannine community is seen not only by comparing them with male figures from the Synoptic tradition but also by studying their place within peculiarly Johannine patterns. Discipleship is the primary Christian category for John, and the disciple par excellence is the Disciple whom Jesus loved. But John tells us in 11:5: "Now Jesus loved Martha and her sister [Mary] and Lazarus." The fact that Lazarus is the only male in the Gospel who is named as the object of Jesus' love ... has led some scholars to identify him as the Beloved Disciple. And so it is noteworthy that John would report that Jesus loved Martha and Mary, who seem to have been better known than Lazarus.[150]

In a note to this passage, Brown writes:

Notice the order of names in 11:5. Moreover, in 11:1-2 Lazarus is identified through his relationship to Mary and Martha. The reason for this may be that the two women were known in the wider Gospel tradition (Lk 10:38-42), whereas Lazarus is a peculiarly Johannine character ... who is introduced into the Gospel by being placed in a family relationship to Mary and Martha. This is not unlike the introduction of the Beloved Disciple into well-known scenes by placing him in a relationship to Peter.[151]

Brown identifies Martha in three important roles in the Gospel of John: as an ordained officer of the Johannine church, as one of the first to confess faith in Christ as the Son of God, and as a disciple loved by Jesus and well known and respected within the early Christian community. His insights regarding her have proven highly influential.

Later commentators have taken two approaches to the Martha material in John. One is to explore her overall importance in the Gospel narrative. Elisabeth Moltmann-Wendel, for example, describes Martha's role as catalytic: it is one of many stories of Jesus in which the

dynamic comes from the women ... They are the active ones who set the process in motion and finally achieve something ... There is a direct relationship between [Martha's] active nature and [Jesus'] passivity ... The vacillator who sometimes seems so passive and takes so much time before he raises Lazarus becomes the one who raises his dead friend as a result of the activity of a woman (John 11.19ff.) ... He draws energy from Martha's doggedness, from her love for her brother, for life.[152]

Not all are in agreement with this interpretation. Turid Karlsen Seim comments that "Martha's opening words in 11:21f are analogous to those of the mother of Jesus at Cana (2:3-5). She indicates the problem without explicitly making a request; the sovereign independence of Jesus is maintained."[153] Sandra Schneiders makes a similar point. She considers Martha's role pivotal only in the sense that her words and actions provide a pretext by which Jesus can reveal himself:

> Jesus' delay in chapter 11 follows the pattern that can be observed in his response to his mother in chapter 2, to the royal official in chapter 4, and to his brothers in chapters 7. The purpose of these refusals and/or delays in Jesus' response is to emphasize the sovereign independence of Jesus action in relation to human initiative. This is especially important in the raising of Lazarus, which is in no way to be understood as a private favor conferred on the distraught sisters but as Jesus' culminating self-revelation on the eve of the passion.[154]

Martha's Confession

A second approach to the Martha material in John—and the more common one—is to focus upon Martha's testimony and its implications.

Various writers have pointed out that there is a "Martha-strand" and a "Mary-strand" evident in John 11:1-46 and 12:1-8. In John 11, the Martha episode is more Johannine than the Mary episode, which, according to Seim,

> may imply that Martha represents the Johannine expansion of a tradition that was more in favour of Mary (cf. the Lukan preference for Mary to Martha in Lk 10:38-42). There are still remnants in Jn 11:1-2 and 45 indicating Mary as the main person. But in the typically Johannine verse 5 where it is related that Jesus "loved" the family in Bethany, Martha is the more important character.

She seems to have expanded in the narrative as a main carrier of the evangelist's distinctive theology.[155]

John Rena elaborates this notion:

Martha's confession that Jesus is the Messiah, the Son of God, the one coming into the world, reaches the lofty goal set for the Johannine readers (20:30-31).[156] Unfortunately, modern paragraph divisions obscure the real ending of the initial Martha episode. Not only is she confessor but she functions as messenger. Her confession is but the prelude to going and telling her sister that Jesus is present and is calling her (11:28b).[157]

Although Rena himself does not make the connection, others have noted the similarities between Martha's calling of Mary, Andrew's call of Simon Peter (John 1:41-42), and Philip's call of Nathanael (John 1:45). Martha, like these disciples, responded to the revelation of the Messiah by witnessing to others and seeking to bring them to Him.

As in the Gospel of Luke, John presents the behaviours of the two sisters as contrasting. Rena continues:

The literary spotlight now shifts to Mary. She responds to the presence of Jesus quite differently than her sister. Unlike Martha, she falls weeping at Jesus' feet. Her initial statement (11:32) is almost identical to her sister's (11:21) but no meaningful dialogue follows. Jesus elicits no confession comparable to Martha's. In fact, after her opening statement, Mary stands closely identified with her mourning compatriots. One wonders why Martha is not included in the group, especially in the summary statement (11:45). Perhaps it is simply because the readers knew Mary better. But maybe John wants to separate the two sisters because they represent two different types of faith. Martha offered her confession without a sign. She qualified for the benediction later pronounced before Thomas (20:29b). Martha models a confessing faith superior to that of her sister, the surrounding mourners, and even Thomas on Easter.[158]

Turid Karlsen Seim's analysis of John 11 cites Brown's arguments regarding the importance of Martha's confession. She then comments,

> it is significant that the confession precedes the miracle. Before the miracle itself takes place, she has through the conversation reached a clarification and understanding that has the effect of making the miracle almost superfluous. Martha believes even before she has seen. The miracle comes as a total surprise to her (v.39); her reaction against Jesus' order to remove the stone shows this very clearly. The actual raising of Lazarus is an addition mainly aimed at the people—and Mary?—standing by (11:42 and 12:9ff).[159]

The similarities between Martha's confession and that of Peter have also been explored. In Elisabeth Moltmann-Wendel's words,

> Jesus responds to Martha's stubborn, passionate faith that he is no ordinary person with the revelation of himself, "I am

the resurrection and the life ... ", and Martha responds with a confession of Christ which stands out as a special climax in the New Testament: "You are Christ, the Son of God, who has come into the world." At most this can be compared with Peter's confession of Christ in Matthew 16.16. Thus John placed the confession of Christ on the lips of a woman, a woman who was known for her openness, her strength and her practical nature. This is a confession of Christ which takes similar form only once more in the other Gospels, where it is uttered by Peter. For the early church, to confess Christ in this way was the mark of an apostle. The church was built up on Peter's confession, and to this day the Popes understand themselves as Peter's successors. However, we must conclude from this story and this confession that Martha is also a leading personality, like the apostles in the early church.[160]

Elsewhere, Moltmann-Wendel suggests that Martha's testimony moves beyond those of Peter and the other disciples. It includes a final addition, absent from all other confessions in John and the entire New Testament: an acknowledgement of Jesus as "the one who is coming into the world."

Now "the one who is coming into the world" is a statement which Jesus often makes about himself in the Gospel of John. He is the light that has come into the world ... The woman takes up Jesus' testimony to himself and in so doing achieves an immediate nearness to him that no other witness to Christ has subsequently achieved. The contrasts which she addresses here could not be greater: on the one hand God—on the other hand the divided cosmos. God hands himself over. The light shines in darkness. God enters the world. Martha makes this statement when she has experienced Jesus as the one who is light in the darkness, who gives life in death and the pains of death: warmth, nearness, hope. She does not make this statement when everything is back to normal and her brother is alive again. She makes it when nothing but the presence of Jesus is the light in her own darkness.[161]

Obviously, Martha's confession, which has long been over-shadowed by that of Peter, deserves to be heard and to be taken seriously.

Martha as Disciple

Discussion of Martha's confession of faith, and the comparison of Martha and Peter, inevitably leads to the consideration of Martha's role and importance in the early church. In her comments on Martha's testimony, Elisabeth Schüssler Fiorenza repeats a number of elements evident in the assessments of others:

Martha, after receiving the revelation and expressing her faith in Jesus' word, goes and calls Mary (11:20), just as Andrew and Philip called Peter and Nathanael. As a "beloved disciple" of Jesus she is the spokeswoman for the messianic faith of the community. She confesses, however, her messianic faith not in response to a miracle but in response to Jesus' revelation and challenge: "Do you believe this?" Her confession parallels that of Peter (6:66-71), but is a christological confession in the fuller Johannine messianic sense: Jesus is the revealer who has come down from heaven. As such it has the full sense of the Petrine confession at Caesarea Philippi in the synoptics, especially in Matt 16:15-19. Thus Martha represents the full apostolic faith of the Johannine community, just as Peter did for the Matthaean community. More importantly, her faith confession is repeated at the end of the Gospel in 20:31, where the evangelist expresses the goal of her/his writing of the Gospel: "but these are written that you may believe that Jesus is the Christ, the Son of God, and that believing you may have life in his name."[162]

She goes on to suggest that

if Robert Fortna is correct that this summary statement concluded the signs source,[163] then it might be possible to conjecture that the evangelist deliberately put these words of his/her source into the mouth of Martha as the climactic faith confession of a "beloved disciple" in order to identify her with the writer of the book. Such a suggestion is not inconceivable since we do not know who the writer of the Gospel was.[164]

As Schüssler Fiorenza notes, this conjecture that Martha may have been the author of the gospel usually attributed to John can neither be proven nor disproven historically. However, it remains an intriguing possibility.

For Schüssler Fiorenza, both Martha and Mary are disciples: Martha is the spokeswoman for the messianic faith of the Johannine community, while Mary is the one who articulates the right praxis of discipleship. Adeline Fehribach accepts Schüssler Fiorenza's conclusions as "a valid interpretation for a reader of the twentieth or twenty-first century" but suggests that "a first-century reader would not have interpreted them in exactly this way."[165] Fehribach approaches the Gospel of John from a historical-literary perspective and argues that the primary purpose of women in the fourth Gospel is to support the portrayal of Jesus as the messianic bridegroom. She concludes that a first-century audience would have perceived Mary of Bethany symbolically as the "betrothed/bride" of Christ on behalf of the Jews. This would automatically make her sister and brother members of Jesus' family within the literary structure of the story.

> ... when Jesus raises Lazarus, it is not just anyone whom he raises from the dead. Jesus raises from the dead a brother of his betrothed/bride, a member of his own extended family, a member of the family of God. In this respect, Mary of Bethany, as betrothed/bride of the messianic bridegroom, represents the community of faith whose "brothers" will see eternal life and Martha of Bethany represents the [Johannine] community of faith in her profession of faith.[166]

Fehribach's overall assessment of the Martha-Mary material in John is that it does not present a positive view of women:

> ... both Mary and Martha are marginalized after they have fulfilled their respective literary roles. First, Mary is marginalized by the shift in focus to Martha, and then Martha is marginalized by Jesus' rebuke and later by the narrator's portrayal of her as one who serves the meal in Jesus' honor. In this respect, Martha is returned to her conventional, subordinate female role after her brother's resuscitation. Mary, however, as betrothed/bride,

really never escapes her female function ... Female characters in the Fourth Gospel ... consistently function in accordance with patriarchal and androcentric expectations.[167]

Fehribach's work forms part of a complex and often contradictory body of recent scholarly literature that examines the issue of the position of women in the early Christian church. The Martha-Mary stories play a central role in much of this discussion. However, the focus in the majority of these studies is not specifically on the significance of Martha's confession of faith set forth in the gospel of John. Rather, the focus is on comparative textual analysis of language used in the account of Martha's service at the meal at Bethany described in Luke 10 (discussed in the previous chapter) and in the descriptions of the work of the disciples and apostles in the book of Acts, which is generally attributed to the author of Luke's gospel.[168]

Various authors have attempted to categorize this corpus of research. For example, Robert Karris suggests,

there are two lines of thought: one maintaining that Luke has a positive view of women, the other that his view of women, especially as leaders, is negative.... . In the contemporary period, it would seem that from 1970 to 1990 or so there had been a fairly wide consensus among certain English-speaking, especially North American, Roman Catholic NT scholars that Luke had a favorable view of women ... The position that Luke has a "negative" viewpoint on women commenced in the early 1980s and has been gathering enormous power since then ... How is one to adjudicate between these differing views of Luke's views of women? It is insufficient to say that one interpretation is feminist, or even radical feminist, while the other is nonfeminist, for one could reasonably argue that proponents of either position are feminist. Further, it is clear that exegetes of either persuasion are reading the same texts. It is equally clear that the cultural climate in North America and the First World in general is providing ocular equipment which previous generations did not have at their disposal. Using this equipment, scholars are now able to see and read details in the text which they may have bypassed in earlier readings. It remains to be seen, however, which view of Luke's view of women has seen more clearly the meaning of the Lucan texts on women.[169]

However, Francis Taylor Gench comments, justifiably, that branding the evangelist Luke as either the "friend" or "enemy" of women greatly oversimplifies the matter; in her view, "the truth lies somewhere in between: Luke's presentation of women is decidedly ambiguous."[170]

It is not the purpose of the present study to reassess the pro- and anti-woman arguments put forward by commentators on Luke's attitude, but rather to consider the views of Martha as a disciple that emerge from these studies. It is obvious that there is a broad spectrum of opinion evident with respect to her importance in the early Christian community.

At one end of the spectrum are analyses that show Martha as a follower whose discipleship consists for the most part in offering hospitality to Jesus and his companions. John Paul Heil begins his discussion of Jesus' meal with Martha and Mary with a reference to Jesus' instructions to the 70 (or 72, depending on the version of the text cited) in Luke 10:6-8. He notes that Martha warmly welcomed Jesus as a guest in her home after he entered Bethany on his way to Jerusalem and comments that "Martha extends to Jesus the kind of hospitality, which implies a meal, that he instructed his disciples to depend upon while on their missionary journeys (9:3-4; 10:7-8)."[171] He goes on to suggest that the Martha and Mary story

> promotes the theme of discipleship in the meal scenes. In the overabundant feeding story (9:10-17) Jesus transformed his disciples, who had been guests at previous meals (5:30-34; 6:1-5; 9:3-4), into his fellow hosts whom he miraculously empowered to serve the crowds a magnificent meal of hospitality as an additional part of their mission of healing and preaching the good news of God's kingdom (9:1-6). But in order for them to become "hosts" who serve Jesus and his disciples, like Martha, they must first become "guests," like Mary, who choose the best portion of his meal, the one necessary dish (10:42), by listening to his word about the necessity of his suffering, death, and resurrection.[172]

He concludes,

> Warmly welcoming Jesus and hospitably serving him as a disciple
> by preparing a meal for him on his way to Jerusalem, Martha
> presents all in the audience, both men and women, with a model
> for them to imitate ... Mary demonstrates to the audience the
> necessity of attentively listening to the word of Jesus in order to
> serve him properly as a disciple ... Indicating the complementar-
> ity of hearing and doing the word of God that Jesus speaks (5:1;
> 6:46-49; 8:15), Martha and Mary demonstrate to the audience
> that women as well as men can become disciples and members
> of Jesus' family, by not only hearing but doing the word of God
> (8:21).[173]

Heil infers that Martha's table service, which in his view involves simply serving a meal, reflects only in part what it means
to be a disciple. Like numerous commentators before him, he
suggests that it is not enough to be just a Martha: one must be
Mary-like as well.

Slightly farther along the continuum of opinion regarding the
nature of women's contributions in the early Christian community are studies that describe Martha not merely as a gracious hostess, but also as a wealthy benefactress. Turid Karlsen Seim notes
that

> as far as the name Martha is concerned, this text [Luke 10:38-42]
> is probably the oldest evidence of this Aramaic female name, a
> feminine form of "mar", that is, "sovereign lady," "ruling lady,"
> "lady." Thus the name helps to emphasize Martha's autonomous,
> well-off, and dominant position. She is the hospitable hostess
> who welcomes the itinerant preacher and performs herself the
> practical tasks which the visit demands. Martha is therefore a
> good example of a patroness in comfortable circumstances.[174]

She cites other New Testament passages (Roman 16:5; 1 Corinthians 16:9; Philemon 2; Colossians 4:15) that suggest women
took on the roles of householders and patrons of the community.
However, she comments that

it is not clear what this patronage further involved. Beyond doubt, the women who were materially able to accommodate the community in their house had thereby also power and influence ... [But] there was not an obvious connection between the status of patron and active leadership, and that there is no terminological evidence that *diakonia* was especially associated with this kind of leadership. Thus even if Martha is a householder exercising hospitality, she is not to be understood automatically, in a presupposed "subtext," to have been the leader of a community.[175]

Martha's service as *diakonia* was discussed briefly in the previous chapter in connection with Elisabeth Schüssler Fiorenza's analysis of Luke 10:38-42. Interpretation of the meaning of this Greek term, whose connotations are widely disputed, is key to discussions of Martha's role in the early church.

John N. Collins has conducted extensive research on the issue. In a 1998 article, he critiques the way in which various recent writers have understood the term, noting that most feminist scholars have taken a lead on *diakonia* from Schüssler Fiorenza, who recognizes this word and its cognates as technical terms for ecclesial leadership in Luke's time. In his view, however, the linguistic basis on which this assumption is made is not entirely clear.[176] He suggests that a majority of these commentators have failed to examine the implications of recent lexicographical work, including that outlined in his own book *Diakonia: Re-Interpreting the Ancient Sources*.[177] Collins himself concludes that the scene described in Luke 10:38-42 "is not and never was about ecclesial ministry. It is about the need to listen to the word of the Lord, a process exemplified here by Mary for all women and men to follow."[178]

On the other hand, Barbara E. Reid, one of the many feminist scholars influenced by the thought and methodology of Schüssler Fiorenza, cites Collins's work but maintains that the term *diakonia* does imply diaconal ministry. She writes,

The conflict represented in the [Martha-Mary] story is one that revolves around *diakonia*, ministerial service (v. 40), performed by women Christians ... this term, by the time of Luke's writing, connotes all manner of ministries, including ecclesial leadership. That there were women exercising a wide variety of ministries, including apostolic work, public proclamation, and leadership, is clear in a number of New Testament texts.[179]

She suggests that

read in the light of the disputes in Luke's day over women's involvement in certain ministries, Martha's complaint to Jesus is not about having too much work to do, but rather that she is being denied her role in ministerial service. In the phrase *periespato peri poll_n diakonian* ("burdened with much serving") the preposition *peri* has the sense "about" or "concerning." Martha is burdened *about* or *with reference to* her numerous ministerial works, not *by* or *with* them. Her distress *about* them is generated by the opposition of those who think she should be leaving them to men. A further possibility arises with closer examination of the verb *perispa_*. Although one of its meanings is "to become distracted, quite busy, overburdened," its primary definition is "to be pulled or dragged away." In other instances where the verb has this meaning it occurs with the preposition *eis* ("pulled toward") or *apo* ("pulled from"); in Luke 10:40 the word alludes to Martha's being pulled away from her diaconal ministry by those who disapprove.[180]

With respect to Martha's complaint about the fact that "her sister" does not take part, Reid comments

"Sister" was the term Christians commonly used among themselves to refer to female members. But it also carries, at times, a further connotation of one engaged in the ministry as her primary occupation (e.g., Rom 16:1; Phlm2). It is possible that part of Martha's anguish is that her sisters, former companions in ministry, have been persuaded that silent listening is the proper role for women disciples, and have left her alone in the more visible ministries.[181]

Reid's analysis leads her to conclude that the forms of *diakonia* sanctioned in the early Christian church as appropriate for women differed from those undertaken by men.[182] Martha's aspirations to participate fully in ministry are frustrated by the patriarchal constraints of her society. Reid concludes that

> the Lukan stories cannot be taught, preached, or passed on un-critically. Luke is a master story-teller and each of his episodes has a powerful identity-forming potential. But unless their patriarchal framework is unmasked and addressed head-on, preachers and teachers will reinforce, rather than challenge, their inscribed gender role divisions ... Choosing the better part would be to read with new eyes against Luke's intent.[183]

While scholars such as Reid argue that Martha, as a female disciple, was limited to certain kinds of activity, some interpreters of Luke-Acts maintain that women did, in fact, play a full and equal role in ministry. Like Reid, Warren Carter was influenced by the thought of Schüssler Fiorenza. He accepts, for example, her arguments that Martha was the head of a house church who welcomed Jesus as an equal into her home and who engaged in a *diakonia* that involved ministry and leadership in the Christian community. He refers to the similarities between the language used to describe Martha's reception of Jesus in Luke 10:38 and the language used in regard to the mission of the Seventy (10:1-20), commenting that

> Martha appears in v. 38 as an embodiment of the positive responses named through chap. 10. In *receiving* Jesus, Martha is a child of peace (10:6) who has encountered God's reign (10:9). She is not subject to the curses and eschatological warnings of 10:12-15. She has "heard" Jesus, not rejecting but accepting the one who sent him (10:16); she has "seen" God's revelation (10:21-25). She is among the blessed disciples who "see and hear" (10:23-24); she inherits eternal life (10:25) ... Martha's *receiving* Jesus signifies her commitment to Jesus' mission and to the God who sent him (cf. 9:48). She appears as a model disciple.[184]

With respect to Luke 10:40, Carter writes that "verses 38-39 highlight Martha's embracing Jesus' eschatological mission and participating in the community of the disciples of Jesus. Given this context, it is more likely that her 'distraction with much serving' pertains to this mission and community and to her particular role in them."[185] He discusses the use of the term *diakonia* in Luke-Acts, noting that "by the end of Acts, Luke's audience has encountered the noun *diakonia* eight times in contexts that concern not kitchen activity but participation with others in leadership and ministry."[186] He concurs with John Collins's conclusion that the word designates "a commissioned spokesperson or agent, a 'go-between' who ministers on behalf of God or the Christian community."[187] When the passage is considered in this context, the reason for Martha's distraction becomes clear:

> She is not distracted by her kitchen duties. Consistently with the actions of the male leaders of Acts denoted elsewhere by *diakonia*, her "much ministry" consists rather of leadership or ministry in the Christian community and on its behalf. By analogy with these uses of *diakonia*, her responsibilities include care for believers, teaching, and preaching, perhaps as a leader of a house church. Furthermore, given the naming of Mary as "sister," the presentation of her positive response to Jesus, and the importance of partnership in the other references to *diakonia* in Acts, it is reasonable to conclude, significantly, that Martha and Mary are partners in this leadership and its tasks ... Martha's "distraction with much ministry" arises, then, from difficulties in her partnership with Mary as leader ... Specifically, her complaint is that Mary has left her to minister alone (10:40b). From Martha's perspective, Mary is not pulling her weight. Martha's prayer to the Lord is the request of a disciple for the Lord's intervention to secure her sister's active participation in their partnership of ministry.[188]

Carter claims that the message in the passage is not directed towards individuals who wish to be in right relationship with Jesus but rather to Christian leaders. He continues:

> In Luke 10:41-42, the Lord responds to Martha's prayer by providing instruction about how to maintain partnership in leadership. The instruction is explicit for Martha and implicit for Mary. Jesus begins in v 41 by naming Martha's anxiety "about many things." ... Anxiety reveals false commitments and distraction

which prevent single-hearted responses to the word made in an attitude full of faith ... The good portion which Martha needs is not to prepare just one dish in the kitchen but to join Mary in listening to Jesus' teaching as a means of overcoming her distraction and regaining her single-heartedness (cf. 10:39). His word to her is not a rebuke but the answer to her prayer concerning her distraction "with much ministry."[189]

Carter concludes that Luke 10:38-42 "celebrates and affirms Martha's and Mary's ministry rather than rendering them silent and invisible," as some commentators have claimed. "Their story (which Luke alone tells) presents an instructive example of crucial aspects of the tasks of ministry and discipleship in the new community."[190]

Carter's interpretation of the Martha-Mary pericope builds on earlier work by Mary Rose D'Angelo. She had argued that Mary and Martha were in fact a missionary couple like Tryphaena and Tryphosa[191] or Evodia and Syntyche.[192] Her conclusions were based largely on an alternate textual reading of Luke 10:39:

> In most of the texts, the verse reads: " ... she [Martha] had a sister named Mary *who also* [h' *kai*] sat at the feet of Jesus." This reading suggests that both women "sat at the feet of Jesus," that is, were his disciples. The Revised Standard Version translates this verse "And she had a sister called Mary who sat ... " This translation is based upon the omission of the relative pronoun in a number of ancient manuscripts. Although the textual evidence for the omission is early and good, there are strong reasons for preferring to include the pronoun. The change from "who also" to "and she" is accomplished by the omission of a single letter, and is quite easy to explain. The expression "sat at the feet of" Jesus came to be less widely understood as an expression of discipleship, and taken as a literal description of the scene, the story made no sense if Martha also was sitting down. The reading "who also" suggests that the author of Luke still understood the story as presenting two women disciples.[193]

D'Angelo also discusses the significance of the term "sister" (*adelph'*) which is applied to Mary, and its relationship to the term "brother" (*adelphos*), both of which are used in connection with those involved in missionary partnerships throughout the Pauline corpus and which do not necessarily imply a blood relationship. From this she concludes that Martha and Mary were women missioners who lived and worked together as a pair, and who may, in fact, have been lesbian lovers. Considering the tenuous evidence on which it is based, this latter conclusion is both highly conjectural and extremely controversial.

The brief survey above has attempted to highlight the diversity of opinion evident in late twentieth-century and early twenty-first–century interpretations of Martha as a disciple of Jesus and as a member of the newly formed Christian community. In many cases the opinions expressed are speculative and reflect decidedly modern perspectives. However, as noted in the introductory chapter, the brief references to Martha that appear in the gospels of Luke and John were not all that was recorded of her in the early Christian period. Her name also appears in a number of extant gnostic and apocryphal texts; these provide additional insights into her role and importance as an early church leader.

Martha in Non-Canonical Early Literature

Gnosticism, a philosophy especially prominent in its Christian form in the second century, incorporated Jewish, pagan, and Christian elements. Different sects developed different kinds of gnosticism, although some features were common to the movement as a whole.

> A central importance was attached to "gnosis," the supposedly revealed knowledge of God and of the origin and destiny of mankind, by means of which the spiritual element in man could receive redemption. The source of this special "gnosis" was held to be either the Apostles, from whom it was derived by a secret tradition, or a direct revelation given to the founder of the sect.[194]

Bultmann, among numerous others, has discussed the relationship between John's gospel and gnosticism:

The Gnostic view of the world starts out from a strict cosmic dualism. Life and death, truth and falsehood, salvation and ruin of human life are anchored in the cosmos. In it the divine world of light and the demonic power of darkness stand over against one another. In the primeval time a part of the light fell into the power of the darkness ... In order to redeem and bring home this lost creature of the light, the good God of life sends the saving knowledge (Gnosis) into the world ... After his completed work of redemption the Redeemer ascends again and so makes a way for the elements of light that follow him ... In John Jesus descends from heaven, like the Gnostic Redeemer, to bring to men the saving message, and he returns to the Father after completing his work. In face of his word light and darkness separate themselves; before him life and death are decided. He who is of the truth hears his voice; to the blind, however, the messenger of life remains hidden.[195]

Raymond Brown's description of the Johannine Martha as the woman to whom "the mystery of Jesus as the resurrection and the life is revealed" is apt in view of the fact that a number of gnostic texts portray Martha as a recipient of the gnosis.

One of the major difficulties in assessing Martha's role in gnostic circles is the relative scarcity of source documents. Much of the gnostic spiritual teaching probably remained unwritten due to its esoteric nature and, undoubtedly, many of the texts that were compiled no longer survive. For many centuries, most of what was known of the various gnostic sects was derived from references preserved in the writings of the Church Fathers, especially Justin Martyr, Hegesippus, Clement of Alexandria, Irenaeus, Tertullian, Hippolytus, Origen, and Epiphanius. During the course of the eighteenth and nineteenth centuries, these were supplemented by the discovery of a few Coptic texts and fragments. However, it was only with the recovery of a corpus of 53 gnostic texts at Nag Hammadi in Egypt in 1945 that a reasonably substantial body of gnostic literature became available to scholars.

Extant sources suggest that Martha's reputation played a prominent role in the religious life and thought of the early centuries of the Christian era. Origen (ca. 185–ca. 254) discusses the various gnostic sects in his *Contra Celsum* and records, "Celsus notes, moreover, certain Marcellians, so called from Marcellina, and Harpocratians from Salome, and others who derive their name from Mariamne,[196] and others again from Martha" (5.62).[197]

Martha's name appears with some frequency in surviving Coptic sources. Salome, Mariamne, and Martha are mentioned in the *First Apocalypse of James* in the Nag Hammadi Codex (V, 3), a text that is thought to have been translated into Coptic in the late third or early fourth century, and that may have been written towards the end of the second century. It is also probable that older material was used in the composition of the document.[198] It describes a dialogue between Jesus and his brother James. While the full context is unclear due to missing sections in the text, James is advised by the Lord, "When you speak these words of this perception, encourage these four: Salome, Mary, Martha and Arsinoe."[199] Presumably the four are to be encouraged to provide interpretations of Jesus' teachings.

The names of these four women are also brought together twice in the *Manichaean Psalm Book*, a text originally written in Coptic and dating from the second half of the fourth century. Manichaeism, derived from the teaching of the Persian Mani or Manes (ca. 216–276), combined influences of gnosticism and Zoroastrianism. It taught that "the object of the practice of religion was to release the particles of light which Satan had stolen from the world of Light and imprisoned in man's brain, and that Jesus, Buddha, the Prophets, and Mani had been sent to help in this task."[200] In one of the Psalms of the Lord Heracleides—one of the Twelve apostles of Mani—Martha is called "a joyous servant," and it is noted that Jesus "gave life to Martha, the breath of discretion."[201]

Martha, Mary (Magdalene), and Salome appear as interpreters in one of the longest extant gnostic texts, the *Pistis Sophia*. This work survives in a Coptic manuscript dating from the late fourth century. It is divided into four sections. The first three were probably composed between 250 and 300 CE, and the fourth

in the early third century.[202] The text purportedly contains the
revelations of the risen Christ to his disciples, given in response to
their questions. Various participants in turn take part in the dialogue: Mary the mother of Jesus, Mary Magdalene, Philip, Peter,
John, Andrew, Thomas, Matthew, James, Salome. Martha comes
forward four times to comment on the revelations of the Pistis
Sophia, a female wisdom figure.[203] Although Martha's role is not
as prominent as that of her sister Mary (Magdalene), who is one
of the principal questioners and interpreters in the work, each
of her explanations is commended for its excellence: by Jesus in
Book I and by the First Mystery in Book II.

Other early sources that are not specifically identified as gnostic also suggest that Martha may have played a more active role
in the events recorded in the gospels than the canonical texts
reveal. The second Greek version of the *Gospel of Nicodemus*[204]
notes that "Martha, and Mary Magdalene, and Salome, and other
virgins" accompanied the mother of Jesus at her vigil at the foot
of the cross.[205] Another fragment, a Coptic version of a text generally known by the title *Epistula Apostolorum*, is of particular
interest. The original, now lost, is thought to have been composed in the Greek language, probably in the first half of the
second century. The content and form suggest Lower Egypt as
the likely place of origin.[206] Some of the traditions recorded in
this work may have been derived from the *Gospel to the Hebrews*, a work contemporary to the canonical gospels (i.e., late first
century) that is considered one of the most authoritative gospels
in Egypt.[207] The text purports to be a letter from the college of
the apostles, enumerated by name, to the churches of the four
regions of the world. It describes revelations of the Lord made
following his resurrection. Both the extant Ethiopic and Coptic
manuscripts record that three women came to the tomb on the
third day after the crucifixion. The Ethiopic version names them
as "Sarah, Martha, and Mary Magdalene"; the Coptic, as "Mary,
the daughter of Martha,[208] and Mary Magdalene." They did not
find the body of Christ.

As they were mourning and weeping, the Lord appeared to them and said to them, "(*Copt*.: For whom are you weeping? Now) do not weep; I am he whom you seek. But let one of you go to your brothers and say (*Eth*.: to them), 'Come, our (*Copt*.: the) Master has risen from the dead.'"[209]

The Coptic version of the text then reports that Martha, not Mary Magdalene, was the first to announce to the disciples that Christ had risen:

Martha came and told it to us. We said to her, "What do you want with us, O woman? He who has died is buried, and could it be possible for him to live?" We did not believe her, that the Saviour had risen from the dead. Then she went back to the Lord and said to him, "None of them believed me that you are alive." He said, 'Let another of you go to them saying this again to them.' Mary came and told us again, and we did not believe her. She returned to the Lord and she also told it to him. Then the Lord said to Mary and also to her sisters, "Let us go to them." And he came and found us inside, veiled.[210]

Only after the apostles touch Christ's body themselves do they understand that he had truly risen.

Such texts, although few in number, suggest that Martha, along with a number of other women, played a leading role in the church of the second and third centuries.[211] However, at the same time, other documents were being produced and circulated that downplayed the importance of women and suggested that their "proper" role was to be subordinate to men.[212] The apostle Paul, for example, acknowledged woman as equals "in Christ Jesus,"[213] but not in social and political terms: they were to "keep silence in the churches" and "be subordinate, as even the law says … For it is shameful for a woman to speak in church."[214] The pseudo-Pauline letters in the canonical gospels (I and II Timothy, Titus) stressed such anti-feminist elements in Paul's views: "Let a woman learn in silence with all submissiveness. I permit no woman to teach or to have authority over men; she is to keep silent."[215] Paul's letters to the Ephesians and Colossians, the first letter of Peter, and the non-canonical first Epistle of Clement of

Rome to the Corinthians emphasized that wives should be subject to their husbands.[216] The letters to both Timothy and Titus noted that bishops and deacons should be "husbands of one wife" and should "manage their households well."[217] As Ruether points out, the fact that such proclamations were considered necessary gives evidence that opposite practices were going on.[218] The *Apostolic Church Order*, a document containing regulations on various matters of moral and ecclesiastical practice and thought to have been composed in Egypt ca. 300 CE, reports on the events at a reputed council at which Mary and Martha were present. John reminds the council members that women had been banned from participating in the eucharist because they tended to behave inappropriately:

> Ye have forgotten, my brethren, that our Teacher, when He asked for the bread and the cup, and blessed them, saying: "This is My Body and My Blood," did not permit these [the women] to remain with us. Martha said (concerning Mary): I saw her laughing between her teeth exultingly. Mary said: I did not really laugh, only I remembered the works of our Lord and I exulted; for ye know that He told us before, when He was teaching: "The weak shall be saved through the strong."

Her argument fails and the male disciples agree that the only fit ministry for women is to "strengthen and keep vigil for those women who are in want."[219]

Unfortunately, proponents of the position that women were not fit to occupy leadership roles in the church came to prevail.

Martha as Role Model in Later Medieval Tradition

As noted in the introductory chapter, the later Middle Ages—the age of chivalry and of courtly love—witnessed a resurgence in the power and influence of women. In ecclesiastical circles and, more importantly, in popular religious tradition, there was a new emphasis on female participation.[220] Elisabeth Moltmann-Wendel has summarized these developments:

From the twelfth century onwards, all over Europe, we encounter religious feminist movements which continued down to the end of the Middle Ages. They were part of the revolutionary religious and social movements, and accorded with the trends of the time, representing a move away from previous hierarchical orders of the church and the unworldly ideals of the cloister towards a new religious life in the world. This religious life was intended to be a true discipleship of Christ, consisting in a renunciation of possessions and active love for one's neighbour. New spiritual communities arose; some, e.g. the Humiliati and the Franciscans, were integrated into the church only after the religious orders ... Women played a central and active part everywhere. Presumably they had a much more active role among the heretics, because there they had far more chance of participation. But even the communities which were accepted by the church could hardly resist the pressure of women.

Many motives prompted these new movements, but the religious unrest among women must also be seen in connection with social causes. For example, because of the high death rate among males as a result of disease and the crusades, there was a surplus of women. The rise of a monetary economy, the beginnings of industry, and the increase in city populations all altered family structures. Moreover, in southern France, where women's movements were very strong and were supported by a large number of noblewomen, changes had been made in the laws of inheritance among the nobility; in order to preserve land-holdings, daughters were barred from inheriting and formed a new class, intent on action.

Thus, more than ever before, women from every class were thrown back on themselves and sought their own purposes in life. Many travelled with the wandering preachers; others looked for firm ties outside the family.

The church had to cope with the problem of women and the flood of women who kept presenting themselves, and to look for new practical and ideal solutions. In the course of time, different forms of community life began to develop: there were both the women's communities who lived without any form of monastic order as, for example, the Beguines, and communities which had fixed rules of life, who attached themselves to the new orders. An introverted image of women was now no longer enough. The activities of women called for a new model.[221]

Martha, with her reputation for both piety and activity, had much to offer in this capacity. Her leadership abilities are abundantly evident in the medieval legends that grew up surrounding her. These qualities are made manifest in different ways: she is portrayed as a missionary, a preacher and evangelist, and as the spiritual director of a community.

Martha, the Missionary

The synoptic gospels all conclude with a reference to Christ's "great commission" to the apostles: to go out to all the world and preach the gospel message.[222] While Martha is not specifically named as one who heard this commandment and acted upon it, the interpretations of both the canonical and non-canonical texts discussed above suggest that Martha may indeed have been among the many women involved in the missionary endeavour following Christ's ascension.[223]

Of the four surviving medieval versions of Martha's life, only one, the *Vita Beatae Mariae Magdalenae*, refers specifically to Christ's final meal on earth and his ascension. The list of participants in these events is worthy of note:

On the fortieth day after His resurrection, when He was about to ascend into heaven, the Saviour wished to see again His own who were in the world, and, wishing to be seen by them, He appeared to them in the holy city while they were eating.[224] And as soon as He was seated at the table, He ate with them, so that through the act of eating He proved that He was truly in the flesh. It was thus a solemn feast of joy, the most memorable meal of all time, a worthy feast for angels and men. The Virgin Mary, his happy and glorious mother, the queen of heaven, sat at the table with the Son of God; and he whom Jesus loved before the others, John, the apostle and evangelist, prophet and virgin;[225]

also, the special friend of the Saviour and his foremost servant, Mary Magdalene; and his hostess, the most devoted Martha; and Lazarus, whom he had recalled from the dead; also Mary Cleophas, and Salome, and Joanna, and Susanna. [Each of the eleven remaining apostles are mentioned by name and epitaph.] And they were most faithful co-workers, although it was said before the passion that not even His brothers believed in Him.[226] The Son of God deigned to eat with them and afterwards reproached them for their disbelief.[227] He said: "I send the promise of my Father upon you. Remain in the city until you are clothed with power from on high.[228] For you will be baptized with the Holy Spirit before many days."[229] He imposed on them the charge to preach, first in Jerusalem, in Judaea, and in Samaria,[230] and then, when the Jews had rejected the Word of Life, to preach the Gospel to all the world,[231] promising to the evangelists the power to perform wonders of all kinds.[232] He said these and similar things, as if He were a king on his couch speaking, as a prince to His people. Then, the meal being finished, He arose. On leaving, He led his table companions outside, to Bethany on the Mount of Olives, which was a mile from Jerusalem, to celebrate the Sabbath.[233] Finally, with the queen of Heaven, her companions the Marys, the apostles and the crowd of disciples standing by, about one hundred and twenty people, He said His final farewell: "Behold I am with you, even to the end of the age."[234] And raising His hand, He blessed them,[235] and at the same time they saw Him rising into the sky, being carried to heaven. Then a luminous cloud appeared and received Him into the sky,[236] while the queen of heaven, the apostles, the beloved of God, and the companion Marys watched.[237]

In this account, Martha is specifically named among those receiving the commission to spread the gospel message. All four legendary texts note that one of Martha's first acts following Christ's ascension was to sell her possessions in order to make material provision for the disciples.[238] The *Vita Beatae Mariae Magdalenae* notes that the disciples resolved to dedicate the home of Martha, Mary, and Lazarus at Bethany as a basilica, since the Saviour himself had blessed it and visited it so often. Subsequently, Lazarus was ordained the first bishop of his own city.[239]

As the persecution of Christ's followers grew more intense, Martha was among the many who were sent into exile. While details vary in the different versions of the legend, it is generally agreed that she was sent off in a boat. The *Vita Pseudo-Marcilia*, Vincent of Beauvais, and the *Legenda Aurea* all describe it as one without sail or rudder that contained no supplies or provisions. Through divine providence Martha and her companions were led to the port of Marseille, on the southern coast of Gaul. These same three versions of the legend state that Martha, her sister, Mary, and their protector Maximinus, Bishop of Aix,[240] moved to the territory around Aix, where they engaged in preaching and miracle-working. According to the *Vita Pseudo-Marcilia*,

> the Lord gave the glorious Martha both the ability to heal all kinds of sickness and to make holy prophecies. She was physically beautiful, elegant and charming in appearance, and highly eloquent and clear in speech. Her sermons were received by kings and nobles. She succeeded in converting a greater number of people than the rest of her companions.[241]

Vincent of Beauvais records that "many thousands of people acknowledged faith in the Christian religion because of [Martha's] worthy preaching, holy way of life and all the miracles she provided, and they freely sought holy baptism."[242]

The *Vita Beatae Mariae Magdalenae* provides a slightly different account. It names Maximinus as the protector of Mary Magdalene only; Martha is said to have placed herself under the protection of Parmenas, bishop of Avignon. She, along with her maidservant Marcella and a number of other disciples—Epaphras, Sosthenes, Germanus, Euchodia, and Syntex, the supposed author of the *Vita Pseudo-Marcilia*—withdrew to Aix, in the province of Vienne. Here

> St. Martha and her companions preached the gospel of the Lord Saviour to the people in the towns of Avignon and Arles, and in the villages near the Rhone in the province of Vienne, giving testimony to the people she saw around her and witnessing publicly to what the Lord Saviour had proclaimed. Whatever she preached of divine power was reinforced with her own miracles.

When occasion demanded, she set about cleansing lepers, healing paralytics, raising the dead, and restoring the blind, mute, deaf, lame, feeble, and ill, through prayer and the sign of the holy cross.[243]

Again, it is recorded that Martha's efforts to convert the inhabitants of the region met with much success.

Martha the Spiritual Leader

Following the account of Martha's most famous miracle—the subduing of a dragon[244]—Martha settled in the area of Tarascon, near Avignon. Eventually, a community grew up around her, and a basilica in honour of the Lord Jesus Christ and the Blessed Virgin Mary was dedicated there. According to the *Vita Beatae Mariae Magdalenae*, it was Martha's own home that was so honoured. Martha's role and function within this community is of particular interest.

In their descriptions of the dispersion of the apostles, the *Vita Pseudo-Marcilia*, Vincent of Beauvais and the *Vita Beatae Mariae Magdalenae* provide long lists of the names of the bishops assigned to various cities.[245] The pseudo-Marcilia and Vincent lists, which include only the bishops of Gaul, reveal only slight differences, probably due to transmission errors. For example, Urcissinus in pseudo-Marcilia is replaced by Austregisulus in Vincent, Gracianus in pseudo-Marcilia becomes Cratianus in Vincent, Ferrucius in pseudo-Marcilia becomes Ferrutionus in Vincent, etc. The listings of bishops and their assigned cities in Gaul differs in both form and content in the *Vita Beatae Mariae Magdalenae*, and a listing of the appointment of bishops for Belgium, Germany and Spain is also included.[246] Such discrepancies can be attributed to variant traditions. However, all versions are consistent in that only males are designated as bishops. Nevertheless, the legendary Martha—despite her sex—seems to function in the capacity of a bishop and shares many of the episcopal attributes.[247]

Various "facts" support this argument. There is no indication that anyone other than Martha assumed responsibility for the spiritual oversight of the settlement at Tarascon, and the medieval legends emphasize her role as a protector. During a time of persecution, she provided sanctuary for the bishops Fronto of Périgueux and Georgius of Velay when they were expelled from their own cities.[248] Pseudo-Marcilia describes her as "a pious mother and nurse to the bishops and all believers at this time. She took care of all, like a mother hen does her chicks."[249] This imagery recalls Matthew 23:37 and Luke 13:34, where Jesus refers to himself using similar terminology.

In hagiographical literature, a confrontation between a saint and a monster is commonplace. In reviewing the medieval legends, it is noteworthy that a considerable number of the saints of ancient Gaul—particularly the bishops—are said to have experienced confrontations with a beast: Marcellus of Paris, Romanus of Rouen, Fronto of Périgueux, Laudus of Coutances, Vigor of Bayeux, Germanus of Auxerre, Paulus of Léon, Nigasius of Rouen, Emilianus of Nantes, Samson of Dol, Tugdualus of Tréguier, Veranus of Cavaillon, Gaugericus of Cambrai, Lupus of Bayeux, Vitonus of Verdun, Audoenus of Rouen, and Julianus of Le Mans, to name but a few.[250] This phenomenon raises some important questions regarding Martha. In conquering the dragon of Tarascon, she fulfills what appears to have been a prerequisite for Gallic bishops. In addition, when confronting the dragon, Martha employs the aspergillum and holy water, items traditionally connected with a male priest or bishop and the rite of exorcism. These items commonly appear in medieval artistic representations of Martha, and serve as attributes by which she can be identified. Both legendary and iconographical material thus imply that Martha had a reputation in the later Middle Ages which was based on achievements in spheres of activity generally considered "masculine."

Martha's Witness

John's gospel presents an image of Martha that differs from that found in Luke: in John she is the one who listens to Jesus, engages in theological discussion with him, and confesses her faith. In addition, textual studies that compare the language of discipleship found in the account of the meal at Bethany in Luke 10 with that found in the book of Acts have led to a variety of conclusions regarding Martha's importance in the early Christian church.

Unfortunately the canonical gospels tell us little more of this aspect of Martha's character. However, extant apocryphal and gnostic literature suggests that Martha—a woman of great strength and conviction—did indeed play a prominent role in church tradition in the early centuries of the Christian era. Memories of this tradition survived into the later Middle Ages, when legends arose which portrayed her as a missionary and spiritual leader. She occupied a position of authority and performed with great renown ecclesial functions traditionally associated with men. The Martha described in these legends provided an extremely positive role model for women in the later Middle Ages, and she offers many lessons for modern women as well.

The medieval legends also present another side of Martha. She is cast in roles more often associated with her sister, Mary: those of the contemplative and the penitent. This facet of her character will be discussed in the next chapter.

4

Martha the Contemplative

She devoted herself diligently to prayer and supplications.
She was always attentive to heavenly things, never shelter on earth.
Her body was on earth but her mind turned towards heaven.
(*Vita Auct. Pseudo-Marcilia,* trans. D. Peters)

A major problem with much of the exegetical literature on Luke 10:38-42 is its tendency to see the protagonists as "types"—in particular, as representatives of "contemplation" and "action." Consequently, it is common to think of Martha and Mary in these terms. As noted in a previous chapter, these "types" are frequently pitted against one another. On the other hand, other interpreters have concluded that the goal of the Christian life should be the integration of the qualities of Mary-like spirituality and Martha-like service.

An examination of the late medieval images and legends of Martha shows that at this time she herself was considered the embodiment of both qualities.

Martha's Spirituality

It is obviously unreasonable to think of Martha as solely concerned with activity. The simple fact that she carries out the task of preparing and serving a meal for what may have been a large number of people shows her to be thoughtful and organized. In addition, it is unlikely that her confession of faith in John 11 was a spontaneous outburst. Her theological discussion with her Lord reflects an awareness and understanding of contemporary Jewish concepts of the resurrection. Both early Christian and later medieval literature attest that Martha's actions—preaching, healing, miracle-working—were rooted in her deep-seated faith.

The literature also describes Martha as one for whom prayer, meditation, and contemplation of the divine were of vital importance. Meister Eckhart[251] considered Martha to have achieved within herself the perfect balance between concern for things temporal and for things eternal. These same qualities are also evident in late medieval artistic representations. For example, the altar paintings in the church in Teifenbronn, created by Lucas Moser about 1431, emphasize Martha's spiritual maturity. In one, Martha is shown in the rudderless boat with Mary, Lazarus and Maximinus. While Mary and the men converse in an animated manner, Martha prays for deliverance. Elisabeth Moltmann-Wendel comments that "Martha is the quiet, tranquil centre in contrast to the over-dramatized Mary Magdalene and the men, who seem somewhat ridiculous and almost superfluous."[252] In another work, Martha is portrayed as a wise virgin and Mary Magdalene as a foolish one. In Moltmann-Wendel's words, "This was a reversal of all previous values. In this way Martha became the woman who attained new recognition and a new sense of her own worth."[253] A few years later, around 1440, the Dominican artist Fra Angelico produced his painting of Christ in the Garden of Gethsemane for the Convent of San Marco in Florence. Here Martha appears with Mary in an antechamber nearby. While Mary reads, Martha is fully alert, keeping prayerful vigil while the male disciples sleep. Her posture echoes that of her Lord. She is the woman who remains faithful during Christ's darkest hour, when all others seem to have forsaken him.

The Life of Austerity

The twelfth- and thirteenth-century legends of Martha are closely linked with those of her sister, Mary, traditionally identified with Mary Magdalene in the Christian West. All versions of these stories emphasize the austerity of the lives of both women after their arrival in Provence.

The Provençal legends surrounding Mary Magdalene show close links with what Magdalen LaRow has described as the "hairy hermit" legends[254]—stories of the hermits of the Egyptian deserts in the fourth and fifth centuries who practised extreme forms of self-discipline as a means of gaining spiritual insight. The most famous of the fourth-century female anchorites was Mary of Egypt.[255] A number of the elements from the story of this other "penitent prostitute" came to be incorporated into Mary Magdalene's life history. According to the later medieval versions of her life, for example, that found in the *Legenda Aurea*, Mary Magdalene spent her last 30 years engaged in solitary reflection:

Blessed Mary Magdalene, wishing to devote herself to heavenly contemplation, retired to an empty wilderness, and lived unknown for thirty years in a place made ready by the hands of angels. There were no streams of water there, nor the comfort of grass or trees: thus it was made clear that our Redeemer had determined to fill her not with earthly viands but only with the good things of heaven. Every day at the seven canonical hours she was carried aloft by angels and with her bodily ears heard the glorious chants of the celestial hosts. So it was that day by day she was gratified with these supernal delights and, being conveyed back to her own place by the same angels, needed no material nourishment.[256]

Contemporary medieval artistic images of the saint often show her clothed in nothing but her long, flowing hair.

The description of Martha's life at Tarascon following the dragon incident is likewise modelled on the experience of the desert ascetics:

After many petitions of the people, St. Martha stayed on there in that country [Tarascon], with the permission of her former master Maximinus and her sister Mary Magdalene. As long as she lived she continued her fasting, vigils, and prayers. What labours, what anguish, what hunger, how many persecutions, how many troubles and sorrows she endured there! Who can estimate the cost? For in the first seven years she ate the roots of raw grasses and the fruits of the trees and the foliage of trees and mushrooms, and they were better to her than a platter of food. Afterwards a community of brothers and sisters came to stay with her, and a great basilica was built in honour of the holy Christ and the blessed Virgin Mary. Martha lived a harsh life there, avoiding meat and all fat, eggs, cheese and wine. She ate only once a day. In the winter she customarily wore a cloak of sheepskin, and in summer a tunic and cloak with goat skin next to her flesh. She went barefoot and wore a turban of camel hair on her head. A belt made of horse hair intentionally tied in knots was around her waist, and often worms came out of her broken and rotting flesh. Stretching out on tree branches or vines, with a stone under her head, she slept on a hair shirt. She devoted herself diligently to prayer and supplications. She was always attentive to heavenly things, never shelter on earth. Her body was on earth but her mind was turned towards heaven. A hundred times a day and as many times at night she bent her knee to the earth in prayer.[257]

At the same time, Martha was ever mindful of those around her:

> She was powerful in all the virtues of faith, hope, and charity. She was always notable for the hospitality which she had practised at Bethany: customarily her table was filled with strangers and guests. Her mouth did not cease from divine praises; frequently the works of her hands were enjoyed. Often she stayed at home with those around her. Often she went to the towns and cities and villages nearby to spread the divine word to the crowds of people. The words which she spoke produced miracles. When she placed her hand on the listeners, they received the Holy Spirit. When she placed her hand on the sick, they received the Holy Spirit. When she placed her hand on the sick, they were made well. Acting in this way, Martha was loved by God and favoured among men. How many thousands of people were converted and baptized through her exhortations to faith in Christ is too long to describe in detail.[258]

The legendary Martha neglects neither the things of God nor the well-being of others. Indeed, she emerges as a much more fully rendered figure than Mary.

Martha, the Penitent

In the descriptions of Mary Magdalene's life in the later medieval legends, the reason behind her ascetic lifestyle is revealed: she is a penitent, seeking forgiveness for her wrongdoings. According to her legend, a priest who had set up a cell near Mary's grotto witnessed her ascent to heaven and fearfully approached her.

> He therefore invoked his Savior's name and called out "I adjure you by the Lord, that if you are a human being or any rational creature living in that cave, you answer me and tell me the truth about yourself!" When he had repeated this three times, blessed Mary Magdalene answered him: "Come closer, and you can

learn the truth about whatever your soul desires." Trembling, he had gone halfway across the intervening space when she said to him: "Do you remember what the Gospel says about Mary the notorious sinner, who washed the Savior's feet with her tears and dried them with her hair, and earned forgiveness for all her misdeeds?" "I do remember," the priest replied, "and more than thirty years have gone by since then. Holy Church also believes and confesses what you have said about her." "I am that woman," she said.[259]

The legends of Martha are of particular interest: while she lives the life of a penitent, no sin is ever attributed to her. In fact, her purity and virtue—from her childhood onwards—are emphasized. Yet, as death approaches, it is recorded that she sees a crowd of evil spirits hovering about her, holding up a list of the evil deeds she has done; she prays that God will not be mindful of "the transgressions of [her] youth and ignorance."[260] Her action serves as a reminder that "all have sinned and fall short of the glory of God."[261] Even those who have led what is considered an exemplary life are dependent upon God's divine forgiveness.

Martha's Deathbed Visions

The legendary accounts of Martha's final year record several visionary experiences. These represent the climax of a life of meditation and receptiveness to the divine presence. As was mentioned in Chapter 1, the time of her death was revealed to her "by the spirit of prophecy" a year in advance.[262] Then, on the eighth day before her death, "Martha heard choirs of angels bearing the soul of her departing sister, Mary Magdalene, into heaven."[263] Finally, as she lay on her deathbed,

behold, the blessed Martha saw her sister Mary Magdalene coming to meet her, holding in her hand a torch from which she relit all the lamps and candles in the place. Scarcely had the one finished calling the other by name when her pious Guest [Christ] appeared and said to her: "Come, my beloved hostess, leave the prison of the flesh and cross over to my palace in heaven, where I will receive you as my guest, and where I am, O my servant, you will be with me.[264] You received me in your home and I will receive you in my heaven. Once I gave my consolation to the desolate, and I will not take it away from you after your death. For love of you, I will hear those who come to your tomb in devotion, complaining bitterly of their need. At when she was about to turn back, quivering, He said: "Stand fast, I will come to you." Hardly were these words spoken when the Lord and Mary disappeared from that place.[265]

The following day, "the distinguished hostess of Christ crossed over into the joy of the angels, where she rejoiced and praised without end her good Guest, the Lord Jesus Christ."[266] In this final reversal of roles, the one who entertained Christ as a guest in her home during her lifetime becomes a guest in his heavenly mansion after her death.

Martha the "Contemplative in Action"

A number of the modern commentators who have attempted to "rediscover," "resurrect," or "re-vision" the Martha/Mary story suggest that in order to derive an adequate role model from the text, the stereotypes the two sisters represent need to be conjoined to create a single Martha/Mary figure who incorporates the positive aspects of both women. For example, as a meditation by a New Zealand pastor suggests,

> Sometimes our faith requires us to be silent like Mary; to think to study, to pray, to learn. At other times, like Martha, we are called to a more active expression of our faith; to even undertake heroic feats for the sake of the gospel. Sometimes the gospel calls us to be pacifists, sometimes activists. Neither one is better than the other ... What is God's call on your life at this time? Do you need to draw on the studious learning of Mary, or the courageous activism of Martha ... or both?[267]

Or, in the words of theologian Dorothy Soelle,

> We have to learn that we need not choose between contemplation and action ... We need not divide the world into doers and dreamers, into gentle, listening, self-surrendering Marys on the

one side and pragmatic, busy Marthas on the other. We need both Mary and Martha, for in fact we ourselves are both sisters.[268]

However, the Martha of medieval legend needs no help in providing a role model for the woman of faith. She has been described aptly as a "contemplative in action,"[269] one whose personal godliness issues forth into loving concern for other's needs.

One of the many ways in which Martha's concern for others was made manifest was through the performance of miracles. This aspect of her character will be explored in the next chapter.

5

Martha the Miracle Worker

*Whatever she preached of divine power
was reinforced with her own miracles.*
(*Vita Beatae Mariae Magdalenae*, trans. D. Peters)

Miracle stories fall into one of two categories: the ordinary, and the fantastic or far-fetched. The former involves rather commonplace situations in which the miracle-worker brings about a totally unexpected outcome. The latter describes highly improbable situations that are believable only when considered through the eyes of faith: for example, the surviving of beheadings or other horrific mutilations. The medieval legends of St. Martha present examples of both types of miracles.

Martha's "Ordinary" Miracles

Most of the miracles attributed to Martha take the form of healings. It is noted that "when occasion demanded, she set about cleansing lepers, healing paralytics, raising the dead, and restoring the blind, mute, deaf, lame, feeble, and ill, through prayer and the sign of the holy cross."[270] Her healing powers continued to be felt from beyond the grave; many came to her tomb and were cured of their illnesses. Reputed to have been among them was Clovis, the first king of the Franks.[271]

One of Martha's healing miracles is described at some length in the *Vita Pseudo-Marcilia*, the *Vita Beatae Mariae Magdalenae*, Vincent of Beauvais's *Speculum Historiale*, and more briefly in the *Legenda Aurea*. This is the account of the healing of a young man who drowned while attempting to come to hear Martha's preaching.

The distinguished disciple of Christ was near Avignon, before the city gates, in a pleasant place beside the Rhone River, preaching and healing the sick who were brought to her. A young man who was on the other side of the river saw the crowds of people listening to the holy one, and he wanted to see and hear her. Having no boat, but enthusiastically eager to cross the river, he began to swim, naked. Then he grew weak in the middle of the river, after encountering a swift current in the raging river. He was carried off and submerged in the depths. To be brief, many came together to help and all that day the citizens searched for him with their boats, but he was not found. On the second day, about nine o'clock, the lifeless body of the youth was discovered and was placed sorrowfully at the feet of St. Martha. Then the maidservant of Christ, her heart moved, informed the people that she would prostrate herself over him and call upon God, asking that He, in His omnipotent strength, would deign to raise the boy from the dead. She prostrated herself in prayer next to the body in the form of a cross and interceded, saying: "Adonai, Jesus Christ, who in your holy and ineffable mercy once raised my brother Lazarus, your beloved, from the dead; who holds the keys to life and death; who commands death and makes it flee; who calls the dead to life: most bountiful Lord, look upon the prayers and supplications of your servant and those standing around, and order the spirit to return to the corpse of this young man, so that those at hand and in the future who see and hear of the greatness of your excellent judgement will believe in you and follow you as their Saviour." Having finished this prayer, the maidservant of Christ rose from the ground, took the young man by the hand, and said: "In the name of the Lord Jesus Christ, O young man, rise up from the dead and resume living." And immediately the boy rose up, healthy and unharmed, and was baptized in the name of the Holy Trinity.[272]

A second "ordinary" miracle of Martha is described in the *Vita Pseudo-Marcilia*, the *Vita Beatae Mariae Magdalenae*, and by Vincent of Beauvais: the changing of water into wine.

The great renown of the most holy Martha and the most sweet odour of her good reputation, like the odour of ripe fields blessed by the Lord,[273] inspired the love of all the souls of the provinces to faith in Christ and in the servant of Christ, throughout all the provinces of Gaul, and especially in Vienne, Narbonne and Aquitaine. Her most holy sister Mary Magdalene, held in great reverence, rejoiced with her and congratulated her, as did the most holy archbishop Maximinus, her protector and the overseer of her contemplative life, who proceeded to go from Narbonne, the second province of Vienne, to Tarascon, in order to see and to speak with the servant of Christ. At the same time, archbishop Trophimus of the city of Arles and bishop Eutropius of Orange both arrived at Tarascon with the same intent and desire, on the same day and hour. None of them suspected the arrival of the others, yet they arrived at the same time, through the inspiration of God, who arranges all things agreeably. The sacred heroine received them with honour, served them with generosity, and urged them to remain. On the sixteenth day from the calends of January, which is the seventeenth day of the month of Casleu, which is called December among the Latins, they dedicated to the Lord Saviour as a basilica the home of St. Martha, famous for her miracles and her virtues and distinguished by her holy way of life. After the dedication of the shrine, when the bishops approached the dinner table, St. Martha served them, with her usual admirable love. Many were gathered together around the table. The wine ran short, so the hostess of the Lord Saviour ordered water to be poured in the name of Jesus Christ and drunk abundantly by all. And when the bishops at the banquet tasted it, they observed that the water was changed into excellent wine. Therefore the bishops established by common decree that the day should be celebrated each year, on account of the dedication of the basilica and the miracle of the changing of water into wine.[274]

The nature of these miracles is particularly noteworthy. First, they are in keeping with Martha's character as revealed in the gospels, where she shows both concern for the physical well-being of others and skill as a hostess. Second, these events parallel miracles ascribed to Christ in the New Testament. In her prayer to raise the young man from the dead, Martha refers to the raising of her brother, Lazarus. Her call for the boy to rise up echoes Christ's calls to Lazarus,[275] to the son of the widow of Nain,[276] and to the daughter of Jairus.[277] Similarly, the story of the conversion of water into wine brings to mind John's account of the miracle that took place at a wedding feast at Cana.[278] Martha's life is presented in the medieval texts as an exemplum for others; she in turn models her life on that of Christ, and her actions imitate his.

Martha's "Fantastic" Miracle

To the modern mind at least, the most extraordinary of Martha's miracles is that resulting from her encounter with the dragon of Tarascon.

There was at this time on the banks of the Rhone between Arles and Avignon a huge dragon, the front half of which was shaped like an animal and the rest of the body like a fish. It killed many passersby who encountered it. It also slew asses and horses, and submerged boats which crossed the Rhone. Therefore great armed crowds of people often came wishing to slay it, but it concealed itself in the river by the forest. It was larger than an ox, longer than a horse, and had the head of a lion. Its teeth were like sharp swords, its mane like a horse. It had a sharp ridge along its back like a pickaxe, hairy scales, six feet, claws like a bear, and a tail like a snake, and was fortified with two twisted plates, one on each side. It could not be killed when attacked by javelins or any kind of arms. It had so much strength that twelve lions or as many bears could neither equal nor conquer the huge cruel beast. None of the inhabitants of that region for some distance could conquer or kill it. They heard reports of the distinguished deeds which the Lord performed through St. Martha and they came to her, humbly asking that she visit their country and free them from the ruinous dragon which bothered them very much. The compassionate saint set out for the designated place, confident in the strength of the name of Christ to drive out the dragon. However, she found it in the forest leaning over a man whom it had just killed, prior to devouring him. The hostess of Christ was unafraid and approached, sprinkling the holy water which she had brought with her on the evil beast and holding out the sign of the cross. The dragon became so weak and stupid that it did not succeed in going forward or showing any fierceness. Thus it stood overpowered, like a sheep, having no strength. Without delay the holy one bound it with her own belt, while all wondered at this victory. Immediately it was overpowered with spears and stones by all the people. This dragon was called Tharascurus by the inhabitants, and afterwards the place was called Tharascurus [Tarascon]. Previously it was called Nerluc, that is "black forest," because it was dense and dark and black there. This dragon of which we speak was considered of the lineage of that which is called Leviathan in Job and had come down by sea from Galatia in Asia, a descendant of Leviathan, a most ferocious aquatic serpent, and of the animal called the Bonachus.[279] The Bonachus was an animal which originated in the region of Galatia, and which drove away its attackers with burning dung which it shot out like an arrow over the range of almost an acre, and everything which it touched was burned as if by fire.[280]

This story so captured the popular imagination that the dragon became the most common attribute of Martha in medieval artistic representations.

Martha is one of two female saints popular in the later Middle Ages whose attribute is a dragon. The other is Margaret of Antioch, who reputedly lived in the early fourth century, during the reign of the Emperor Diocletian. After rejecting the advances of the prefect Olybrius, she was denounced as a Christian, tortured, and imprisoned. While in prison, the devil appeared to her in the guise of a dragon. According to one version of the legend, she made the sign of the cross and the monster vanished. According to another, more picturesque, tradition, Margaret was devoured by the dragon but escaped when she pierced its abdomen with a holy cross. In artistic portrayals, Margaret is generally shown with a dragon and a cross. However, in the surviving versions of the Martha legend, the cross is also an instrument by which the miracle is performed, and in the *Vita Beatae Mariae Magdalenae*, only the cross—and not the holy water—is mentioned. Thus it is possible that some works identified as images of Margaret because of the presence of the dragon and the cross are, in fact, intended to be portraits of Martha.[281]

The legend of Margaret describes an individual's confrontation with the forces of evil, represented by a dragon. Martha's battle is of a more complex nature, and in its basic outlines has more in common with that of the most famous dragon-slayer of the Middle Ages, George of Cappadocia.[282] Both Martha and George face a dragon that has terrorized the countryside and against which the general populace is powerless. Both arm themselves with the cross and with prayer before battling the beast. In the Martha legend, the saint herself subdues the dragon by binding its neck with her belt. George, on the other hand, strikes the monster with his sword and then instructs the princess who was to have been the dragon's next sacrificial victim to bind its neck with her girdle.[283] In both legends, the people are terror-stricken, but the saint calms them and invites them to be baptized. At this point in the Martha legend, the people slay the beast, while in the George legend, it is George himself who kills the monster. In both legends it is noted that a great basilica is built on the site in honour of the Blessed Virgin. Subsequently, Martha continues to serve the poor and needy in that place, while George moves on to other adventures after distributing among the poor the reward money given to him. It is because of the similarities between the two legends that Martha is sometimes called a "female St. George."

The theme of a confrontation with a dragon or other monstrous beast is common in the folklore and mythology of most ancient societies. Consider, for example, the numerous Oriental legends, the Babylonian tale of Marduk and Tiamat, the Greek myths of Apollo and the serpent of Delphi, or Heracles and the Hydra. The legend of St. George and the princess may have been rooted in the Greek story of Perseus and Andromeda. In Judeo-

Christian tradition, the serpent of Genesis 3 was the instrument that brought about the downfall of humanity. This serpent came to be identified with the "great dragon, actually the Devil or Satan" who had battled Michael and his angels and been cast out from heaven.[284] The Scriptures also make several specific references to the sea-serpent known as Leviathan, the name given to the progenitor of Martha's dragon.[285] It is recorded that on the day of his judgement the Lord will "punish Leviathan the fleeing serpent, Leviathan the twisting serpent ... the dragon that is in the sea,"[286] and that God alone has the power to combat Leviathan's strength.[287]

Dragons and monsters, particularly sea monsters, were seen as symbolic of evil, sin, and paganism in many forms. Iconographically, they appear in different contexts. From the fourth century certain passages from the Psalms—including 74:13-14, which refers to "the breaking of the heads of the dragons in the waters"—were incorporated into the baptismal liturgy. As a result, dragons often appear in baptismal scenes, where their watery abode represents the chaos and death from which the baptized emerge triumphant.[288] The snake or dragon is also sometimes introduced into Crucifixion scenes, with the cross resting on the beast or Christ's blood dripping onto it: this emphasizes Christ's victory over death and the fulfillment of the curse placed upon the serpent in Genesis 3:15.[289] For similar reasons, the serpent may appear in scenes of Christ's resurrection.

Confrontations between saints and monsters occur frequently in hagiographical literature. These monsters might be specifically identified as a guise of Satan or the forces of evil, as in the Margaret of Antioch legend, or generally understood to have such connotations—as in the legends of Martha and George. Such encounters occur, for example, in the legends of the apostles Philip and Matthew; of popes Sylvester and Leo IV; of bishops Donatus of Epirus and Clemens of Metz; and of numerous lesser saints such as Briocus, Theodore, Mevennus of Brittany, and Beatus of Switzerland.[290] With respect to the Martha legend, it has already been noted that a considerable number of the saints of ancient

Gaul are said to have confronted a fierce beast, and that such an act seemed almost a prerequisite for Gallic bishops.[291]

Contemporary Assessments of Martha the Dragon-Tamer

In recent years, the legend of Martha and the dragon has been rediscovered by a number of theologians.[292] In most scholarly studies, the dragon/serpent imagery is examined from a feminist perspective. According to this line of thought, the serpent is not seen as something intrinsically evil but rather as symbolic of the earth and the forces of nature. Its capacity to shed its skin is interpreted as a sign of regeneration and rebirth. In the traditions of many ancient cultures, the serpent is associated with mother goddesses. Similarities between the medieval cult of the Virgin and characteristic devotion to pagan goddesses have been noted by many historians: Mary is omnipotent, omniscient and immortal, and she functions in the roles of saviour, protector, and promoter of fertility.[293] As has been shown, the legendary Martha fulfills similar roles.[294]

Elisabeth Moltmann-Wendel has suggested that there may be a number of specific links between the origins of the Martha legends and the ancient matriarchal subcultures:

> First, there may have been influences from Egypt, where dragons, snakes, and crocodiles were regarded as holy and protected for much longer than in patriarchal cultures.[295] Second, there is the possible influence of the spiritualist group called the Cathari ... Conceivably the Cathari had feminine concepts of God. As with other Neoplatonic systems and various medieval sects, there may have been feminine emanations of the Deity such as Sapientia (Wisdom), Fides (Faith), and Justitia (Justice). Third, the phenomenon of dragon-taming with holy incense is reminiscent of the great goddesses of the Mediterranean area who used poppy as a drug [to tame dragons] ... A fourth possibility—which seems to me important and also never recognized before—is that the Martha tradition is connected to the Celtic cult of the mother deity. Just as the Celtic spring goddess Bridget was changed

into the Saint Brigitte and the *Matres* (Mother) cult in southern France occurs again in the cult of the three Marys, it also appears that the Martha cult contains within it elements of a Celtic cult veneration of a goddess. There are several reasons for saying this. First, according to the original French legend, retold in the nineteenth century by the Romantic poet Frédéric Mistral, Martha strikes water at a springhead.[296] This is the typical function of a locally venerated Celtic spring goddess. Second, Martha's unusual way of dealing with the dragon is reminiscent of the goddess, who, for a long time among the Celts, remained the mistress of the animals, birds, bears and snakes … Third, the word Martha, from a purely linguistic point of view, is linked with the surviving *Matres* or *Matrae* cults, which in the fifth century were already widespread and often integrated into Christian traditions. These cults were syncretistic venerations of three goddesses, a Celtic tradition supportive of women … Fourth, an oft-recurring addition to the *Matres* cults is cake or bread. In accordance with these medieval concepts, Martha feeds with bread, whereas Mary feeds with milk. Fifth, and finally, one of the oldest depictions of Martha—Martha at the grave of Lazarus, from the twelfth century, at Autun—shows Martha with neither bread nor dragon nor keys but instead with her arms raised and bent. According to Erich Jung, this is the posture of both blessing and ruling, taken mainly by goddesses and gods.[297]

Moltmann-Wendel also provides an interpretation of the Martha story—one heavily influenced by Jungian thought. She compares it with that of St. George:

The new element in the Martha legend is that it is not a man here who is armored, armed, a hero, a soldier, who conquers the dragon: it is a woman. Another new element is that the victory is friendly, without violence. Martha conquers the dragon by spiritual means, without weapons, without armor, and in bare feet, and binds the dragon with her girdle, the sign of purity in a patriarchy and the symbol of eros and power in a matriarchy … In the matriarchal consciousness the dragon is a source of power which is in bondage; it represents elements that are unconscious, driving and impassioned—all of which are positive and are to be integrated into human existence … To make it understandable for us personally, and to put it in modern terms, the dragon is what we fear and therefore hate and normally try to suppress. The other, non-violent way to get along with our fear is to integrate it, to accept it as part of our personality.[298]

Or, as Moltmann-Wendel states elsewhere, in the Martha legend "a woman symbolizes the victory over the unconscious, death, the threat, and she has conquered the dragon in a new way. She has not trampled it down, but bound it. Martha marks the symbolic beginning of another way of dealing with evil: not its annihilation but its redemption."[299]

Such an interpretation is obviously contemporary. It may be considered theologically controversial by some. Yet it does present an example of how the legends of a medieval saint can present new insights into human nature and an enduring model of the empowered woman. In the words of theologian Dorothy Soelle,

> I always think of [Martha] when I see the strong women of my generation who act unflinchingly and struggle against the dragon that controls us. They have broken openly and unequivocally with the racists in South Africa; they stand in front of the big stores and they talk with the people in the little shops on the corner; they call on the bank directors; they say loudly and unambiguously what they think. In these groups of women who for years have been organizing the boycott, "Don't buy the fruits of apartheid," I see a lot of Marthas together, just as in the women who put a girdle around the other big dragon who lives in the Pentagon and began to act against it. That is the Martha whom Meister Eckhart saw, the one the people of southern France pictured as a dragon-slayer, who, according to folk legend, crossed the sea with her sister Mary in order to teach and to preach.[300]

Martha, the ancient heroine, continues to serve as an inspiration for women of conviction, such as the activists described by Soelle who seek to change the world at large. She also provides a model for those who aim simply to restore peace and harmony in everyday life. Rosemary Radford Ruether states,

> Perhaps we might think of Martha, the dragon-tamer, as the type of good pastor, politician, or homemaker who does not respond to conflicting forces with military might or crusades to annihilate the other by force, but rather uses persuasive reason to win the others into friendship. How much better our world would be today if we had more such Marthas, more dragon-tamers and less crusading warriors![301]

Pastor Maureen Ryan makes a similar point in her whimsical retelling of the Martha legend, *An Alternate Strategy for Dealing with Dragons* (to be read with an Irish brogue!):

Now this you understand did not happen in my mother's time nor in her mother's but happen it did and it happened here in the County Galway. There was a village, hard by the Atlantic, where silver fish jumped into the nets and the cows gave nothing but pure yellow cream morning and night but not a smile would you see, walking the length of the street. And that on account of the dragon living under the mountain time out of mind and he with a terrible hunger for virgins.

The villagers thought they would contact St. George to seek his help, but "hadn't fame gone to his head entirely and without they gave him silver pennies and gold coins and himself on a page in the Book of Kells he wouldn't come next or nigh them." However, the priest announces that he has heard St. Martha is in Dublin and the villagers seek her out. They ask if she would be willing to come to their aid, and after helping them with the washing up, Martha goes off to find the dragon. She addresses the beast:

"Did you ever hear tell 'twas wrong to kill?" says she.

"Would you ever tell them to stop hating me? says he.

"I will," says she, "If you'll love your neighbour as yourself and turn the other cheek." Then doesn't she see the blood trickling down the self-same cheek. "Well, the creature!" says she. "Would you look at them scales. Like a thousand in-growing toenails all yellow and crusty, cutting into your poor body every second of the day. Why wouldn't you be roaring?" And with that she rolls up her sleeves and it was out with the rags and oil and she polishes each scale till it's as soft as the leather on the shoes of the Archbishop above in Dublin. And, as she oiled, she sang the Agnus Dei and, as she sang, didn't the dragon roll over on his back with his four scaly little legs waving in the air and purr!

After a few days the villagers came visiting. Some stayed "to polish a scale or two," while others brought silver fishes and milk for the dragon

till the day came when he himself would fly down to the village to pass the time of day as civil as you like. Then it got that he'd be there on wash day to heat the river with his breath and he'd burn the furze on the bog for them too. He'd heat the young ones' curling tongs and give them grand rides round the mountain on his back till they'd mount up with wings like eagles.

"Isn't he a pet after all?" they said. And weren't they terrible glad that St. George had stayed across the water and that St. Martha didn't have a sword at all?[302]

Ryan's message is obvious: Martha's way, which focuses on kindness and understanding, is much more effective in "dealing with dragons" than violence and confrontation.

Martha and the Virgin Mary

In considering the implications of the Martha/dragon imagery, it should be noted that two other prominent female figures were associated with the serpent or dragon in later medieval Christian thought. The first was the woman in Revelation 12—often interpreted as a personification of Ecclesia, the Church. The second is the Virgin Mary, who, on the basis of the interpretation of St. Bonaventure and others, is sometimes identified with the woman of Revelation 12.[303] Mary is likewise often depicted standing over a serpent or dragon. In this guise she is recognized as both Ecclesia and as a second Eve, predestined to bring about the redemption of humanity, which was lost due to the actions of the first Eve described in Genesis 3.[304] This imagery may also have been derived more directly from the words of Bernard of Clairvaux, who called Mary "the conqueror of dragons."

The notion of a cross-identification between Martha and the Virgin will be explored more fully in the next chapter.

6

Martha the Church

St. Martha, the follower of Christ, is considered a type
of the holy Church because of her piety.
(*Vita Pseudo-Marcilia*, trans. D. Peters)

It was earlier suggested that in order to fully appreciate Martha, it is necessary to move beyond traditional stereotypes that depict her as someone whose life and actions are at best acceptable but on the whole not worthy of commendation. Previous chapters have explored various activities and symbols associated with Martha. At this point it is useful to examine a little known stereotype of Martha that reflects the fully developed character described in canonical and non-canonical texts and in the late medieval accounts of her life. This is the image of Martha as the Church.

Origins of the Image

The Martha/Church linkage can be traced back many centuries. Specific reference to Martha in this context appears in what is probably the earliest of the medieval versions of her life, the *Vita Pseudo-Marcilia*, dating from the early to mid-twelfth century. It begins with the following comments:

St. Martha, the follower of Christ, is considered a type of the holy church because of her piety, and her life would require a great volume for the understanding of its mystical sense. Therefore we will write briefly of the declarations of the Gospel regarding her distinguished life, forgoing discussion of her as reflecting types, in order that an extended account of her life will not be distasteful to readers or onerous to the memory of hearers, but rather that it may be an exemplum for pious imitation for the minds of the faithful.[305]

Despite the author's proclaimed intention not to dwell on Martha's typology, a number of later passages suggest how and why Martha can be seen as representative of the Church.

The roots of this image of Martha are probably even more ancient. In the later fourth century, Ambrose of Milan wrote of a woman who symbolized the church in his treatise *On Penitence*.[306] This woman was the one described in Mark 5:25-34:

A great crowd followed [Jesus] and thronged about him. And there was a woman who had had a flow of blood for twelve years, and who had suffered much under many physicians, and had spent all that she had, and was no better but rather grew worse. She had heard reports about Jesus, and came up behind him in the crowd and touched his garment. For she said, "If I touch even his garments, I shall be made well." And immediately the hemorrhage ceased; and she felt in her body that she was healed of the disease. And Jesus, perceiving in himself that power had gone forth from him, immediately turned about in the crowd, and said, "Who touched my garments?" And his disciples said to him, "You see the crowd pressing around you, and yet you say, 'Who touched me?'" And he looked around to see who had done it. But the woman, knowing what had been done to her, came in fear and trembling and fell down before him, and told him the whole truth. And he said to her, "Daughter, your faith has made you well; go in peace, and be healed of your disease.[307]

In another sermon attributed to Ambrose, *De Salomone*, Christ's benevolence towards the family at Bethany is noted as follows: "Christ dried up a copious flow of blood in Martha, expelled demons from Mary and reunited the body and life spirit in Lazarus."[308] By the later Middle Ages, the identification of Martha of Bethany and the hemorrhissa was firmly established. It was included, along with the attribution to Ambrose, in some later medieval "lives" of the saint, most notably the *Legenda Aurea*:

> Eusebius, in the fifth book of the *Ecclesiastical History*, refers to a woman with a hemorrhage, who, after she was healed, made a statue in the image of Christ with a fringed garment, as she had seen Him, in her courtyard or garden. And it was greatly revered. The herbs growing up around the statue, which had previously had no power, were of such potency when they touched the fringe of the garment that they subsequently cured many illnesses. Ambrose said that this woman with a hemorrhage whom the Lord healed was Martha. Jerome relates, and it is also found in the *Tripartite History*, that afterwards Julian the Apostate took away the statue which the woman with a hemorrhage had made and put in place one of himself, which was destroyed by a bolt of lightning.[309]

However, if Jacobus de Voragine's sources are examined in more depth, his assumptions do not stand up to close scrutiny. Eusebius does record the following in his *Ecclesiastical History* (Book VII, chapter 18):

> But since I have come to mention this city [i.e. Caesarea Philippi or Paneas], I do not think it right to omit a story that is worthy to be recorded also for those that come after us. For they say that she who had an issue of blood, and who, as we learn from the sacred Gospels, found at the hands of our Saviour relief from her affliction came from this place, and that her house was pointed out in the city, and that marvellous memorials of the good deed, which the Saviour wrought upon her, still remained. For [they said] that there stood on a lofty stone at the gates of her house a brazen figure in relief of a woman, bending on her knee and stretching forth her hands like a suppliant, while opposite to this there was another of the same material, an upright figure of a man, clothed in comely fashion in a double cloak and stretching out his hand to the woman; at his feet on the monument itself a strange species of herb was growing, which climbed up to the

border of the double cloak of brass, and acted as an antidote to all kinds of diseases. This statue, they said, bore the likeness of Jesus. And it was in existence even to our day, so that we saw it with our own eyes when we stayed in the city.[310]

However, this source, written by a close contemporary of Ambrose, makes no mention of a commonly held belief at that time that the woman with the issue of blood was Martha, nor do the references to the statue in Jerome or the *Tripartite History*.[311] It is likely that the association was of late derivation; consequently, the sermon is attributed to Ambrose. Of possible relevance to their dating are legends surrounding a tenth-century St. Martha, an abbess of Mombasia in Laconia, which note that this Martha was miraculously cured of a debilitating hemorrhage after a vision of John the Evangelist.[312] It is conceivable that "Ambrose's" description of the healing of "Martha of Bethany" was derived from the story of this other St. Martha.

Martha and the Old Testament Progenitors of the Church

It is likely that the conflated image of Martha of Bethany and the hemorrhissa was known to the author of the *Vita Pseudo-Marcilia* and inspired discussion of Martha as a type of the Church. In "explaining" this typology, the author compares Martha to a number of Old Testament figures who are also seen as "types" of the Church, in that their lives and actions foreshadow pivotal people and events in the New Testament.

It is noted that Martha's hospitality "is not destined to be forgotten. For just as Abraham and Lot and Joshua and many others had pleased God and likewise welcomed angels as guests, so was the diligent and most pious hostess attentive to all."[313]

The reference to Abraham recalls Genesis 18:1-19, where the Lord, in the form of three men (or angels), appears to Abraham as he sits at the door of his tent by the oaks of Mamre. Abraham offered his visitors food and drink, and washed their feet. In return, they offered him two promises: that he would be the father of a great nation, and that the Lord would not destroy the city of Sodom if only ten righteous people could be found there. In Genesis 19:1-29, it is recorded that Lot welcomed two angels into his home in Sodom, and provided them with lodging, even offering his daughters as substitutes to a group of Sodomites who wished to rape the visitors. As a result of his actions, he was saved when the city was consumed. The reference to Joshua is less straightforward, but is likely intended to recall Joshua's reverence towards the holy visitor who confronts him in Joshua 5:13-15.

· Abraham's hospitality, and its similarity to Martha's, is mentioned again at several points. Later, in the same section of the *Vita Pseudo-Marcilia* as was cited above, it is coupled with an allusion to Job 8:7-9:

> One greater than he whom Abraham received as a guest, namely God and man; this great King of Kings and Lord of Lords, who alone encloses all in the palm of his hand; whom Job described as higher than the sky, broader than the greatest land, deeper than the sea; whom many prophets and kings wished to see and did not see, to hear and did not hear: she [Martha] received and fed this Guest.[314]

In the section of the *Vita Pseudo-Marcilia* describing the raising of Lazarus, Martha is compared to various figures from the Old and New Testaments, including, once again, Abraham and Job. While Abraham "welcomed three angels as guests, because of faith in the Holy Trinity," Martha "received into her home this God, three in one, and what is more, God and man."[315] Later in this passage, she is said to be comparable to Job on the basis of her confession of faith; in Job 19:25-26, "the blessed Job ... said 'I believe that my Saviour will rise up on earth on the last day, and even though my skin be destroyed, in my flesh I will see God,' and Martha, believing in the future resurrection, said: 'I know that my brother will rise in the resurrection on the last day.'"

A final parallel between Abraham and Martha is drawn in the section "How His Own Were Sent Away." Martha and her companions were not destined to have an inheritance in the city of Jerusalem, but in a better place; the same was true for Abraham, who was told "Leave your land and your family and come into the land which I will show you, and I will make you grow into a great nation."[316] Here it is emphasized once again that Martha has much in common with the first of the renowned Hebrew patriarchs of the Old Testament.

In line with the medieval practice of interpreting scripture in an allegorical or typological manner,[317] the angels who met Abraham were understood as a symbol of the Trinity, and their prophecy was considered a prefiguration of the Annunciation. In both the Old and New Testaments, Abraham is presented as the prototype of the faithful believer, the elect of God.[318] The story of the destruction of Sodom was seen as an Old Testament "type" of the damnation of the wicked at the Last Judgement. In addition, the New Testament describes Lot as the righteous one rescued by God from the midst of sin and idolatry.[319] Joshua, whose name is a variant of "Jesus," was considered one of many Old Testament prefigurations of Christ. As a faithful leader who brings his people to the promised land and exhorts them to serve God alone, Joshua provides a further prototype of the role of the Church. Likewise, from the early Christian period, Job was seen as both a type of the suffering Christ and a model of faith.

Martha and Peter

The similarities between the confessions of faith made by Martha and Peter were discussed at some length in Chapter 3. The author of the *Vita Pseudo-Marcilia* also draws several parallels between the two figures.

In the introductory section, it is noted that both Peter and Martha were chosen to receive special attention from Jesus:

> She [Martha] began to love the Lord, and she received him. And He who loves all, and who singled out St. Peter from all of us asking, "Peter, do you love me,"[320] He loved her so much that He preferred her home to any other lodging.[321]

Peter's name also appears in the section "How Lazarus was raised by her prayers," where the confessions of faith of Peter and Martha are said to be comparable. Elsewhere, there are references made to Peter's arrest during the persecution of the Jews following Christ's ascension and to the fact that he had personally ordained Fronto of Périgueux, the bishop who played a prominent role in the account of Martha's burial.[322]

In ecclesiastical tradition, Peter is considered to be the founder of the Church. In Matthew 16:18, he is specifically described by Christ as the rock on which the church would be built. In artistic portrayals, Peter's special attribute is a key or keys. These reflect Christ's commendation in Matthew 16:19: "I will give you the keys of the kingdom of heaven, and whatever you bind on earth shall be bound in heaven, and whatever you loose on earth shall be loosed in heaven." The same artistic attribute is also sometimes used to identify Martha.[323] According to traditional interpretations, the key is linked with Martha's "domestic" role: she is the mistress of the household, the chatelaine.

There may also be a possible link between the key and the dragon imagery since in Revelation 20:1-2, an angel holding "the key to the bottomless pit" seizes "the dragon, that ancient serpent, who is the Devil and Satan" and binds him for a thousand years. It is noteworthy in this respect that some versions of the *Legenda Aurea* refer to Peter as a dragon-tamer, if only indirectly. The account of the life of Silvester, who served the church as pope from 314 to 325 CE, includes discussion of an episode in which the emperor Constantine approaches Silvester and asks for his help in overpowering a dragon that has been killing more than 300 men a day with his breath. In modern editions of this work, it is noted that Silvester prayed for assistance "and the Holy Ghost appeared to him."[324] However, according to medieval tradition it was Peter who came to him and offered advice. For example, William Caxton's early printed edition of *The Golden Legend*, originally published in 1470, records:

> S. Peter appeared to him and said: Go surely to the dragon and the two priests that be with thee take in thy company, and when thou shalt come to him thou shalt say to him in this manner: Our Lord Jesu Christ which was born of the Virgin Mary, crucified,

buried and arose, and now sitteth on the right side of the Father, this is he that shall come to deem and judge the living and the dead, I command thee Sathanas that thou abide him in this place till he come. Then thou shalt bind his mouth with a thread, and seal it with thy seal, wherein is the imprint of the cross. Then thou and the two priests shall come to me whole and safe, and such bread as I shall make ready for you ye shall eat. Thus as S. Peter said, S. Silvester did … Thus was the city of Rome delivered from double death, that was from the culture and worshipping of false idols, and from the venom of the dragon.[325]

In the medieval mind, the key and dragon imagery were linked to the figures of both Peter and Martha. This lends further support to the notion that in the later medieval period, both were considered symbols of the Church.[326]

Martha and the Virgin Mary/Eve/ Woman of Revelation 12

In the previous chapter it was noted that dragon imagery is associated not only with Martha, but also with the Virgin Mary. In the later Middle Ages, the Virgin Mary was commonly considered a personification of Ecclesia, the Church.[327] This type of imagery came to be associated with the Virgin as a result of exegesis that associated her with both Eve and with the Woman Clothed in the Sun in Revelation 12.

Since the time of the early Church Fathers, the curse of the serpent in the Garden of Eden after the fall of Adam recorded in Genesis 3:15, a verse sometimes called the *protoevangelion* or "first Gospel," has been interpreted as the original prophecy of a Redeemer. In Jerome's Vulgate translation it reads: "I will put enmity between thee and the woman, and thy seed and her seed: she shall crush thy head, and thou shalt lie in wait for her heel."[328] As early as the second century, reference had been made to Mary as a second Eve:

He [Christ] became man by the Virgin, in order that the disobedience which proceeded from the serpent might receive its destruction in the same manner in which it derived its origin. For Eve, who was a virgin and undefiled, having conceived the word of the serpent brought forth disobedience and death. But the Virgin Mary received faith and joy, when the angel Gabriel announced the good tidings to her that the Spirit of the Lord would come upon her, and the power of the Highest would overshadow her ... And by her has He been born, to whom we have proved so many Scriptures refer, and by whom God destroys both the serpent and those angels and men who are like him.[329]

In subsequent discussions of the Virgin and original sin, this victory was seen as proof that from the beginning of creation, Mary was predestined to become the vehicle by which sin was overcome.

The passage in Revelation 12 further developed the image of conflict between a woman and a serpent/dragon:

And a great portent appeared in heaven, a woman clothed with the sun, with the moon under her feet, and on her head a crown of twelve stars; she was with child and she cried out in her pangs of birth, in anguish for delivery. And another portent appeared in heaven; behold a great red dragon, with seven heads and ten horns, and seven diadems upon his heads ... And the dragon stood before the woman who was about to bear a child, that he might devour her child when she brought it forth; she brought forth a male child, one who is to rule all the nations with a rod of iron, but her child was caught up to God and to his throne.[330]

Artistic representations of the Apocalyptic Woman are found from the ninth century onwards. In many of the early versions, she is identified only with the Christian Church. However, in eastern tradition, this Woman of Revelation 12 had been linked with the Virgin Mary as early as the fifth century; the theme was developed at some length by the Greek philosopher Oecumenius in the early sixth century. In the West, Bernard of Clairvaux applied the Apocalyptic image to Mary in the twelfth century in his *Sermon on the Twelve Stars*[331]; its implications were explored further by later writers.

The image complex that associated the Virgin Mary, Eve, and the Woman of Revelation 12—in turn derived from the association of all three with a serpent or dragon—may also bear some relationship to Martha images. For example, one of the carvings on the door of the ancient church of St. Martha at Tarascon shows a woman with a dragon at her feet.[332] It is usually described as a depiction of Martha's victory over the Tarasque, and can undoubtedly be understood as such. Much of the other imagery on the doorway, however, is derived from the book of Revelation: for example, Christ enthroned in judgement and the symbolic representations of the four evangelists as man, eagle, ox, and lion. Thus it is conceivable that the woman/beast symbolism also alludes to the passage in Revelation that, in turn, was related to the powers of the Virgin.

In the *Vita Pseudo-Marcilia*, the parallel between Martha and the Virgin Mary is related not to their common association with dragons, but to the fact that both, in different ways, offered shelter and hospitality to Jesus:

> [Martha] proved to have a common part also with the holy Virgin; for the glorious Virgin Mary received God and man in her holy womb, and Martha received God and man as a guest in her own home. The divine body of the former [Mary] nourished that which is most blessed in her holy womb; the holy hostess Martha cared for Him in her own home. He whom the one begot, the other cared for. Therefore she proved to have something in common with the divine Virgin, but they were different. Their worth is different: for the former is blessed among all women[333] and nothing is similar in worth. In her chaste virgin womb she received the Son of God. The latter [Martha] received Him devotedly in her earthly home. The former cared for a small boy, the latter a man of thirty years.[334]

Later, when describing the visit of Fronto and Georgius to Martha's home, the author of the Pseudo-Marcilia text makes no specific comparison of Martha and the Virgin Mary, but does emphasize the former's maternal qualities: she is the "pious mother and nurse" and the "mother hen who shelters her chicks under her wings."[335] The latter image brings to mind the medieval artistic portrayals of the Madonna Misericordia, in which the Virgin as Ecclesia is shown with her protective cloak spread over her people.[336] Similar portrayals of Martha also exist: for example, in the Martha church in Carona in the Tessin district of Switzerland.

Unfortunately, the richly evocative image of Martha as the Church has been largely forgotten. While its implications are explored at several points in the *Vita Pseudo-Marcilia*, the earliest of the surviving medieval lives of the saint, reference to the association does not appear in derivative texts which were likely more widely known. This symbol of Martha is not one that has been developed to any extent in later literature, although occasional allusions can be found. For example, James Martin, in his 1964 article "History and Eschatology in the Lazarus Narrative John 11.1-44," comments:

> The succeeding question of Jesus [i.e. the one following his revelation of himself as the revelation and the life] and the reply of Martha (11.26b,27) have a double reference: to the death of Lazarus and to the situation confronting the Church in the interim. "Do you believe this?" is the question of Jesus to the Church mourning her dead this side of the Parousia. Martha, representing the Church, confesses the firmness of her faith (perfect tense). In terms of John's bifocal historical vision, the confession is that of Martha herself in her bereavement, and the titular form *ho erchomenos* is meant to refer to the presence of Jesus before her. In the other historical focus Martha represents the Church and the *ho erchomenos* reflects the hope of the Parousia; it is analogous to the *palin erchomai* of John 14.3.[337]

However, Martin does not expand on the notion of Martha as a type of the Christian Church.

Martha and the Ship

One of the comparatively few ancient visual symbols associated with Christian figures or Christian themes that has survived in modern times is that of the Church as a ship. A number of the early Church Fathers and apologists, from the time of Tertullian (ca.160–220) onwards, likened the Church to a boat in which the faithful found safety and were borne to salvation. Images of Noah in the ark, thought to express this notion, are found from the beginnings of Christian art, in scenes from the Roman catacombs. In medieval art, the ship is an attribute of several saints, including Peter, the fisherman called by Christ to become a "fisher of men."[338] Even today the ship is commonly associated with the Church, in particular with the ecumenical movement and the World Council of Churches.

In this connection, the coat of arms designed for the Sisters of St. Martha in Antigonish, Nova Scotia, in the 1930s holds particular interest. A pamphlet produced by the congregation describes the crest as follows:

The Coat of Arms consists of two shields. The first bears the Constantine monogram, the most ancient symbol of Christ. The golden field symbolizes the wealth made available for mankind through the death of Christ. The color, red, is symbolic of Christ's love for St. Martha and of Jerusalem where the actual shedding of Christ's blood took place. The Jerusalem Cross surmounting this shield is a further reminder of Jerusalem's role in the drama of our redemption.

A second shield, imposed on the first, proclaims the union between Christ and the virgin [Martha]. The colors, silver and blue, indicate the virgin as the pure bride of Christ. Her shield is parted at the honor point to show she has fought against the enemy of Christ (the dragon), and conquered him by use of blessed water.

The sailless boat whose only identification is the Cross of Christ[339] symbolizes the consecrated life of a Martha, a life which can be summarized in the motto at the base of the Coat of Arms.

DEO SOLI – FOR GOD ALONE[340]

A book seeking to explore the contemporary relevance of Martha in the life of the congregation explains further that "the legend of the exile and boat trip were taken by the Sisters of Martha as a symbol of Martha's strength, arising from her faith in God, and God's guidance of her."[341]

While a boat does appear in artistic narrative scenes showing Martha's voyage to Provence with Mary Magdalene, Maximinus, and others, there is little evidence in either literature or art that the ship was ever associated symbolically with Martha in the medieval period. However, in light of the traditional links between Martha and the Church, the decision to apply this ancient symbol of the ship to Martha seems apt.

An Old Stereotype for a New Age

What does it mean to suggest that Martha can be seen as a "type" of the Christian Church. In particular, is she relevant to the Church today?

The preceding chapters examined various aspects of Martha's character. A remarkable figure emerges once one looks beyond some of the more negative assessments of her worth. She is a faithful servant of Christ who places the welfare of others above her own. Her stalwart belief, even in the face of great sorrow and adversity, never waivers. She is unafraid when facing tasks that others find daunting, since her strength comes from her absolute belief in the power and goodness of her God. She is a leader who sets an example through her combination of pious behaviour, forthright witness, and social concern. At the same time, she remains humble and ever dependent upon divine guidance. She is, in short, a woman of strength and character well deserving to represent those in the modern world—both women and men—who seek to follow God.

7

Martha and the Creative Imagination

Martha breaks down her own stereotype:
the lesser soul in its lower sphere of the workaday world.
(Mary Lou Sleevi, "Martha")

In 1573, the Italian painter Veronese was summoned before the Inquisition, charged with sacrilege as a result of certain details in his painting of the Last Supper that hung in the refectory of the Monastery of San Giovanni e Paolo in Venice. It has been recorded that Veronese responded to his accusers by stating that "painters take liberties, the way poets and lunatics do."[342]

Some of the most thought-provoking commentators on the biblical stories of Martha are not ministers, theologians, or scholars, but artists of various types. Mention has already been made of certain works of visual art featuring Martha, such as Fra Angelico's painting of *Christ in the Garden of Gethsemane*, which shows Martha in a nearby antechamber keeping prayerful vigil while the male disciples sleep.[343] The purpose of the present chapter is to examine a selection of literary reincarnations of Martha and to consider how the creative imagination serves to move beyond the biblical texts and to bring her character alive.

As noted previously, there has been a tendency among commentators on the Lukan Martha to focus on the contrast between her life of action and service and the behaviour of her more "spiritual" sister, Mary. The same focus is evident in many poetic interpretations: Martha is frequently portrayed as the stereotypical fuss-budget and complainer. For example, a poem by early nineteenth century Italian poet, Giuseppe Gioacchino Belli (1791–1863), famous for his satirical sonnets written in Romanesco, the dialect of Rome, expands upon the Lukan conversation between Martha and Jesus in his *Marta e Mmadalena*, written in 1836. Belli's Martha confronts Jesus, emphatically proclaiming that she can no longer stand her sister. Mary Magdalene occupies herself solely with rosaries, masses, and novenas, then chastises Martha when she says anything. Martha claims that she works day and night, fettered by her many cares, while Magdalene—a "painted saint"–can only be found at mealtimes. Jesus is unsympathetic. He informs Martha abruptly that Mary has chosen the better path and he refuses to provide any further explanation. Martha's retort is equally pointed. She tells Jesus she isn't convinced that he is right and that without her efforts the household would fall apart. The tone of the poem is antagonistic, and neither Martha nor Jesus is portrayed in a good light. Both come across as rude and unforgiving. [344]

The American poet Annie Johnson Flint (1866–1932) adopts a gentler manner, but still chastises Martha for her over-concern with the material:

Martha was busy and hurried,
Serving the Friend divine,
Cleansing the cups and the platters,
Bringing the bread and the wine;
But Martha was careful and anxious,
Fretted in thought and in word,
She had no time to be learning
While she was serving the Lord,
For Martha was "cumbered" with serving
Martha was "troubled" with "things"—

Those that would pass with the using
She was forgetting her wings.

On the other hand,

… Mary was quiet and peaceful,
Learning to love and to live,
Mary was learning His precepts,
Mary was letting Him give—
Give of the riches eternal,
Treasures of mind and of heart;
Learning the mind of the Master,
Choosing the better part.

Flint concludes that

Service is good when He asks it,
Labor is right in its place.
But there is one thing better—
Looking up into His face.[345]

While somewhat sympathetic towards Martha, it is clear that Flint considers Mary's way preferable.

British author Rudyard Kipling (1865–1936) recognized the irony in the traditional interpretations of Martha. Although she is considered inferior to her sister, without Martha and her heirs the necessary work of the world would not go on. Kipling's 1907 homage to labourers entitled "The Sons of Martha" presents a compassionate view of Marthas past and present:

The Sons of Mary seldom bother, for they have inherited
    that good part;
But the Sons of Martha favour their Mother of the careful
    soul and the troubled heart.
And because she lost her temper once, and because she was
    rude to the Lord her Guest,
Her Sons must wait upon Mary's Sons, world without end,
    reprieve, or rest.

It is their care in all the ages to take the buffet and cushion
    the shock.
It is their care that the gear engages; it is their care that the
    switches lock.
It is their care that the wheels run truly; it is their care to
    embark and entrain,
Tally, transport, and deliver duly the Sons of Mary by
    land and main.

    …

And the Sons of Mary smile and are blessèd—they know
    the Angels are on their side.
They know in them is the Grace confessèd, and for them
    are the Mercies multiplied.
They sit at the Feet—they hear the Word—they see how
    truly the Promise runs.
They have cast their burden upon the Lord, and—the Lord
    He lays it on Martha's Sons![346]

Kipling's is probably the best known "Martha-inspired" poem. Since 1922, it has been connected with the Ritual of the Calling of an Engineer, also known as the Kipling Ritual or the Iron Ring Ceremony, designed for students about to graduate from an engineering program at a Canadian university. This ritual was created by Kipling at the request of H.E.T. Haultain, a professor of mining engineering at the University of Toronto, who wished to improve the image of the profession by instituting a ceremony similar to that in which young doctors take the Hippocratic Oath. Kipling had long been a literary hero to engineers, on the basis of such published works as the short story "The Bridge-Builders" of 1893 and the poem "The Sons of Martha" of 1907. A description of the Ritual of the Calling on the University of Alberta Faculty of Engineering website notes that "the ritual is designed and executed in order to give engineers a strong sense of their responsibility to the public, their peers, their profession, and themselves."[347] The symbol of this responsibility is an iron ring worn on the little finger of the working hand, a symbol that these modern-day "sons and daughters of Martha" wear proudly.

It has been pointed out that many recent biblical interpreters recognize that active Marthas abound in today's society, and that it is wise to attempt to salvage Martha's reputation by "re-telling" her story in new ways. One approach has been to avoid interpretations that see Martha-like and Mary-like behaviour as contradictory and opposing paths, and to consider the sisters as representative of different facets of contemporary women. This trend is also evident in poetry. Consider, for example, "Mary, Martha, Mary: Variations on a Theme by St. John," composed in the 1940s by American Roman Catholic author John Gilland Brunini (1899-1977). It begins:

> Oh, Mary, Martha, not so bound in roles
> That Martha may not Mary be,
> Or her sister she![348]

Today's Mary will do Martha's work tomorrow. Contemplation leads to action, which in turn inspires further reflection.

British Columbia poet Susan McCaslin (b. 1947) considers the sisters from Bethany as representative of the inherent tensions in the lives of modern women:

> Martha minds the child,
> wipes rice flung on floor and cupboard,
> dances attendance on unexpected houseguests,
> keeps guard over her tongue while
> the microwave beeps—one, two, three.

> Mary is upstairs in her study
> composing poems into the personal computer—
> freeing unicorns and roses from the machine.
> They leap like sheep over a stile
> and fly out the window over suburban lawns.

> Mary and Martha battle for ascendancy
> within the woman who sits,
> rises, bears some other name.[349]

In another of her "Martha" poems, McCaslin speaks of the power that results when action and contemplation are united:

Without Mary, Martha's industry
is the social order gone mad,
its purpose blunted by routine.

Martha accusing Mary is society
threatened by the dreamer's
silken bag of essential dreams.

　...

But if Martha unites herself to Mary
light pours from the multiple heavens
into the kingdoms of the world;
And in the writing of the poem
Martha's arm curves to execute in time
the words and images danced in Mary's eye.

Then Mary rests in the household of her soul,
dreaming, brooding over fields of sleep
where Martha gathers wool and jewels

to screen them through her sieve like dust-
refracting light.[350]

In her afterword to an anthology entitled *Poetry and Spiritual Practice: Selections from Canadian Poets*,[351] McCaslin discusses the importance of mystical experiences as sources of poetic inspiration. She then speaks of the 2001 terrorist attacks in New York and Washington and goes on to ask, "What possible relevance can the contemplative poet offer a world torn by hatred and violence?" She concludes:

Contemplation, like poetry, requires scrutiny into the depths of the self. The seeds of destructiveness as well as the seeds of peace-making reside in each of us. Poets' words of healing grounded in this silence can do more than at first appears to shift the weight of the world toward peace ... Contemplation is needed as a basis for political action, since, without this ground of deepening, our acts of charity and attempts at social-political transformation can be hollow or misplaced. Many of the great mystics and saints were both contemplatives and activists. Poetry itself is both a form of contemplation and a form of action—a going inward in order to express or communicate something transformative to others.

Though both modes of authentic being (contemplation and action) may have ascendancy over each other at different times in a writer's life, the most felicitous situation seems to be when they enter into a fruitful juxtaposition ... Contemplation is not merely passive, and creative expression merely active, but both part of a dialectic in which the active and the receptive cohere.[352]

McCaslin's *A Canticle for Mary and Martha* consists of a total of 22 poems inspired by the gospel story recorded in Luke 10:38-42 and by the two women traditionally regarded as "types" of the active and the contemplative lives. In a review of the book in which these poems were originally published,[353] Michael Lythgoe notes that "To McCaslin, Mary and Martha offer models for life, for art, for the love of God ... McCaslin's compositions remind us of the higher goods, the transcendent ... Literature like this can open Christianity, or open the human heart to Christianity."[354] Clearly, the two sisters from Bethany were a source of inspiration and meaning for McCaslin,[355] and her work in turn serves as an inspiration to others.

In her 1989 poem "Martha," American poet Mary Lou Sleevi returns her subject to a biblical setting. Her inspiration is the story of the raising of Lazarus in John 11. She describes how Martha slips away from the other mourners following the death of her brother, goes out to greet Jesus—characteristically, taking a jug of water to quench his thirst—and proclaims that if he had been there Lazarus would not have died. The significance of Martha's confession of faith is highlighted:

Amid bare desolation,
blazing skies herald the encounter
between Jesus and Martha
that opened the way for God's glory to be revealed.

The Word's self-revelation
as Resurrection and Life

was made in this private moment
with just a Martha. …

Martha's spontaneous profession of faith,
perhaps the strongest in the gospels,
may have surprised her.

She sealed her faith and her future
in the Life who came Late
even then and there.[356]

Sleevi goes on to suggest that Martha's example allowed even
Jesus to be fully himself, both human and divine:

Martha showed the workings of faith
not so much by believing in miracles
but by sticking her neck out …

The assertiveness of Martha
was home-grown.
She was never passive.
She leaped
and she was fed.
She was the first in the house
to wake up in the morning
just to get a headstart on each day.

But her house was so open to the Spirit
that Jesus could be fully human,
Fully God,
at the grave of a brother.[357]

She concludes:

Martha breaks down her own stereotype:
the lesser soul
in its lower sphere
of the workaday world.
If there lived a saintly symbol somewhere
of lesser virtue,
little influence,

limited resources,
the name wasn't Martha.

She combines activism and access to God,
using her initiative
to bring them together.[358]

Like McCaslin's Martha-Mary figures, Sleevi's Martha provides within herself a model of one who combines the positive qualities of both action and spirituality.

The account of the raising of Lazarus in the Gospel of John has given impetus to some of the most moving and thought-provoking Martha poetry. In such works, the focus is most often on the dramatic moment of Lazarus's resurrection and its immediate aftermath.

British poet Ursula Wood (1911–2007), later the wife of composer Ralph Vaughan Williams, described the events of John 11 in her "Lazarus," written in the 1940s. The poem describes the situation from the perspective of the disciples and other spectators.

We waited in the quivering heat for his return.
None of us had seen a miracle before but we believed
in the man, and his accredited acts. We were not deceived.
He did return.

The sight of the resurrected Lazarus invokes a reaction that the onlookers did not anticipate:

We had thought, simply that we should all rejoice,
gathering around him, strangely unchanged by the days
he had been dead in the dark, then go on our various ways
having heard his voice.

But when he came it seemed cold as night, and we fled,
having seen fear in his terrible eyes, and great despair.
We could not break into his isolation, nor did we dare
hear what he said.

Wood's words aptly convey the sense of awe and terror that the event must have generated in the hearts of most in attendance. However, her assessment of Martha and Mary's response is disappointing:

> But his sisters stayed unguessing, being blinded with joy,
> they took his hands and kissed them, and led him inside.
> In a day or two they forgot he had ever died
> Or had changed since he was a boy.[359]

The suggestion that the raising of their brother from the dead had no lasting impact on his family seems unrealistic. Moreover, the implication that the women did not have the capacity to appreciate the significance of the scene unfolding around them is frustrating.

The "Lazarus" of American poet Edwin Arlington Robinson (1869–1935), originally published in 1920, focuses on the impact of the resurrection on Lazarus and his sisters. Many of Robinson's poems describe a topsy-turvy world in which things are not what they seem; compare, for example, his "Richard Cory," in which a man who is handsome, rich, admired, and envied by all, "one calm summer night, went home and put a bullet through his head." In "Lazarus," a man who has been given back the gift of life and restored to his family emerges as the picture of loneliness, despair, and confusion, since he has seen what lies beyond death. His sisters are terrified as well, and react to the event in ways that contradict their traditional stereotypes. Mary is the one who takes the lead:

> Mary, who felt her sister's frightened arms
> Like those of someone drowning who had seized her,
> Fearing at last they were to fail and sink
> Together in this fog-stricken sea of strangeness,
> Fought sadly, with bereaved indignant eyes,
> To find again the fading shores of home
> That she had seen but now could see no longer
> Now she could only gaze into the twilight,
> And in the dimness know that he was there,
> Like someone that was not. He who had been

Their brother, and was dead, now seemed alive
Only in death again—or worse than death;
For tombs at least, always until today,
Though sad were certain ... "Better the tomb
For Lazarus than life, if this be life,"
She thought; and then to Martha, "No, my dear,"
She said aloud; "not as it was before.
Nothing is ever as it was before.
Where Time has been. Here there is more than Time;
And we that are so lonely and so far
From home, since he is with us here again,
Are farther now from him and from ourselves
Than we are from the stars.[360]

Martha cowers in fear, while Mary takes on a maternal, protective role, saying:

If you remember what the Master said,
Try to believe that we need have no fear.
Let me, the selfish and the careless one,
Be housewife and a mother for tonight;
For I am not so fearful as you are,
And I was not so eager.[361]

There is a sense that Martha blames herself for the situation in which Lazarus finds himself:

... Tears again
Flooded her eyes and overflowed. "No, Mary,"
She murmured slowly, hating her own words
Before she heard them, "you are not so eager
To see our brother as we see him now;
Neither is he who gave him back to us.
I was to be the simple one, as always,
And this was all for me." She stared again
Over among the trees where Lazarus,
Who seemed to be a man who was not there,
Might have been one more shadow among shadows,
If she had not remembered. Then she felt
The cool hands of Mary on her face,
And shivered, wondering if such hands were real.[362]

Martha seems to recover her senses somewhat, rises up, and goes with Mary to the door. She then urges Mary to speak to their brother, to try to comfort him. In the end, neither Lazarus nor his sisters learn what it means to experience death; Lazarus suggests that it is Jesus who has gained the most insight as a result of what has happened:

"I cannot tell you what the Master saw
This morning in my eyes. I do not know.
I cannot yet say how far I have gone,
Or why it is that I am here again,
Or where the old road leads. I do not know.
I know that when I did come back, I saw
His eyes again among the trees and faces—
Only his eyes; and they looked into mine—
Long into mine—long, long, as if he knew."[363]

The biblical account of the raising of Lazarus is so well known that modern readers often forgot the impact such an event must have had on those present. Poems such as Robinson's, with their haunting imagery, inspire us to think more closely about how we respond to the momentous events in the Gospel record.

The human side of Martha, evident in poems such as Robinson's "Lazarus," is also revealed in certain works that are totally imaginative creations, not linked to the biblical accounts. Chilean lyric poet Gabriela Mistral (1889–1957, under the pen name of Lucila Godoy y Alcayaga), the winner of the Nobel Prize in Literature in 1945, highlights the close relationship between the sisters from Bethany:

They were born together, lived together,
ate together—Martha and Mary.
They closed the same door,
drank from the same well,
were watched by one thicket,
clothed by one light.[364]

She contrasts the activities of the two during their lifetimes, portraying Martha as the bustling keeper of the household and

Mary as quiet and reflective. Finally she describes the death of
Mary and the aged Martha's speechless grief:

One golden-eyed noon
while Martha with ten hands
was busy reshaping old Judea,
without a word or sign, Mary *passed on.*

... Martha went to crouch
in Mary's corner
where with wonder and silence
her mouth scarcely moved ...

She asked to go to Mary
and toward her she went, she went
murmuring, "Mary!"—only that,
repeating, "Mary!"
And she called out with such fervor
that, without knowing, she departed,
letting loose the filament of breath
that her breast did not protect.
Now she left, ascending the air;
now she was no longer and did not know it ... [365]

The two sisters, inseparable in life, are finally reunited in
death. Mistral's deeply touching portrayal of sisterly devotion
and love evokes strong emotions in her readers as well.

More unusual in theme, but no less poignant, is "Mary Passed
This Morning: Letters from Joseph to Martha," by African-Amer-
ican poet Owen Dodson (1914–1983). It consists of a series of
brief "letters" ostensibly written by the aged Joseph, the earthly
father of Jesus, following the death of the Virgin Mary. Joseph's
grief is palpable as he describes the funeral:

Dear Martha,
we laid her flat in the earth
where lilies of the valley
and poppies grew with grass;
then there was the laying on
of hands: Peter touched Mary's

face, then the disciples kissed
his hand in equal turn like prayer:
then in equal turn they bowed to me
(Judas was not there)
all the disciples bowed to me.
Mary seemed to smile.
A hallelujah crossed the air.
Some bird began to cry.
I picked some poppies and some lilies:
it was all I could do,
to sprinkle over her.
The bird wept on like a child.
We left her lying there.
Oh oh Martha.
       signed Joseph[366]

This epistolary relationship apparently went on for some time, although Martha's replies to Joseph are not included. In other "letters," Joseph reports that he is sending Martha some of Jesus' garments for Lazarus; he offers advice to Martha on how to deal with her rheumatism and arthritis; he describes his weariness as the years pass. A relationship between these two people has no basis in either the biblical record or in later legend, but it is in keeping with Martha's traditional character that this practical, hard-working, dependable woman would continue to serve as a friend and confidante to Jesus' family even after his death.

The Provençal legends of Martha have also attracted the attention of a number of poets. British writer Charles Causley (1917–2003) composed his epic "St. Martha and the Dragon" in the early 1970s.[367] Written partly in rhyme, partly in blank verse, it is essentially an extended retelling of the dragon-slaying episode found in the medieval stories of the saint. The beast has been terrorizing the countryside, and at the request of the townspeople, Martha goes forward to meet it, bearing holy water and the cross. However, in his account of the vanquishing of the dragon, Causley introduces a new element. Martha addresses the tyrant, stating that she doesn't come to "spill [its] blood or crack [its] golden spine." Instead, she wishes to prove that she is able "without sword or buckler" to win over the dragon by the power of human love. The beast is taken aback, and stands motionless while Martha sprinkles its brow with holy water and ties her horse-hair belt around its head. Her gentleness and compassion cause a tear "big as a boulder" to fall from the dragon's eye. It renounces its sins and Martha proclaims that it has been freely forgiven. The dragon then "plunged like an otter in the sounding river" and was seen no more. In Causley's version of the legend, the beast is conquered not through God's might alone, but through repentance for sin and the power of both human and divine love.[368]

Scottish-born poet Alice Major has been a resident of Edmonton, Alberta, since 1981. Aside from its title, her "Saint Martha and the Dragon"[369] bears no resemblance to the poem of Charles Causley. It consists of what she describes as five brief "monologues," each based on an episode from the saint's life. The first, "Bethany," presents a charming reminiscence of her childhood ("Mary was as happy to play house as I ... "). "The Kitchen" describes Martha's reaction to Jesus' visit to her home ("I wanted to be in there too, hearing about the crowds in restless Jerusalem. But someone had to think of dinner for those poor men who'd walked the length of Samaria"). "The Ointment" refers to the incident in John 12:1-3 where Mary pours oil on Jesus' feet ("All three of us cried out to see his cracked and blistered feet. He came so far to heal our brother and could not heal himself").

The fourth "monologue," entitled "Provence," is of particular interest. Martha is portrayed as one who grows weary of her work and seeks to escape:

That foreign country smelled of sea-mud
and salt. The years went by, wearing
their path to our door.

All the feet that came to us,
all the seekers and penitents and
visiting bishops. All the prayers
and sermons, and the mouths
that chattered and had to be fed.[370]

She implies that "the dragon" that she faces and ultimately flees is her abundance of work and her sense of responsibility for dealing with the cares of the world:

It was a great dragon winding
in and out of the house, and me alone
to feed its ever-lengthening gut.

The worm was eating up my life,
and one day, at last, I told myself
"The worms will have enough of you
all too soon."

and the bread can rise in peace.
So I came away to find a place
where the scent of rosemary blows
through my window.[371]

This image runs contrary to the usual portrayal of Martha in literature dealing with either her biblical or her legendary life. In her afterword to the collection in which the poem appears, Major writes that she "took the bare bones of biographical events and built [her] own stories around them."[372] In this case, the way in which Martha is presented diminishes her impact as a role model.

Major's effort is nevertheless admirable for her creative skill. The fifth and final monologue, "The Hermitage," is at once whimsical and moving. Major turns full circle and picks up once again the theme of Martha's relationship with her sister. She refers to the stories of Mary's life of penitence in the wilderness of St. Baume, displaying the same Celtic sense of whimsy and humour evident in Pastor Maureen Ryan's account of dragon-taming cited in chapter five:

I hear tales of Mary in the wilderness.
They say she's nourished on celestial food
and carried up to heaven daily
by angels.

And have to laugh. That's where they all
think food comes from—that magic cook-pot
in the sky. While someone else is off
chopping garlic and squeezing lemons
to sustain the heavenly illusion.[373]

However, the tone changes as Martha speaks of the harshness of her sister's life:

She lives a long way off. I visit when I can.
She is careless of herself
so I take dried fruit and strips
of fish, jars of sour-bitten plums.

Last time, I also took a balm to soothe
the rubs and blisters raised
by the rough garments she wears
so passionately and
absent-mindedly.

  ... I patted oil on her back—so slight. So
unexpectedly familiar. Words
uncoiled suddenly, a phrase
alive in my inner ear:
    My
    little
    sister

  ... Tears stung me
as if I breathed through smoke
and my throat ached
as I inhaled
the dragon's
perfumed
breath.[374]

In this final section of the poem, Major persuasively weaves together various themes that permeate the various parts: the sisterly bond, the exasperation of the sister who is left to do the work, pungent fragrances of various kinds, the ever-present demands of "the dragon." Unfortunately, however, on the whole Major's Martha comes across as a rather unwilling and unexemplary saint.

While Martha has been represented often in poetry, she also appears as a protagonist in various longer works of fiction.

The theme of two contrasting siblings—one practical, one more thoughtful and sensitive—has frequently been taken up in literature. Perhaps the best-known example is that of the Dashwood sisters, Elinor and Marianne, in Jane Austen's *Sense and Sensibility*. In some of these works the characters bear a minimal connection with the biblical sisters from Bethany, if only in the fact that the latter lend their names. For example, the titular characters in the 1925 novel *Martha og Maria* by Danish writer Johannes Anker Larsen (1874–1957)[375] have little else in common with their biblical counterparts, although Christian themes do appear in this story of two young girls growing up in post–World War I Denmark. Canadian author Veralyn Warkentin's 1994 play *Mary and Martha*[376] also considers Christian, and, in particular, Mennonite, identity in its discussion of events surrounding the closing in 1959 of the "Mary-Martha Home," a fictional Mennonite girls' home. The focus of the play is the interaction between the two sisters, Martha and Emma, who have run the home since its inception.

Martha and Mary also appear in works that bear some relationship to the biblical texts, although only with respect to certain details. For example, in British writer Marina Warner's short story "Mary Takes the Better Part,"[377] two of the principal characters are the sisters Martha and Mary. Martha is the practical one, who always comes to the rescue when Mary calls (Martha comments that Mary is "so openly hopeless, you can't fail to feel genuinely and desperately needed. And there's something pleasurable in resisting the natural resentment her demands inspire. She paints a halo round your head").[378] Mary, an art school graduate, has taken up a rather unsuccessful career as a fabric designer. The events in the story bear some similarity to the Lukan account of the meal at Bethany. Martha is asked to come and help prepare a meal for an assortment of Mary's guests. When Martha seeks Mary's help, one guest, Geraint—a decidedly unChristlike figure—echoes Jesus' words in Luke 10:41-42, telling her: "Martha, Martha, you worry too much! You worry about everything. And there's only one thing that's needed, and Mary knows it." However, the "one thing needed" in this case is "Enjoy yourself!"[379] In her analysis of the text, Mary Conde points out:

> A knowledge of the New Testament story is not essential to a reading of "Mary Takes A Better Part," but the title itself alerts the informed reader ... [The story] is an episode from Christ's life told entirely without authorial comment from Luke, unlike the parables which Christ himself told which are more rigidly attached to some explicit moral judgement.[380]

She also notes that Warner based the character of Mary on a man, and that "Warner's story has as much to do with concepts of masculine and feminine as it has to do with relationships between sisters."[381] Warner's use of the language of the Authorised Version of Luke's story "[tempts] us into the error of seeing Martha and Mary as the clichés of their respective attributes in the original, and this makes Warner's argument against the oppressions and follies of stereotyping more compelling."[382]

A story such as Warner's uses the pretext of a scriptural passage to explore ideas that have little to do with Christian spirituality. However, the Lukan and Johannine accounts of Martha and Mary of Bethany have also more directly inspired a number of examples of biblical fiction. Such works allow a broad scope for character development and provide reflection on ways in which Jesus may have been seen by his contemporaries.

In her *Martha, Martha: A Biblical Novel*,[383] written in 1960, American author Patricia McGerr suggests that certain stereotypical aspects of the characters of Martha and Mary were evident from an early age. The book begins with an account of the bar mitzvah of Lazarus at the age of thirteen. His sister Mary is eleven and described as "spoiled by her father, vain, pleasure-loving, and self-willed." Martha, aged seventeen, is described as the "little mistress of the household"; she has borne responsibility for looking after her widowed father and her two younger siblings since the death of her mother six years earlier. Throughout most of the book, Martha is portrayed as a person preoccupied with her sense of duty, someone who stubbornly insists on doing what she believes to be right. She becomes moody, bitter, and demanding when those around her fail to accept her point of view. Her behaviour results in misery in her household, and is shown to be a contributing cause to the fact that her sister, Mary, who comes to be known as Mary of Magdala, falls into immorality.

By the central section of the novel, Martha and her siblings have become followers of Jesus. However, in Martha's case, she joins the entourage not so much because she is a believer herself, but because Lazarus and Mary have become believers, and she, as the ever-attentive "mother hen," feels she must watch over them. Martha finds an ally in Judas of Carioth, a Judean like herself. These two find fault with many of the actions of Jesus and the other disciples. They see them as simple Galileans lacking in knowledge and in concern for the keeping of the Temple laws— as men who, in many respects, are unlikely candidates to serve as leaders in the Messiah's earthly kingdom. Judas comes often to visit Martha; they become "companions in discontent." Both feel they have been saddled with the burdens of management and that their contributions go unrecognized.

It is only after Lazarus's death that Martha briefly lays aside her activity and takes time to meditate on her brother's last words to her: the one thing needful in life is love. She begins to question whether her acts of service are performed as an expression of real concern for others or whether they are self-serving. When Jesus finally comes to Bethany, Martha goes forward to meet him and confesses her belief that he is the Christ, the Son of God. However, it is not until some time later, after Lazarus is restored to life and Jesus returns to Bethany to celebrate the Passover with his friends there, that Martha comes to a full realization that his word is truth.

The book concludes with an account of Jesus' passion and death, and the news of his resurrection. Mary, who has gone ahead of the other women coming to anoint the body, returns and reports that the tomb is empty. The others hurry off to confirm Mary's story. However, Martha has no need of visual proof: she remembers Jesus' words to her that he is the resurrection and the life, and that he will rise on the third day. She heads back to Bethany to begin preparations for his return. Over the course of the novel Martha develops from a person who believes in the righteousness of works to one of deep faith. In keeping with her essential character, her faith continues to be made manifest in practical service.

In her retelling of the Martha and Mary story, American writer Joyce Landorf spends little time on preliminaries. She plunges immediately into the drama. *I Came to Love You Late*, written in 1977, begins with a graphic and tension-filled account of the deathwatch for Lazarus.

Background is provided through flashbacks and reminiscences. We learn of Martha's childhood, family life, and education, that she had been married at the age of fourteen to her cousin Benjamin, and that he and her father had been killed only two months later by a runaway Roman carriage careening through the streets of Jerusalem. She enjoys a special and long-standing friendship with the disciple Andrew, who came from Capernaum, the birthplace of Martha's mother. The accounts of how the family from Bethany met Jesus, his frequent visits to their home, and even the memorable meal where Martha lost her temper and complained to Jesus in frustration about her sister are all described in retrospect.

Landorf's characterizations of the sisters from Bethany once again reflect their traditional stereotypes. Martha, age 32, is efficient and forthright; it is noted that she "had the vexing ability to speak, command, and delegate authority much like a Roman centurion."[384] However, she also has a good heart, gets things done, and has a reputation for "healing hands." She began to carry out adult responsibilities from the age of five, when her mother died giving birth to Mary, and she "became the self-appointed guardian and mother to both her brother and infant sister."[385] Mary, age 27, is the sensitive dreamer. In Landorf's retelling of the story, Mary of Bethany is not identified with Mary Magdalene, who makes a cameo appearance near the end of the book.

When she finally takes a break from her nursing duties at Lazarus's bedside, Martha vents her frustration with God for his lack of intervention on behalf of her brother. Mary, who has been absent from the death room, appears and indicates that she has spent the day in prayer. Mary feels that they should send for their friend Jesus, who has a reputation for healing, but Martha is reluctant. She claims that she does not wish to take advantage of their friendship or to put Jesus in danger. However, Mary points out that another underlying reason is that Martha does not have true faith in Jesus' power; she tells her sister: "You believe Jesus can do *certain* things, like healing people, but only up to a point or under the right circumstances. You think of Jesus as another Simeon, the magician—a person who can do *some* magic tricks, but not all. You've turned our Master into a magician, and a limited one at that!"[386]

As in McGerr's novel, a major focus of *I Came To Love You Late* is Martha's transformation from a follower who struggles to believe to a deeply committed disciple of Jesus. In the initial chapters, she is angry and bitter over Lazarus's death and rails against God, whom she feels has abandoned her. Later her anger is directed against Jesus for his failure to come to the family in their hour of need. Martha is thoroughly confused by Jesus:

> ... her exasperated thoughts kept coming. We love Jesus. He is our friend. We have asked nothing of him before. He is such a puzzling, mysterious friend ... He is godly and quite literally filled with heavenly power like the prophets of old. Yet he walks among us, eats with us, and is so amazingly human that I sometimes cannot envision him as the Messiah.[387]

When he finally does arrive following Lazarus's death, "unspoken reproach fills her soul" but "even with her dark well of thoughts, [she] gleaned a vague measure of hope" because she knows that God will grant Jesus whatever he asks. The text continues:

> She had faith in him, but it was a faith with some reservations. Mary had been right when up on the roof she had accused Martha of limiting Jesus' powers. But a change was taking place within her, and standing here, looking at what Andrew and the others called the "long-awaited Messiah," Martha's faith increased, and her thought process began a bending toward a new direction.[388]

Following the raising of Lazarus, Martha comes to a realization. She observes,

"I have admired and loved Jesus as a friend. I have served him, sometimes too diligently, but obediently, and I have believed in him. But after today's proof I find I have not loved, served, and believed him completely and wholly without reservation. I need to see that my devotion to him and my serving him must not only be done because he is my friend but because he is my Lord." The truth—the whole truth of God—began to illuminate each dark little corner of her mind. *I must serve him not out of duty alone but cheerfully, willingly, and out of love.* Her thoughts astounded her. The incredibility of knowing Jesus for the better part of three years and missing his lordship, his divine saviour-hood, his true identity poured over her soul. *How could I have been so blind?*[389]

She goes on to confess that while she does not know why she came to love Jesus so late, she does love him. She now knows who he is—her God, her King, her Saviour, and her Messiah.[390]

Subsequently, Martha's general attitude changes. For example, after Mary anoints Jesus' feet at the Passover meal in the home of their neighbour Simon,

Martha saw the whole drama played out before her with new eyes of love. Mary, with her dazzling beauty, her bell-like singing voice, and her creative hands was always the center of attention. For years, Martha was known only as "Mary's sister," and some-times, when she stopped to think about it, she felt a few shivers of resentment as they crept about in her mind. But everything inside her had changed that day at the tomb. It was as if her love for the Lord had been a smoldering, smoky ash heap that instead of dying out, had suddenly erupted into a blazing flame. She was free to love—especially Mary—as she had never been able to before … Martha found herself acquiring a surprising taste for patience, and for the first time she began to understand her desire to be of comfort to the sick and dying instead of merely applying a poultice or brewing a herbal remedy. But most of all she had discovered some brand-new characteristics in herself: like singing the song which bubbled within her, or feeling a new development which involved a risk—that was the decision to give herself in love to others. She became more tolerant of people, and to her surprise, she began to accept them as they were without imposing on them her frantic desire to change them.[391]

In an interesting side note to the account of the Last Supper, Landorf's Martha and Mary are invited by the disciple Peter to go to Jerusalem to supervise the Passover meal preparations at the home of Joseph of Arimathea. The two sisters slip away from the kitchen long enough to eavesdrop as Jesus distributes the bread and wine to his disciples and utters his final teachings to them. They realize that Jesus is actually about to die, and "their hearts are filled with sad questions and uncomfortable doubtings."[392] They return to Bethany, and two days later the word comes to them that Jesus has been crucified.

Just before daylight the next day, Martha and Mary head back to Jerusalem to complete the burial preparations. En route they encounter an injured child, and Martha reaches out to him, telling Mary she will take the boy to their home while Mary goes on to assist with the anointing of Jesus' body. As Martha tends to the child's wounds, Mary returns to Bethany with the news that Jesus is alive. Martha is at first reluctant to believe, even when Andrew and Lazarus confirm Mary's message. Confusion reigns as others come to her home to discuss the event. Finally, Martha escapes to the silence of the rooftop to ponder what she has heard, and slowly comes to understanding and acceptance.

> Quietly she said to the night. "My Jesus is not dead. He is alive."
> It was a knowledge that did not sweep over her soul with flashing joy as it had with Mary, Lazarus, and Andrew, but one that came softly and gradually. The assurance that he was alive came like an early-morning mist which glides and steals over the hillsides unnoticed by anyone. Martha didn't see it coming until the truth of Jesus' resurrection completely covered her.[393]

Some time later, Landorf's Jesus makes a post-resurrection visit to Martha in the courtyard of her home. He visits the child she has rescued from death, and tells Martha that the path which he wants her to follow is to care for little ones such as this. Jesus then disappears from her sight as quickly as he had appeared, only to reappear a few moments later. He ascends a hill near Bethany, and Martha and her household join the crowds who witness his ascension into heaven.

A variety of subsequent events are described briefly in the two final chapters of Landorf's book. Lazarus and Andrew go off on a mission to Cappadocia and Scythia. Mary marries the Roman centurion Claudius, who is a convert to Christianity, and they have a daughter. Martha becomes a surrogate mother to a variety of unwanted children who find their way to her doorstep. On the final page, Lazarus and Andrew return to Bethany, and the possibility of a romantic liaison between Martha and Andrew is suggested. However, this concluding section comes across as a not overly successful attempt by the author to tie up loose ends, and provides an anti-climactic conclusion to Martha's journey of faith.

In her 1991 novel *Martha and Mary of Bethany*, American writer Gloria Howe Bremkamp takes the same "raw materials" as those found in the works of McGerr and Landorf—the scriptural accounts of the meals at Bethany and the stories of the wedding at Cana, the death of John the Baptist, and the resurrections of Lazarus and of Jesus—and creates characters that are in some ways similar, but in others quite different. Once again, her title characters both reflect elements of their traditional stereotypes. Bremkamp's Mary, who, like Landorf's, is not identified with Mary Magdalene, is the sensitive younger sister, who enjoys solitary walks and periods of reflection. Her elder sister, Martha, is practical, outspoken, and demanding at times. It is suggested that her aggressiveness is attributable in part to stress and worry over the illness of her husband, Simon, a figure who does not appear in McGerr's novel, but who has been linked with Martha by some biblical commentators.[394] Simon and Lazarus are both silversmiths who gain much of their livelihood creating commissioned works for Herod and members of the Roman hierarchy.

Unlike McGerr and Landoft, Bremkamp does not focus on Martha's gradual evolution from skeptic to believer in Jesus. Her Martha is drawn to Jesus from the time she first hears of his powers, recognizing him as one who has the capacity to heal her husband of leprosy. The main journey towards faith described in the novel is undertaken by Simon. He refuses to see Jesus when he first comes to his home in Bethany, but Jesus assures Martha that "in his own time, he will come." Eventually, Simon is ready and he seeks out Jesus. At that point "rebellion faded to reluctance. Reluctance gave way to the greater need of healing. Tears of surrender poured from his eyes. He dropped to his knees and said, 'Lord, if you will, you can make me clean.'" His vulnerability and fear are revealed, and the power of Jesus' compassion overwhelms him. Jesus accepts Simon's confession without judgement or condemnation, and puts forth his hand to heal him. Subsequently, Simon provided constant witness to Jesus' great power.

Bremkamp's handling of the Lukan story of the meal in Martha's home is of particular interest. When Martha, overwhelmed by her work of preparation, notices Mary sitting at Jesus' feet, she is envious and tells Jesus that Mary should be helping her. When Jesus responds that only one thing is needed in life and Mary has chosen the better part, Martha is dismayed. She suggests that Jesus doesn't understand, and laments, "Obviously you've never tried to feed two dozen hungry people at the same time!" However, an odd smile crosses Jesus' face, and Martha recalls the story she has heard about how Jesus fed five thousand people with a few loaves and fish. Her anger disappears, replaced by embarrassment. Later, Martha apologizes to Jesus for her rudeness and asks his forgiveness. He replies: "You owe me nothing. But you owe yourself the freedom from resentment and jealousy. Be at peace."[395] Again, there is the suggestion that the power to change and to experience healing comes about as a result of individual choice.

The meaning of the "one thing needed" to which Jesus had alluded becomes clear to Martha only in the final chapter. Martha, Simon, Mary, and Lazarus have been forced to flee Bethany following the raising of Lazarus because their lives are in danger. On Jesus' advice, they travel to Joppa. From there, they plan to go to Cyprus, where they will be safe from the powers of the Jewish Sanhedrin and the Roman authorities. While in Joppa word is brought to them that Jesus has been crucified. Under questioning from their host, a friend of Joseph of Arimathea, Martha affirms her belief that Jesus is the Son of God and that God is eternal. She recalls Jesus' words to her, his promise that he would be resurrected just as he had resurrected Lazarus, and she "[begins] to understand what Jesus meant by the better part and how important it was to tell others about him and about the ongoing of life he represented."[396] She realizes that the "one thing needful" was belief in Jesus' teachings and in the power of the resurrected Christ.

In contrast to inspirational literature based on the gospel texts are stories that treat biblical characters or those derived from church tradition in a much more flippant and irreverent manner. Mary O'Connell's *Living with Saints* explores the parallels between various Roman Catholic saints and modern young women. One review of O'Connell's book describes it as "ten tales sure to enchant some readers and enrage others."[397] Another commentator writes,

> O'Connell creates a world in which the saints do everything from smoking to swearing to running tattoo parlors while they do what needs to be done: conferring grace on the earthbound … O'Connell's fiction reclaims the radical orneriness of these God-obsessed women. These saints aren't clever send-ups or sappy parables. No cheap laughs here, no complaints devoid of ideas for reform. Faith may have some cheesy trappings, but these trappings are exactly what hold the faith and its mysteries together.[398]

It is difficult to see how such generalizations apply to her tale of Martha of Bethany, which has been variously described as either "the least successful of the stories"[399] or "the gem in the collection."[400]

While most of O'Connell's saints are placed in contemporary contexts, her account of Martha retains its ancient setting. She describes a woman pining over Jesus:

I wanted to be the physical bride of Christ. I wanted Jesus to gaze upon me, Martha, and shudder with tormented desire. I wanted the King of the Jews to dust the disciples and spend sunny afternoons with me, gathering daisies and wild blue veronica in the bright fields north of Bethany. I wanted to stare at the face of the messiah—my Jesus!—all day long.[401]

O'Connell's Martha is a woman in love: she even sacrifices her own lamb Fuzzy for Jesus' dinner, hoping that Jesus would "reflect upon her sacrifice as he feasted."[402]

Martha's love is unrequited; indeed, Jesus goes so far as to dismiss her efforts. She asks him to tell Mary to help her with the serving, but Jesus replies:

Martha, don't bother your sister. Can't you see that Mary and I are having a conversation? She has chosen to nourish the soul, not the body ... Mary honors me greatly. You in turn, should do the same. Do you understand nothing about my teachings?[403]

Martha wakes the next morning "craving death." The sting of Jesus' rebuke leaves her feeling "in limbo, floating between despair and despair."[404] As in Patricia McGerr's novel, it is Judas who befriends Martha, offering her comfort and reassurance. He alone comes back to her home to thank her properly for the meal and criticizes Jesus for his ill manners.

In the account of the death and raising of Lazarus, O'Connell strips Martha of her words of hope and confession found in the biblical text. Mary is the one who admonishes Jesus for not coming earlier to save their brother. Jesus weeps, falls to his knees, and asks the women directly: "Do you believe I am the savior? Do you believe I am the messiah?" Both Martha and Mary reply yes, but note parenthetically that they "were mostly humoring him."[405]

The conclusion of the story deviates sharply from its scriptural sources. Judas comes to inform Martha of Jesus' death. He reports that the Pharisees planted a bag of silver coins on him "to make it look like [he] revealed him as the messiah, to make it look like an inside job."[406] He bemoans the fact that he has been made to appear a traitor. Martha and Judas run off to the anonymity of Egypt, and do not find out about the resurrection and ascension of Jesus for some time. They make a new life for themselves in Egypt, where they have two children, Sarah[407] and Ezra. Martha notes,

> We did not raise them as Christians, because to be a Christian—to follow Jesus—was to perpetually hunger for your own miracle, waiting for thrills, redemption, the bright promise. There was marvel and beauty in the waiting, but I never wanted my children to be that hungry. Jesus Christ was the folly of my vain girlhood, and as a woman, I had no use for him.[408]

Reviewers who take a positive view of O'Connell's *Living with Saints* suggest that the author's ability to exploit the humanity of her subjects allows her to reach out to contemporary readers, showing the divine at work in even the most mundane of lives. Lynda Sexson, for example, describes O'Connell's Martha as a woman inflamed by carnal desire for Jesus, saying that "the erotic and the sacred are two peas in a pod." Martha's desire was her flaw, and "Christian myth celebrates divine flaws: a broken suffering God, a virgin birth, a crowd that doesn't get the story."[409] However, this argument is difficult to follow. This Martha—who never quite overcomes her lust for Jesus, and who, like Alice Major's Martha, deals with adversity by fleeing from it—seems too human. There is little of the divine evident in her.

It has been suggested that a collection like O'Connell's is most likely to appeal to teenagers and young women who are more or less lapsed Roman Catholics—or to "those with a yen for Catholic kitsch."[410] The audience for biblical novels such as those of McGerr, Landorf, and Bremkamp consists largely of conservative Christian women. In both cases, the readership is fairly restricted. Ironically, it is probably among readers of classic detective novels, science fiction, and fantasy literature that the name of Martha of Bethany is most widely recognized.

Anthony Boucher (1911–1968), pen name for American writer William Anthony Parker White, wrote six detective novels in the late 1930s and early 1940s. Two—*Nine Times Nine* (1940) and

Rocket to the Morgue (1942)—were published under the byline of H. H. Holmes, the real-life pseudonym of nineteenth-century mass murderer Herman W. Mudgett. One of the main characters in these two novels, Sister Ursula, was created in the tradition of G.K. Chesterton's Father Brown. The sister is a middle-aged Roman Catholic nun who serves the Order of Saint Martha of Bethany. In each book, she assists her police contact, Lieutenant Terence Marshall, in solving a locked-room murder. The sleuthing nun also appears in several of Boucher's short stories from the later 1940s. Boucher's Order of Saint Martha of Bethany is described as "an order that does the dirty work." Some members are nurses, some work with the blind, many do menial housework for poor invalid mothers. The sisters salvage clothes, help to establish hostels for youth and the homeless, and "glorify God by doing even unto the least of these all the good that [they] can."[411] They take the usual triple vow of poverty, chastity, and obedience, but are not subject to canon law; that is, they are lay sisters. What is most unusual about them is that they take their vows for only a year at a time, and there is a one-day gap just before the feast of their founder, Mother La Roche, before their vows are renewed. As Sister Ursula explains, "For twenty-four hours we are theoretically free from all vows. Of course, no one ever does anything about it, but it's nice to think you could if you wanted to."[412]

American science fiction writer Poul Anderson (1926–2001) paid tribute to Boucher in his short story "Kyrie" (1968), which also features the fictional Order of Saint Martha of Bethany. The plot focuses on the reasons why his protagonist, Eloise Waggoner, joins the Order and retreats from the world. The story takes place far enough into the future that there is permanent settlement on the moon. At least one non-human intelligent race exists, and human telepaths like Eloise communicate with them. Anderson sets the stage:

> On a high peak in the Lunar Carpathians stands a convent of St. Martha of Bethany. The walls are native rock; they lift dark and cragged as the mountainside itself, into a sky that is always black. As you approach from Northpole, flitting low to keep the

force screens along Route Plato between you and the meteroidal rain, you see the cross which surmounts the tower, stark athwart Earth's blue disc. No bells resound from there—not in airlessness.

You may hear them inside at the canonical hours, and throughout the crypts below where machines toil to maintain a semblance of terrestrial environment. If you linger a while you will also hear them calling to requiem mass. For it has become a tradition that prayers be offered at St. Martha's for those who have perished in space; and they are more with every passing year.

This is not the work of the sisters. They minister to the sick, the needy, the crippled, the insane, all whom space has broken and cast back. Luna is full of such, exiles because they can no longer endure Earth's pull or because it is feared they may be incubating a plague from some unknown planet or because men are so busy with their frontiers that they have no time to spare for the failures. The sisters wear space suits as often as habits, are as likely to hold a medikit as a rosary.

But they are granted some time for contemplation. At night, when for half a month the sun's glare has departed, the chapel is unshuttered and stars look down through the glaze-dome to the candles.[413]

Interestingly, even in this intergalactic world, the life and mission of the Marthas reflect their historical roots.

It is in her role as the legendary conqueror of dragons that Martha of Bethany is most widely recognized in contemporary youth culture. Her name appears frequently on websites devoted to fantasy literature and dragon lore.[414] Martha's dragon is even better known in the fantasy world than Martha herself. The tarasque is featured in the novel *A Crewel Lye: A Caustic Yarn,*[415] part of the Xanth series by British fantasy writer Piers Anthony (b. 1934). The beast (usually spelled in this instance as *tarrasque*) also appears as a powerful and dreaded monster in the Dungeons and Dragons fantasy role-playing game. The tarasque is found in other cyber games as well, such as Anarchy Online; a similar monster, known as the Torrasque, is found in Starcraft. Aficionados of such games probably have little awareness or understanding of the connections with the legendary St. Martha, however.[416]

Having examined ways in which Martha has inspired various modern-day creative writers, the final chapter will now consider Martha's place in contemporary Christian circles: among religious orders dedicated to her, among theologians, and among the general population.

Martha Today

Therefore we ... are informed of this holy one, whose life we call to memory,
for one who is mindful of her will be remembered by God.
(*Vita Pseudo-Marcilia*, trans. D. Peters)

In earlier chapters, Martha has been put forward as a worthy role model for the contemporary church. Her potential in this respect remains largely unrecognized. For the most part, the focus of modern Christian literature is the Lukan image of Martha. Little attention is paid to the significance of the Johannine Martha, and the medieval legends surrounding her have had little general influence, due to both their relative inaccessibility[417] and to the rather incredible nature of much of their contents. For the most part, the attitude towards Martha reflected in published materials of the past few decades varies according to the constituency in which it originates.

Martha Among the Religious Orders

Within the Roman Catholic Church today, a number of religious congregations and associates around the world are dedicated to Martha and to the values she represents. Such groups can be found in Canada, the United States, and Europe, including Tarascon, France, where the Sisters continue to care for the ancient Church of St. Martha. The calling of these women lies in areas of Christian service, including work in social agencies, health care, teaching, and domestic work, especially in colleges and seminaries.

In Canada, the Sisters of St. Martha of Antigonish in Nova Scotia were formally established as a religious congregation in 1900. The women received their formation from the Sisters of Charity in Halifax. In co-operation with Saint Francis Xavier University, the sisters were involved initially in the Christian education of youth and the training of young men for the priesthood. Soon after the founding of the congregation, the Marthas were called to respond to other needs within the Diocese of Antigonish and in the dioceses of central and western Canada. In 1906, they opened their first hospital. Care of neglected and homeless children began in 1917, followed by care of unmarried mothers and, later, by family social services. Teaching in rural schools began in 1925.The group had a history of long-standing involvement with the Antigonish Movement, which began in the late 1920s under the auspices of the Extension Department of St. Francis Xavier University in Antigonish. This movement focused on adult education as a vehicle for social improvement and economic reorganization. Despite declining numbers in recent years, the sisters continue to minister in the areas of teaching, social service, and health care; the retreat centre at the congregation's mother house in Antigonish offers hospitality and the opportunity for spiritual renewal to hundreds of visitors each year.[418]

Within two decades of their founding, the Sisters of St. Martha of Antigonish also responded to a call from Henry O'Leary, the Bishop of Charlottetown, Prince Edward Island, to assist him in the establishment of a similar institute in his diocese. The Congregation of the Sisters of St. Martha of Prince Edward Island was founded in 1916 for work in the Diocese of Charlottetown. Later, work was undertaken in several parts of Canada and the United States, in addition to missionary work in Central America. Today the Prince Edward Island sisters focus on a wide variety of ministries, including both the traditional (religious education, nursing, spiritual direction, hospitality, and home making) and more contemporary concerns (bioenergetics therapy, earth ministry, arts and music, and creative self-awareness programs).[419]

Currently, Roman Catholic communities of the Sisters of St. Martha are located across Canada, including Calgary and Lethbridge, Alberta; Regina, Saskatchewan; St-Hyacinthe, Quebec; and at various centres in Nova Scotia, Prince Edward Island, and Newfoundland.

In 1986, the General Chapter of the Sisters of St. Martha in Antigonish set up a committee to engage in research designed to lead the Sisters to identify more deeply with Martha in her faith in Jesus and to formulate a comprehensive spirituality/theology of Martha. One of the outcomes of the project was the production of a book, *The Search for St. Martha*, written by Irene Doyle, CSM, which was published by the congregation in 1993. In the book's general introduction, General Superior Sister Joan Fultz writes, "Martha speaks to us, women religious in today's world of faith-filled companionship with Jesus in community for mission. She challenges us to be authentic witnesses to 'resurrection and life' as women in church and society."[420] Individual chapters briefly survey Martha's story in the New Testament, Martha in post-resurrection times and in the tradition of the church, and Martha in the experience and spirituality of the Sisters of St. Martha. One of the final chapters explores the question "Is Martha Relevant Today?"

A major emphasis in this latter section is on varying images of Martha evident in the artwork that graces the buildings and grounds of Bethany, the congregation's mother house in Antigonish. In the early 1920s, shortly after Bethany was built, a statue of Martha and the dragon was placed on the lawn. More common, however, are images from the 1930s, 1960s, and 1980s depicting Luke's Martha serving Jesus at the table, a scene that has remained dominant in the consciousness of these sisters throughout their history.[421] However, much of the discussion in Sister Irene's chapter on Martha's relevance for today focuses on a different image, one that was introduced in the 1950s and that has grown to hold increasing significance for members of the order—

that of Martha holding a jar of oil. This image is found in statuary, in paintings and on holy cards produced for the congregation.

The image of Martha with a pot of oil is somewhat unusual. In Christian art, the pot of oil more commonly serves to designate images of Mary Magdalene. In Western ecclesiastical tradition, the Magdalene came to be identified with the unnamed woman of Luke 7:36ff who anointed Christ's feet, and with Mary of Bethany. This composite figure in turn came to represent the repentant sinner.[422]

In the medieval period, Martha was identified through a number of artistic attributes, some of which have been discussed more fully in previous chapters. These fall into two categories.[423] Martha's "domestic" attributes include a cooking pot, often accompanied by a soup ladle and broom.[424] These items are clearly derived from her image in Scripture as the sister who assumes responsibility for serving guests.[425] Among Martha's more "masculine" attributes are those connected with the incident of primary importance in her legendary life in Provence: the slaying of the dragon known as the Tarasque. The dragon itself is the primary attribute in this category. However, various versions of the medieval legends note that holy water was the instrument by which the dragon was conquered; it is for this reason that a pot of holy water and the aspergillum are frequently introduced into artistic depictions of Martha.[426]

If one considers the two seemingly disparate categories of attributes that distinguish Martha, it is evident that the cooking pot/ladle and small broom and the pot of holy water/aspergillum represent images that are very similar in appearance: in fact, some items that are interpreted by art historians as cooking pots may have been intended originally as representations of pots of holy water. Louis Réau goes so far as to suggest that the identification of Martha as the patroness of cooks and housewives may have originated in "an iconographic misinterpretation," in which the bucket of holy water that she held in her hand to sprinkle on the Tarasque might have been mistaken for a household utensil.[427] It should, however, be kept in mind that the medieval viewer, accustomed to seeing symbolically rather than in concrete terms, may have considered Martha's pot as representative of her activity in two spheres, on the domestic front and in the world at large, and not one or the other exclusively.[428]

In some artistic representations, the vessel Martha holds also bears a striking resemblance to the vessel of oil more commonly associated with Mary. Sister Irene follows the lead of Elisabeth Moltmann-Wendel in interpreting Martha's vessel in this way:

> In the [medieval] cult of Martha we find an expression of people's wishes for an awareness among women of their femininity, for sovereign motherhood, and for the integrative sagacity and wisdom of the woman. The Martha of this period often has a vessel in her hand. This is the famous jar of oil, which did not really go with her but with her sister, who was thought to have anointed Jesus. However, the jar of oil has become a vessel, a symbol, of the woman. Her body is a vessel. Her implements are vessels. Martha, the "great mother," becomes the embodiment of the mature, powerful, creative woman who fulfils herself and makes her own contribution.[429]

She goes on to comment,

> It is interesting that in addition to the symbolic vessel, its contents, the oil for anointing, is considered part of the representation of Martha. The anointing of Jesus' head by an unnamed woman in the Gospel of Matthew (26:6) and Mark (14:3) is interpreted as an act pointing to his Messiahship. It would seem that this medieval image of Martha incorporates symbolic actions of other women of the New Testament associated with Jesus.

> On another level, oil is symbolic of the good works attributed to Martha in the Middle Ages. Its use is a sign of joy. Oil used in healing dates back to antiquity. In Mark 6:13 the apostles healed many when they "anointed them with oil." Commentators say, " … Anointing is not merely a medical remedy, but as in Mark (6:13) it symbolizes the healing presence and power of the Lord Jesus."[430]

Because of the broad range of associations suggested by the image of Martha with the vessel of oil, it holds significant symbolic meaning for the modern-day Sisters of St. Martha in Antigonish. It identifies a mature and caring woman, who recognizes Jesus as Lord and who uses her powers and skills for the benefit of others.

In recent years, the sisters have begun to ritualize some of their community events using Martha's jar of oil as a focal point. Sister Irene writes, "at our General Chapter in 1994, one of the Sisters acted out the role of St. Martha presenting us with the jar of oil. Each morning someone poured a bit of oil into the jar, symbolizing the oil of the day—hope, joy, healing, etc."[431]

Part of the ritual involved proclaiming various "oils of scripture."[432] Later, this Martha ritual was repeated at regional meetings. Individual Martha jars were presented to other communities, which were invited to give the jar a place of honour and to pour out its oil in celebration of consecration, blessing, healing, strengthening, and missioning. In the ritual response a vow is pronounced:

> We receive with gratitude this Martha jar
> containing the oil of our Chapter experience.
> We claim our identity as women of faith;
> We believe that the Risen Jesus empowers us;
> And so we commit ourselves, to the best of our ability,
> To live simplicity, as the core of our charism and identity,
> To respond to critical human needs,
> To live quality community life as mission and for mission,
> To respond to the call to live simplicity more visibly.[433]

Faithfulness, belief in Christ's power and his gift of empowerment, devotion to a simple lifestyle, responsiveness to those in need, a life of Christian witness—in all these things modern-day Marthas strive to follow in the footsteps of their patroness.

A contemporary Sister of St. Martha has summed up her reflections on the scriptural stories and legends of Martha in the following terms:

What struck me most about Martha was her faith. Her whole being, thought, feeling, and activity were in God ... I admired

Martha in her convictions and in not being afraid to state them.
I believe this takes a certain amount of maturity and belief in
oneself, plus inner strength and connectedness with the Presence
within ... I believe that the qualities in Martha which struck me
can also be meaningful to the Congregation as a whole. What is
more important in our service than being inner-connected, being
real, having convictions and not being afraid to profess them? ...
It is easily seen why the feminist movement of the Renaissance
chose Martha as a symbol. For this same reason, I can see how
Martha can be a source of strength to women today struggling
for their place in society and the Church.[434]

Martha and the Theologians

It is not surprising that the biblical texts, legends, and artistic
images associated with Martha of Bethany hold a particular interest for a congregation created under her patronage. In recent
years Martha has also been "rediscovered" by a number of prominent theologians, some of whose efforts have been discussed in
earlier chapters of this study.

Some writers have followed the lead of Raymond Brown, who
identified Martha as an ordained officer in the Johannine church,
as one of the first to confess faith in Christ as the Son of God,
and as a beloved disciple of Jesus, well known and respected in
the early Christian community.

A few, such as Mary Rose D'Angelo and Warren Carter, have
offered speculations regarding Martha's role as a missionary in
the early church.

Others, particularly Elisabeth Moltmann-Wendel and various
female theologians influenced by her thought, have been drawn
to the legendary Martha who subdued dragons, and have drawn
analogies between this figure and modern women who fight oppression and injustice in the church and in society.

Still others, including a number of feminist and liberation
theologians, and especially those influenced by the work of Elisabeth Schüssler Fiorenza, have found in the Martha/Mary story

support for women's full partnership in the life of the contemporary church.

Some especially interesting studies in this latter regard are those emanating from non-Western theologians and based on analysis of the biblical texts dealing with Martha found in Luke 10 and John 11. In many of these works, the stories are discussed in a developing world context, but the overall assessment of Martha is similar to that found in Western commentaries. For example, in her consideration of the Lukan story of Martha and Mary, Pakistani scholar Christine Amjad-Ali notes,

> Martha, it seems to me, has received a bad press. She is no silent serving housewife, effacing herself in the background, she is an independent woman, of some social standing. She owns her own house and she runs her own household. She is a follower of Jesus, calling him Lord, and when the opportunity arises she is ready to take the initiative so that she may have the honour of offering the hospitality of her house to the Lord.[435]

However, she then goes on to describe Martha's "faults":

> Martha takes the initiative, and against all notions of proper behaviour goes out – as a single woman – to meet Jesus – who is a single man – and then invites him back into her house … Mary's behaviour upsets her sister Martha to the point that Martha again violates the canons of good manners and bothers a guest with an internal family dispute … Abruptly, and not at all with the traditional deference a woman should show to a male guest, Martha asks, "Lord do you not care that my sister has left me to serve alone? Tell her then to help me."[436]

Jesus intervenes, but not in the way Martha expects:

> He does not quiet the family storm by restoring the traditional order and telling Mary to return to her family responsibilities and help Martha. Rather he moves from a position of tacitly supporting Mary to one of openly championing her. Instead of rebuking Mary for her dereliction of duty, he rebukes Martha. The loving use of Martha's name (Martha, Martha) softens the tone of Jesus' words and takes some of the sting out of what he

says, but nonetheless the content of his reply is uncompromising. Martha is in the wrong not Mary. According to Jesus, Martha is worried and bothered about irrelevancies and not about what is necessary. Mary, in contrast, has chosen the good part. Jesus' final words are absolute and totally unambiguous. Mary's "good part"—her claim to be a disciple on the same level and in the same way as Jesus' male disciples—will not be taken away from her.[437]

A similar point is made by Dorothy Ramodibe, a South African theologian, who writes of the oppressive structures in her society, especially with respect to women, and then comments,

Jesus treated women in a remarkable way. He was a symbol of what equality means insofar as men and women are concerned. Jesus did not see a woman's place as in the kitchen. He allowed women to sit at his feet ... Jesus encouraged women like Mary to participate in his work rather than just prepare meals (Lk 10:48).[438]

While it is not stated explicitly, Ramodibe implies that Mary of Bethany is superior to her sister, Martha, as a role model for Christian women. This conclusion can create problems. Another African theologian, Musimbi Kanyoro from Kenya, writes:

Sometimes even a "women's reading" of the Bible does not answer the questions that bother us. Take the Martha and Mary story (Luke 10:38-42; John 11:1-44). In that story we have found liberation in the affirmation by Jesus of Mary's desire for knowledge. That is good. But what about Martha? A majority of women in Africa are Marthas. We live on a continent stricken with all sorts of calamities. Hospitality and service are the true hope for the millions of starving and dying. We are a continent where more than 60 percent of women are illiterate, and no change in this seems in view. This means that for us celebrating Mary's privileged position of learning is very painful.[439]

While Western women may find negative assessments of Lukan Martha offensive, the difficulties inherent in "traditional" interpretations of the Martha-Mary story are particularly acute for women in the developing world.

Various theologians from the non-Western world have also presented positive views of Martha, based on the picture painted of her in John's gospel. Lee Oo Chung from Korea notes the similarities between Martha's confession of faith in John 11:27 and that of Peter in Matthew 16:16. Chung suggests that the former has received little attention only because Martha is a woman.[440] Ana Maria Tepedino from Brazil also acknowledges the importance of Martha's confession of faith; in Tepedino's words,

> when we reflect on Martha's reply to Jesus' revelation, we see a summary of all the christology of the Gospels: election, adoption, the incarnation. In fact, Martha's proclamation contains the whole core of faith—Jesus as the revelation descended from the heavens, the message of God so all humanity may have life.[441]

While the conclusions of these two women echo those commonly found in the texts of Western writers on John's pericope, both situate their discussions in their own cultural contexts. Both maintain that women's capacity to relate to Jesus' message and his sacrifice is a result of their closeness to the realities of their everyday lives, and that the lived experience of women in their countries is one of pain, persecution, oppression, and social injustice. This notion that women have a special understanding of suffering due to the cultural conditions under which they live appears in the writings of women theologians from across South Asia, India, and Africa.

In her book *Mary & Martha: Women in the World of Jesus*,[442] feminist theologian Satako Yamaguchi, a co-director of the Center for Feminist Theology and Ministry in Japan, re-examines the stories of the sisters from Bethany with a focus on their role in the gospel of John. She notes that

> the retelling of old stories and the telling of new stories with various cultural and contextual reflections can assist in re-visioning Christian identities. The process should not abandon our histori-

cal heritage but rather build on it, ethically transforming it in our own historical contexts.[443]

Her own "retelling" aims to "emancipate our spirituality from later doctrinal interpretations of the Bible as well as from a modern Western dualistic mind-set that exclusively identifies Western culture with the 'pure' Christian tradition."[444]

In a more recent article,[445] Yamaguchi discusses the role of women in the Japanese church and the difficulties they face. The section entitled "Women in Ministry: Meeting Martha Again for the First Time" describes Martha as one "commemorated in [biblical] stories as a woman leader figure, but marginalized, erased, and distorted into a 'kitchen woman' or 'a chided complaining woman' in the later process of biblical writing, editing, and interpretations."[446] Yamaguchi concludes that

> to restore or "re-member" into our communal memories images of biblical women leader figures that have been distorted and erased is to seek justice both for ancient and contemporary women in ministry. Our struggle to stop all kinds of discrimination against "women ministers" in our church and to build up better conditions for women ministers to work to their full potential is something for which we can claim a firm grounding in the spirituality and praxis in our Christian origins.[447]

Yamaguchi spent a number of years studying in the United States, and her work has been strongly influenced by that of Elisabeth Schüssler Fiorenza. While Yamaguchi discusses the Japanese cultural context, her methodology is based on Western feminist practice. On the other hand, the work of Ranjini Rebera, a Sri Lankan–born feminist theologian now living in Australia, has also been influenced by the thought of Schüssler Fiorenza but her methodology is grounded in South Asian tradition. In her article "Polarity or Partnership? Retelling the Story of Martha and Mary from Asian Women's Perspective,"[448] Rebera combines Schüssler Fiorenza's "hermeneutic of suspicion" with traditional Asian storytelling techniques. She comments:

My own experience in using a combination of these two methods to release women from androcentric interpretative processes has been both challenging and exciting. The process I use incorporates elements of all four stages of Schüssler Fiorenza's framework—suspicion, remembrance, proclamation, and creative actualization. It is, however, in the last stage of being able creatively to identify with the women in the biblical story by placing them side by side with our own experiences and identities that the participants in workshops have obtained the greatest degree of inspiration and learning.[449]

Rebera describes her experiences in developing workshops with other Asian feminist theologians that use communication techniques indigenous to various sub-regions of Asia and that are designed to encourage participants to feel safe in articulating their views on the texts. She notes that "in such situations participants felt secure in abandoning traditional insights derived from Sunday school teachings, Sunday sermons, and conventional Bible study groups."[450]

Rebera discusses the role-playing that took place in the re-telling of the Martha-Mary pericope as a South Asian story, and presents some of the viewpoints which emerged. For example, she writes,

The ownership of property is an indicator of social standing and status in Asia. For women to be recognized as owners of property *despite the presence of a male sibling* is a double affirmation of the woman, particularly in South Asia ... As the owner of her home despite the presence of a brother, Martha had the right to be viewed as a woman of authority who is also the head of a household. Such a view of Martha would make her an icon for authority, rather than an icon for home-making and serving, within the life of the church. Unfortunately, the more traditional view of Martha, as one who was tied to domesticity and who becomes the role model for women extending their domestic role into the life of the Church, continues to be the predominant image for most Asian women and men. Her status as a woman of means continues to be overshadowed by interpretations introduced by early missionaries and that continue to be in vogue today.[451]

Further,

A role-play of this [Martha-Mary] pericope by a group of Indian women led to significant insights. Once again the sisters had been portrayed as being in a close sibling relationship. Both Martha and Mary were portrayed as disciples-in-training. This factor gave each sister the independent right to seek approval from their *guru*, Jesus. Therefore, when Jesus responded to Martha he was not seen as pitting one sister against the other, but as supporting Mary in her choice with what was best for her. He was accepting of Mary's desire to be different in her apprenticeship. He was also seen as understanding of Martha's "mother-figure" concern for the welfare of her younger sister. Martha's worry and distraction were connected to the reputation of the younger sister ... Jesus' response was seen as an assurance that being apprenticed to him was "a better thing" than following the traditional dictates of society that often confined and limited women in public and private roles.[452]

Rebera also notes that in discussion, many women drew attention to the role of unmarried women in ministry in India.

In a rapidly developing technological India, singleness among women is growing. The right to choose marriage and/or a profession is becoming a visible phenomenon in urban, middle-class India ... Viewing these verses from the perspective of single women, choosing to build their own journeys in their own manner, and reading Jesus' response as a validation of that right, adds weight to the argument that the right choice is not a gender-based prerogative but a human right.[453]

Rebera had explored a similar notion in an earlier article:

To study the familiar biblical story of Mary and Martha from the South Asian perspective ... was to see two single sisters, living with their brother. A familiar family scene to South Asian women. To re-learn the Mary-Martha story as one that portrays single women breaking the social norms of protection and dependency to claim their individual identities as two strong leaders, was to release the two sisters from the confines of traditional theological interpretation into the freedom of being human.[454]

Rebera acknowledges that the feminist perspectives she presents are by no means the norm in Asia, but they are indicative of the struggle for Asian scholarship to establish its own genre in the field of biblical scholarship. For Asian women, retelling biblical texts from the basis of their personal realities is significant. The practice places the culture of biblical women side by side with the culture of Asian women and allows them to relate to the biblical characters and events. Concepts of discipleship such as those revealed in the retelling of the Martha-Mary story assist Asian women in reclaiming Asian traditions that have been lost through influences from outside the region. Insights derived from storytelling move the focus from polarizing women in the church to one of partnership. Allowing the patriarchal Asian church to hear the voice of women as initiators of change reopens doors that closed when Euro-centred education became accepted as the only vehicle for learning and research. Finally, through the process of retelling these stories, Asian women are led to reclaim their identities in patriarchal societies where women continue to be defined by their relationships with male figures. In Rebera's words, "it is through the reclaiming of our identity as Asian women who are different from each other, as Martha and Mary were different, that we can claim the right to be equal in all aspects of discipleship and the right to be equal partners within the community of faith."[455]

In her commentary on Rebera's *Semeia* article, American theologian Antoinette Clark Wire suggests that the practice of retelling a biblical story in another cultural context has the potential to offer significant insights for all biblical researchers, and for Christian women generally:

> Though such use of the Bible has been disparaged in Western academic scholarship, I consider that the recovery and hearing of women's stories will be at the foundation of future biblical scholarship. When we learn to respect the oral generators of our tradition, read the texts to hear them and appreciate the authors for preserving and elaborating their work, then we will conceive the synoptic problem and Christology and ethics in new ways more faithful both to the tradition and to ourselves.[456]

The work of scholars such as Rebera highlights Martha's importance as a disciple of Jesus, a partner in the church, and a role model for contemporary women. Nevertheless, despite this interest shown in Martha by various modern scholars in both the Western and the non-Western world, the number of those who have studied her life and recognized her significance remains limited. Their research appears, for the most part, in the form of articles, book chapters, or conference papers. In these studies, Martha is usually discussed within a broader context, such as the role of women as disciples of Christ, rather than serving as the focal point. It is noteworthy that Martha of Bethany—a woman described by Elisabeth Moltmann-Wendell as one of the three most important female figures in the New Testament, alongside Mary, the mother of Jesus, and Mary Magdalene[457]—has never been the subject of a full-scale scholarly monograph.[458]

Martha and Popular Christian Culture

Martha occupies a rather ambiguous position in the popular imagination. The legendary Martha continues to be celebrated in southern France. The tarasque is featured on the coat-of-arms of the city of Tarascon, and each year a festival is held in late June in the city in honour of the famous dragon. During the festivities, a large mechanical model of the beast is paraded though the streets. This celebration, inaugurated by King René, Duke of Anjou and Count of Provence, dates back to 1474.[459]

Outside of this relatively restricted geographic area, Martha is not widely known. As discussed in the previous chapter, reference to the Martha of legend appears in a few twentieth-century literary works. However, the name of her dragon, the tarasque, is probably more widely recognized than that of Martha herself, in particular among readers of fantasy literature and players of cyber games.

In Christian circles, Martha remains generally unappreciated. Various denominations still maintain "Martha Leagues" or "Martha Groups" that focus on the practical but unglamorous tasks necessary to the operation of a congregation or congregational

outreach: cleaning, providing meals for the homebound or for funerals, knitting or sewing for the needy, and so on. For the most part, contemporary Christian literature on Martha continues to focus squarely on her Lukan image, to compare her to her sister, and to cast her in a negative light. Christian bookstores feature self-help titles such as *Having a Mary Heart in a Martha World: Finding Intimacy with God in the Busyness of Life*,[460] *Martha to the Max!: Balanced Living for Perfectionists*,[461] and *Martha, Martha: How Christians Worry*.[462] All are designed to help modern-day Marthas become more Mary-like. Sermons and meditations bear titles such as "Martha of Bethany: A Woman Who Didn't Have Her Priorities Straight."[463] They include comments such as these:

The way Martha worked painted a portrait of a person who was so concerned about doing a great job on relatively little tasks that she had no time for the absolutely important one. She worked hard for Christ without being truly Christ-centered. Martha was diligent, but she lost the point ... She was like a musician so obsessed with tuning her instrument exactly right that she didn't have the time to actually play it.[464]

In some cases, it is not just her activity but her entire personality that is denounced:

Martha is not actually a very appealing character. As I see it, there are two problems with this woman: First, she is a whiner and she is a triangulator. Wouldn't it have been better had Martha gone directly to Mary and said something like, "Say, Mary, when you get to a stopping place, could you make up the salad dressing and put out the place mats, then we can all talk to the Messiah after we have some lunch?" But, no she goes to Jesus to complain about Mary. That is called triangulation. ... There is nothing direct about triangulation—it never results in truth being told directly to the person who needs to hear it! Triangulation is indirect, evasive, and contributes nothing to genuine communication. And [Martha] is a whiner. You can almost hear the whine in her voice. Make her help me, come on, fix this up for me ... Whining is attractive in neither a style or content of communication. That aspect of Martha's personality is incredibly unappealing.[465]

While negative assessments of Martha appear most frequently in Christian popular literature, it is also possible to find recent sermons, meditations, and books that affirm Martha[466] or at least present a sympathetic view of her situation.[467] As one pastor reminds us,

We 21st-century North Americans understand Martha's predicament well. It isn't only matters of hospitality that distract us and pull us in many directions; it's the unrelenting nature of our schedules. Oddly enough, it seems less complicated to plow ahead and attempt to keep up with the calendar than to make a change.

However,

The good news is that Jesus the host grants permission for all distracted, frantic people to sit down and eat their fill of word and promise. When we join them and nourish ourselves at the table, we'll be ready to put hands and feet, hearts and minds to work.[468]

The point of her message—undoubtedly an important one—is that prayer and meditation should inform our actions. In other words, Mary-like contemplation should precede Martha-like activity.

Roman Catholic Archbishop Stanislaw Rylko, President of the Pontifical Council for the Laity in Vatican City, considered the relationship of contemplation and action from a slightly different angle in his celebration of the Holy Mass for volunteers at the World Youth Day pilgrimage held in Cologne, Germany, in August 2005. He proclaimed:

> This Eucharistic celebration is the starting point of your important mission of service that you are preparing to give to young people like yourselves … For the next few days Cologne will be the "world capital" of young pilgrims coming from all corners of the earth in answer to the Pope's invitation … Thank you for choosing to live this World Youth Day experience in the fraternal service of others! …
>
> Christ is the heart of the great spiritual adventure of World Youth Day that we shall experience together during the next few days! It is important that none of you, my dear volunteers, should lose sight of this fact. Only if you have your gaze fixed on him, can your service towards your fellow young people be complete and authentic.
>
> In the Gospel there are several characters who can help you to understand the importance of your mission as volunteers. Of course you remember Martha of Bethany, the sister of Mary and Lazarus, close friends of Jesus (cf. Lk 10:38-42). Thanks to Martha's generous and attentive work, Mary could sit leisurely at the feet of Jesus to listen to his words. In the Church, there

is always a need for Martha! There is always a need for people to put themselves at the service of others to help them to find Jesus—people who create conditions for this encounter to take place under the best possible conditions. This is the mission that you young volunteers are called to discharge during this World Youth Day: Martha's mission! ... Each aspect of your service, even the most insignificant and simple, may or may not be received as a testimony of your faith, as a testimony of your humanity.[469]

This message brings the matter full circle. Those who are filled with the Spirit of Christ go out in loving service; this in turn creates conditions under which others may be brought to Christ.

Concluding Thoughts

The twelfth-century *Vita Pseudo-Marcilia*, a work that outlines the many facets of Martha of Bethany's life and describes her numerous accomplishments, concludes by stating that it is fitting for readers to call to remembrance the life of Martha—"for one who is mindful of her will be remembered by God."[470]

Just as she did in the later Middle Ages, Martha provides a contemporary model of the faithful servant, of one who professes the Christian gospel, of a leader who sets an example through her piety and social concern. As Archbishop Rylko has suggested, Martha's mission is the mission of the Christian Church.

Appendix A

E. M. Faillon
and the Provençal Cult of Martha

Étienne-Michel Faillon, a Roman Catholic Sulpician priest, professor, and historian, was born in Tarascon, France on December 29, 1799. Faillon was ordained in 1824, and stayed a year in the novitiate at Solitude d'Issy-les-Moulineaux near Paris, where priests who were to work in the grand seminaries were prepared. Faillon taught at the Grand Séminaire de Lyon from 1826 to 1829, and in 1829 was appointed a professor at the seminary in Paris. In 1837, Faillon left Paris to become director of the Solitude. Faillon made three trips to Canada, remaining about seven years in total, from October 1849 to June 1850, from May 1854 to September 1855, and from November 1857 to June 1862. As assistant general of the society, he was responsible for visiting Sulpician houses in North America.

In addition to his teaching and administrative duties, Faillon was a prolific scholar and writer. His works included a number of historical and biographical works published in Europe. His two-volume account of the life of Jean-Jacques Olier, founder of the Séminaire de Saint-Sulpice in Paris, published in Paris in 1841, was particularly influential. Various other works were inspired by his Canadian experiences. These included biographies of several notable women of New France: Marie-Marguerite d'Youville, founder of the Sisters of Charity of Montreal, Quebec; Marguerite Bourgeois, founder of the Congrégation de Nôtre-Dame de Montréal; and Jeanne Mance, founder of the Hôtel-Dieu de Montréal. Faillon's major achievement was his *Histoire de la colonie française en Canada*, which appeared between 1864 and 1869, when he was in Rome serving as procurator-general of the Sulpicians. He returned to Paris in 1869, and died during the disturbances of 1870.[471]

In 1848 Faillon produced one of the most extensive accounts of the Martha cult, as part of his *Monuments inédits sur l'apostolat de Sainte Marie-Madeleine en Provence et sur les autres apôtres de cette contrée, Saint Lazare, Saint Maximin, Sainte Marthe, les Saintes Maries Jacobé et Salomé, etc., etc.*, which was published in Paris by J.-P. Migne. This two-volume text includes both commentary and a Latin edition of the *Vita Beatae Mariae Magdalenae et Sororis Eius Sanctae Martha*, with French translation.[472] The title page notes that it was intended to serve as a supplement to the *Acta Sanctorum*, or Acts of the Saints, published by the Bollandists, a group of Jesuit theological scholars in Belgium who had begun publishing hagiographical works in Latin in the early years of the seventeenth century. The work of the Bollandists was halted in 1788 following the suppression of the Jesuit order. However, a new Society of Bollandists was formed in France in 1836, and hagiographical work resumed. The first volume published after the resurrection of Bollandism appeared in 1845. [473]

In his 1848 text, Faillon claims to offer "proofs" of certain Provençal legends of the saints from Bethany and their companions. He maintains that the tomb of Martha was probably venerated at Tarascon from the time of her death in the late first century.[474] It was held in special renown after the late fifth or sixth century, when Clovis I, a convert to Christianity who had heard of the miraculous powers of Martha's tomb, visited Tarascon and was himself healed of an internal disorder.[475] He subsequently accorded a privilege consisting of a parcel of the surrounding lands to the church of Martha.[476]

Although Faillon argues at length in support of his claims, they are for the most part unconvincing due to the nature of his documentation. He provides a facile explanation for the scarcity of evidence, suggesting that most was destroyed at the time of the Saracen invasions of Provence.[477] This claim is not supported by others. Leclercq, for example, denies that the scarcity of documentary evidence of an early cult is due to Saracen destruction, noting that in other areas invaded by the Saracens no conscious attempts were made to totally obliterate the evidence of local religious practices. In addition, surviving martyrologies written in the area of what is now southern France during the pre-invasion period make no mention of local cults of the saints from Bethany.[478] Likewise, John Cassian, who used the examples of Mary and Martha as "types" of the active and contemplative lives,[479] founded the monastery of St. Victor at Marseille around 400 A.D. but made no mention in his writings of the existence of cults of either saint in the area at that time.

Much of Faillon's documentation is archaeological. He admits that the original (alleged) tomb of Martha at Tarascon, which supposedly still contained Martha's relics, was concealed in 1653 within a marble enclosure adorned with a carving of the saint on her death bed.[480] A cast iron replica of the sarcophagus was placed in the church sanctuary. It is this replica which Faillon describes in detail. However, it is unclear as to whether or not Faillon has seen even the replica first-hand. He notes that at the time he wrote an earlier book *Monuments de l'Église de Sainte-Marthe* he relied on "un dessin fort inexact"—an inexact drawing—for his description of the tomb.[481] He does not indicate whether his later change of opinion regarding the theme of some of the carvings resulted from a personal visit to the gravesite. In his later book he refers to an engraving published by Aringhi when discussing the style of Martha's sarcophagus.[482] One suspects that he was still working from secondary sources when writing in 1848.

The subjects represented on the tomb are ones which appear frequently in ancient Christian art: the miracle of the loaves and fishes, an orant, the miracle at Cana, the denial of Peter, the resurrection of Lazarus. Faillon's conclusions regarding the sarcophagus are ambiguous: his stylistic analysis suggests that it dates from the time of the persecutions of the early Christians, and he concludes that because it is so old it must prove that the cult of Martha is equally ancient.[483] He does not elaborate as to why the presence of an antique Roman-style sarcophagus in Tarascon should suggest a connection with Martha, other than perhaps the implication of a possible affirmation of "tradition." Faillon, despite the fact that he lived in a more enlightened age, seems to fall victim to many of the same assumptions as his medieval predecessors! Because he hopes to "prove" the existence of an early cult of Martha in Tarascon, the discovery of an ancient tomb is assumed to be that of the saint in question, with little justification.

Many of Faillon's claims are based on similar convoluted arguments. He describes (again in detail) the ancient doorway of the church of Martha in Tarascon. He notes that it predates the construction of the present church, consecrated in 1197—ten years after the "discovery" of Martha's remains—citing a bull of Pope Urban II from 1096 which mentions a church of Martha.[484] He is apparently unaware that even earlier references to a "terra sancte Marthe" or "sancta Martha" at Tarascon appear in charters dating from 964 and 967.[485] Among the images carved on the doorway are the resurrection of Lazarus, which was a common prototype of the resurrection of Christ in early Christian art and would not necessarily assume a literal connection with the raising of the saint, and a scene which Faillon describes as "Martha's victory over the dragon, commonly called the Tarasque."[486] He concludes that the doorway of the church is a witness to the belief of the ancient citizens of Tarascon that their forefathers were converted to the Christian faith by Martha.[487] However, there are undoubtedly other possible explanations of the woman/dragon scene. Much of the imagery on the door is derived from the book of Revelation, e.g., Christ enthroned in judgement and the symbolic representations of the four evangelists (as man, eagle, lion, and ox). It is possible that the woman/beast symbolism is also derived from this source.[488] The gates of hell were frequently represented by a devouring monster in the art of the medieval West, and the imagery may simply represent an allegorical interpretation of the victory of the Christian church (*Ecclesia*, which was often represented by a woman) over the powers of evil. It is not certain when the legend of Martha and the dragon originated. The story of a monster subdued by a local saint at Tarascon may have predated the Martha cult and was subsequently incorporated into her Life. In addition, even if Faillon's interpretation of the woman/beast imagery on the doorway is accepted, it is hardly "proof" of the existence of an early cult of Martha, when the dating of the door itself is uncertain. Similar comments can be made regarding Faillon's claim that ancient municipal seals from Tarascon depicting Martha as preacher or Martha and the dragon "prove" an early cult, when, once again, the dating of the originals is not firmly established. In addition, Faillon's text suggests that he is aware of only "une empreinte" of the seals and that he has not personally examined the seals themselves, if, in fact, the originals still existed, which he does not indicate.[489]

In addition, many of the "facts" which Faillon presents do not hold up under scrutiny. The suggestion of a patronage relationship between Martha and Clovis I, although well documented in literature from the twelfth century and later, is questionable. The major source for historians on the life and reign of Clovis, King of the Franks from 481–511, is Gregory of Tours' *History of the Franks*, written in the late sixth century.[490] Neither Gregory nor any other contemporary sources suggests that Clovis personally visited Provence. Although the area was attacked by a joint force of Franks and Burgundians in 507, it was successfully defended by Theodoric the Great, the Ostrogothic king of Italy.[491] Gregory's account suggests that it was to Martin of Tours that Clovis owed his allegiance.[492] Historians note that the cult of Martin gained prominence in greater Gaul only after being adopted by the Merovingians as their patron saint following Clovis' conquest of Aquitaine in 507.[493] However, Martin's cult scarcely infiltrated the Rhone watershed area in which Tarascon is located. In this area a "parallel but different form of monasticism, much more aristocratic in its associations, more carefully disciplined, and more directly related to the Eastern monastic tradition" developed, and adherents of the two traditions were suspicious of one another.[494]

It seems unlikely that Clovis, whose conversion to Christianity was probably motivated more by political than spiritual considerations,[495] would express allegiance to both Martin and Martha. Interestingly, even Faillon, the arch proponent of an early Martha cult in Provence, admits that some elements of the Martha legends may have been derived from those surrounding Martin, just as some aspects of Mary Magdalene's legendary life were derived from that of Mary the Egyptian. In his *Commentaire historique et critique* on the *Vita Beatae Mariae Magdalenae*, Faillon notes the similarities between the descriptions of the two saints' funerals, and suggests that these may possibly be the result of the "réssemblance de nom entre Martin et Marthe."[496]

Faillon's suggestion that Martha's grave in Tarascon was a notable centre of healing and pilgrimage in the early Middle Ages is also open to question. While a settlement of some kind existed at Tarascon from the time of the Romans, it was not a centre of any size or importance until the eleventh century. It was only during a time of economic prosperity in the later twelfth century that the town began to flourish.[497] The church of Martha which exists today was constructed after the "discovery" of the saint's relics in 1187. It was probably built on the site of an earlier church, possibly one dedicated to a Martha, but the identity of this earlier saint is unclear. In hagiographical literature confusion between saints with the same or similar names is common. Among the early church leaders of Provence, the early fifth century bishop Lazarus of Aix could easily have been confused in later centuries with Lazarus of Bethany, and likewise, saints named Maximin, Sidonius, and Marcella—later claimed to be the companions of the saints from Bethany—were known to have existed in the early Middle Ages in southern Gaul.[498] Thus, confusion between Martha of Bethany and another similarly named saint is highly probable.

Despite Faillon's imaginative reconstruction, concrete evidence suggests that no cult of Martha of Bethany existed in Provence until the twelfth century, when one was "manufactured" by the monks of Tarascon in response to claims being put forth by rival monasteries. In the twelfth century it was generally accepted that Lazarus and Mary Magdalene had travelled to Provence. The former was honoured as the first bishop of Marseille, probably, as noted earlier, because of a confusion of names between Lazarus of Bethany and the fifth century Bishop Lazarus of Aix. Mary Magdalene's cult had been centered at Vézelay, in the diocese of Autun, from the time of the Cluniac monk Abbot Geoffrey in the early eleventh century. However, according to legend, her body had been brought to Burgundy from Provence to avoid the ravages of the Saracens. Later, in the thirteenth century, both Saint-Maximin near Aix and Sainte-Baume laid claim to the possession of the "true" relics of the saint.[499] The inhabitants of Tarascon concluded that Martha probably accompanied her siblings to Provence, although no other town had "laid claim" to her remains. The fact that Tarascon already possessed a church dedicated to a St. Martha reinforced their cause: a search was undertaken, and in 1187 the body of "Martha of Bethany" was discovered.

Appendix B

The Life of St. Martha
Compiled by Pseudo-Marcilia

O f the four extant texts of the medieval Martha legend, three appear to be closely related. Vincent of Beauvais, in his *Speculum Historiale*, confirms his indebtedness to the pseudo-Marcilia version by neglecting to change the first person reference to "I, Synthex," the author who reputedly transcribed the life of Martha written by Marcella into Latin. The *Legenda Aurea* also notes that Marcella was the author of the work. The latter, although a much abbreviated account, contains a number of verbal echoes of the pseudo-Marcilia/Vincent texts. On the other hand, the most extensive account of Martha's life, the *Vita Beatae Mariae Magdalenae et Sororis Eius Sanctae Marthae*, differs significantly in a number of respects from the others, although certain passages contain verbal echoes. David Mycoff's studies of the Magdalene legends concluded that "there is no evidence that Vincent of Beauvais knew VBMM directly, but much that suggests that *Speculum Historiale* and VBMM shared a few common sources."[500] One of these sources was probably the pseudo-Marcilia life of Martha.

The four texts differ in their intent and their complexity. The shortest of the four, the *Legenda Aurea*, provides only a brief outline of Martha's life. The Martha chapters in the *Speculum*

Historiale provide some additional commentary, but again are essentially "factual" descriptions of the saint's background and activities. They are interspersed in the text among chapters describing the lives of other saints, in particular Mary Magdalene. The lengthy *Vita Beatae Mariae Magdalenae* can be described as a "storyteller's account." It includes some commentary, but for the most part the author's concern is to embellish the stories of the saints from Bethany with additional narrative detail.

The *Vita Pseudo-Marcilia* is in many respects the most interesting of the medieval "lives" of Martha. The author is interested not only in preserving "biographical" details, but in commenting upon Martha's significance.

The following translation of the *Pseudo-Marcilia* text, which has not been previously published, is based on the version found in the Bibliotheca Hagiographica Latina 5546a, as published in Boninus Mombritius, *Sanctuarius, seu Vitae Sanctorum*, Mediolani: ante 1480, reprinted Paris: Fontemoing, 1910, 231–239.[501]

A Life of the most glorious Martha, the hostess of Christ, first produced in Hebrew by St. Marcilia, her maid and little daughter[502] and afterwards translated into the Latin language by Sinticus[503]

St. Martha, the follower of Christ, is considered a type of the holy church because of her piety,[504] and her life would require a great volume for the understanding of its mystical sense. Therefore we will write briefly of the declarations of the Gospel regarding her distinguished life, forgoing discussion of her as reflecting types, in order that an extended account of her life will not be distasteful to readers or onerous to the memory of hearers, but that it may be an exemplum for pious imitation for the minds of the faithful. In short, Martha, the blessed and venerable hostess of Christ, a descendent of royal stock, lived in the village of Bethany, near the city of Jerusalem. Her father was Syrus, her mother Eucharia. Her siblings were St. Mary Magdalene and Lazarus, whom Christ, the true Friend of all generations, raised from the tomb.

Noble antiquity passed from the parent to the offspring. Now a more noble bearing waits in heaven.[505]

From her childhood, she loved greatly the Creator of all things, was highly skilled in Hebrew, and conformed to the precepts of the law. She was physically beautiful, and beautifully educated in the works appropriate to women. She was outstanding among all the pious noblewomen for her morals, and distinguished for her understanding and her works, especially her abundant charity, and her great purity. She avoided all contact with men. Nowhere is it written that she had a husband or that she had entered into marriage with a man, although her father was a distinguished governor of Syria and of many maritime regions. After the dispersion of the disciples of the Lord, he was a most faithful preacher in the city of Athens. Martha, along with her aforementioned brother and sister, possessed three towns which they had inherited by legal right from their mother, namely, Magdala and Bethany and part of the city of Jerusalem. Martha had authority before all her relatives because she was more capable and had a greater abundance of intelligence and honesty. The famous table companion gave freely of all the greatest riches to the soldiers and her household servants. She was greatly skilled in administering a banquet. As the Holy Scriptures claim, one of those invited to the banquet was the Lord, and He attended. Martha served, as was customary, because of her love of the Lord. When the Lord Jesus was in Bethany in the home of Simon the Leper, they prepared there a great banquet. Martha served with honour the one who had raised Lazarus, and in one place it is said that Martha troubled herself with much serving.[506] Such hospitality among us is not destined to be forgotten. For just as Abraham[507] and Lot[508] and Joshua[509] and many others had pleased God and likewise welcomed angels as guests, so was the diligent and most pious hostess attentive to all. She received both members of her household and strangers. Thus it happened that, acting in this way, she began to love the Lord, and she received him. And He who loves all, and who singled out St. Peter from all of us asking, "Peter, do you love me,"[510] He loved her so much that He preferred her home to any other lodging. As the Gospel relates, on days when Jesus was preaching in Jerusalem He returned late to Bethany where his friend Lazarus lived with his sisters Mary and Martha, and He was received there.[511]

How Christ received shelter

Afterwards it happened that the Lord was preaching in the towns and cities on a day described in Luke and, tired in body after a day's journey, He entered into a certain house and this woman named Martha welcomed Him in her home,[512] fulfilling the prophecy which says: "He is like a stranger in the land, and like a wayfarer who turns aside to tarry for a night."[513] O truly happy and glorious one, who deserves to have such a Guest, who serves the bread of angels and on which she was fed! How happy and glorious this woman, whom Jesus loved so much that He wished to be welcomed and fed by her. She received a great and wonderful Guest, whom angels and men welcome and feed. She fed Him who feeds all creatures. One greater than he whom Abraham received as a guest,[514] namely God and man; this great King of Kings and Lord of Lords, who alone encloses all in the palm of His hand; whom Job described as higher than the sky, broader than the greatest land, deeper than the sea;[515] whom many prophets and kings wished to see and did not see, to hear and did not hear: she received and fed this Guest. It is a great and praiseworthy thing to welcome the Lord into a house. Each of the two sisters, namely Martha and Mary, chose to perform her own ministry, which pleased God greatly. Mary, sitting before the feet of the Lord, heard the words of His mouth,[516] as if feasting on that which she preferred to eat. But Martha occupied herself greatly with the preparation of the feast,[517] and because she received so distinguished a Guest in her home, she was eager to serve with the greatest of care: cleaning the house, setting the table, preparing the food. But it did not seem to her enough: it seemed that all the household was unable to give sufficient service and that her sister should come to help her with the preparations. She wished that all her household would prepare the feast. Therefore she stood before the Lord astonished, and complaining about this thing, she said: "Lord, do you not care that my sister leaves me to serve alone? Tell her to help me."[518] But He who is not a respecter of persons[519] loved the different forms of service which were offered to Him: He received and praised the service of the one but did not condemn that of the other: "Martha, Martha, you are anxious and troubled about many things. On the other hand, one thing is needful. Mary has chosen for herself the better part, that is the spiritual life, which will not be taken away from her.[520] She will reap eternal life. Together your service which you choose completes and makes well. She strives for the health of the soul, you, in truth, work for the health of the body. Complete what you have begun, and you will do well. The promise of a crown awaits those who persevere in good works, and their praises will be sung at the end." This is clear: the active life which Martha symbolizes in the holy church is not at all able to continue as active or to please the highest King without the contemplative life which Mary signifies. Wherefore the merciful Guest conceded to each of these holy women her office and choice. In short, with happy spirits in festive custom, they ate, stayed in the home and rested on that day. From that time, the Saviour was customarily freely welcomed as a guest in the house of St. Martha.

How Lazarus was raised by her prayers

How many good benefits were agreeable to the Guest because of the good hospitality! Martha received the needy with a diligent and cheerful spirit when they appeared at her home. The hospitality of this woman was rewarded: for because of the friendship and hospitality of St. Martha, the Lord raised her brother Lazarus from the dead. For the Evangelist says that the Lord Jesus loved Martha and Mary her sister and Lazarus.[521] O happy and praiseworthy generation, which Christ loved more than others! Although the wise words of the Father say: "I love those who love me,"[522] yet rarely is it found in the Scriptures where the faithful whom the Lord loved are mentioned especially by name. And because St. Martha knew her holy Guest loved her, and did not doubt that it was possible for him to do anything, and because she heard that He had raised the daughter of the synagogue ruler[523] and the widow's son,[524] she complained bitterly to the Lord when he returned to Bethany about the death of her brother. She said: "Lord, if you had been here, my brother would not have died. But I know that even now, God will give you whatever you ask."[525] O the unwavering faith of this holy woman! She believed in God, three in one: she saw the Son concealed in human flesh; she did not see the Father, but did not doubt that he would fulfill the requests of the Son; and she believed in the Holy Spirit, who formed an indestructible bond of love between Father and Son, and through whom the Father, at the request of the Son, would raise her brother. On that account the Lord said to the believing woman: "Your brother will rise."[526] Martha immediately replied: "I know that he will rise on the last day."[527] Clearly this holy woman was acquainted with the basic tenets of the law: she had read of the resurrection of the dead in the prophets; she believed in a final and universal resurrection. But she doubted that she would see her brother at the present time and near at hand, and because of this, the Lord said to her: "I am the Resurrection and the Life. He who believes in me, though he were dead, yet he will live. And all who live and believe in me will never die. Do you believe this?"[528] And she said, "Yes, Lord." O, what great faith abounded in this holy woman! She said: "I believe that you are the Christ, the son of God, who came into this world."[529] Martha proved herself to have much in common with Peter, the chief of the apostles, with Job, with Abraham, and with the Holy Virgin: with St. Peter, who, because he believed in the Father, Son, and Holy Spirit, said: "I acknowledge that you are the Christ, the Son of the living God,"[530] and Martha likewise confessed: "You are the Christ, the Son of God, who came into the world"; in common with the blessed Job, who said: "I believe that my Saviour will rise up on earth on the last day, and even though my skin be destroyed, in my flesh I will see God,"[531] and Martha, believing in a future resurrection, said: "I know that my brother will rise in the resurrection on the last day"; in common with Abraham, who welcomed three angels as guests, because of faith in the Holy Trinity,[532] and Martha received in her home this God, three in one, and what is more, God and man. She proved to have a common part also with the holy Virgin; for the glorious Virgin Mary received God and man in her holy womb, and Martha received God and man as a guest in her own home. The divine body of the former [Mary] nourished that which is most blessed in her holy womb; the holy hostess Martha cared for Him in her own home. He whom the one begot, the other cared for. Therefore she proved to have something in common with the divine Virgin, but they were different. Their worth is different: for the former is blessed among all women[533] and nothing is similar in worth. In her chaste virgin womb she received the Son of God. The latter [Martha] received Him devotedly in her earthly home. The former cared for a small boy, the latter a man of thirty years. And therefore she believed in her heart the faith of the prophets, and the confession of the apostles, and was occupied with good works, and truly, as a consort and participant with them, she shared in the kingdom of heaven. And she who believed that all things were possible deserved to receive what she asked of the Lord. He heard her desire, and raised her brother from the dead: when the voice of the Lord decreed: "Lazarus, come out," he was restored to life after four days.[534] Meanwhile a ceremony of great joy was celebrated and a banquet made by the faithful Jews in the house of Simon the Leper; and Martha served. There was no doubt that a miracle had taken place, for Lazarus took his place at the table.[535] From that time on, it was believed that the Lord had raised the brother of St. Martha from the grave because of her holy prayers, and it happened that penitent sinners called upon her, and out of the goodness of her heart she entreated God on their behalf. Her holy Guest, out of love for her freed them from their sin and made them whole. The Ruler of heaven most humbly loved St. Martha, so much that it pleased Him to hold the noble virgin in great honour, so that, avoiding the royal palaces, He was pleased to lodge in her home, to be fed and cared for, and to rest in her holy home. He instituted and made evident the whole religion of all the religious and the sacraments of the holy church. In her sacred home the holy church was formed. The pious women Mary and Martha, representing the contemplative and the active lives, rejoiced in the favour of the Saviour, and He equipped them and showed their successors in the Christian churches how to live uprightly. In these two lives all the doctrines of the laws of all the religious of the Old and New Testaments have their meaning and are fulfilled. By which all the saints and elect of God come, and will come, to the highest kingdom by loving their neighbours as themselves. Let us persist in the active life with Martha by fulfilling in all necessary ways whatever is required in it. By loving God over all and disregarding earthly love, and looking towards the heavens, let us rejoice in the contemplative life with Mary. Thus are the practices of earth, which will not be lost in heaven. Thus we cross over through temporal goods so that we do not lose eternal ones, and thus terrestrial things are not lost because of celestial things nor celestial things lost for terrestrial. By these things also we deserve to fully enjoy the benefits given to us by God. Let us be worthy to possess the kingdom of Heaven. So much let us say of the holy hostess of Christ, according to the testimony of the evangelists: let us move on to treat briefly the rest, namely her life and end.

How His own were sent away

In short, with all her heart St. Martha heard and understood the teachings of the Lord when he said: "All who leave their father and mother, wife and children and lands, in my name will receive a hundredfold, and will possess eternal life."[536] She divided all her material resources into three parts. She gave the first part to her sister Mary Magdalene, to supplement the resources from which she supplied the living expenses and clothing for the Lord and his apostles. The second part she gave to her brother Lazarus. The third part she kept, and on it she lived and entertained the Saviour and his disciples when they came to her home. Whatever remained after the ascension of Christ into heaven—when the multitude of believers were of one heart and one soul and no one set apart anything of his own, but they had all things in common[537]—she placed at the feet of the apostles. And it was in common for the believers because, as the philosopher said, "It shines clearly for all when goods are drawn down in common."[538] And Martha proved herself an apostle among apostles and a disciple among disciples. At that time the growing number of disciples aroused against themselves the hostility of the Jews, so that in the end they were expelled.[539] They took Peter and the other apostles into public custody[540] and killed James.[541] Without reason they were taken away and escaped, sailing in a vessel without sail or rudder or any provisions at all. But in the end the raging fury of the Jews was overthrown. Divine providence enriched them in a better region. It enriched them with villages and towns and cities. It made them rich with many treasures. It enriched them with churches. It multiplied their servants and honours. And, moreover, it would give them heavenly mansions. It gave to each one a city and homeland: Arles to Trophimus; Narbonne to Paulus; Toulouse and Vaucogne to Saturninus; Poitiers to Martialus; Saintonge and Aquitaine to Eutropius; Le Mans and Brittany to Julianus; Bourges to Urcissinus;[542] Tours to Gracianus;[543] Lyons to Irenaeus; Besançon to Ferrucius; Orange to the other Eutropius; Périgueux to Fronto; Velay to Georgius; all of Gaul to Dionysius. Each one was given his own village. See how much the mercy of God continued to be evident in foreign regions. When they were dead, requests were made by the people before the holy ashes and bones and tombs, and they came to the aid of the living. The sick coming to their tombs were healed, the blind given sight, the lame restored, those with demons freed, and those in mourning comforted. The guilt of sinners was forgiven. Therefore God did not wish to give them an inheritance in the city of Jerusalem, for he gave them a better one elsewhere. Similarly, God did not wish to give men a perfect inheritance except in the heavenly kingdom which he made for them. Thus he said to Abraham: "Leave your land and your family and come into the land which I will show you, and I will make you grow into a great nation."[544] Thus God first made man. He transferred him out from paradise into this world, and from there into the ground, and after that He will take him into heaven. Thus it happened that the sons of Israel crossed the Red Sea from Egypt into the promised land.[545] Thus it happened that Christ descended from the bosom of the Father, descended into the womb of the blessed Virgin, and from there He came into the world, and then into the tomb, and then into the ground, and after the resurrection He returned to heaven. Similarly, our Lord will supply three mansions for each one of us, and it is right to go across from one to another: He gives the world in which we stop off, He gives the grave in which the body decays, and He gives heaven in which we remain finally. Bitter death is our companion in the world, worms in the grave, angels in heaven. Thus St. Martha, his hostess, was taken away and enriched with her own treasures in foreign regions.

How she crossed the sea with St. Maximinus, bishop of Aix, who was one of the seventy disciples[546]

Just as the Lord united His glorious mother with St. John the Evangelist, even so the Holy Spirit united Martha and Mary Magdalene with St. Maximinus, who once baptized them. He led them to the kingdom of heaven by the example of his good conduct. They entered into a ship with many others, and after praying for a safe trip, they reached the port of Marseille, under the Lord's guidance. Then they approached the territory of Aix. After fasting and fervent prayers they converted the unbelieving people to faith in Christ by means of miraculous signs and prophecies. The Lord gave the glorious Martha both the ability to heal all kinds of sickness and to make holy prophecies. She was, as we say, physically beautiful, elegant, and charming in appearance, and highly eloquent and clear in speech. Her sermons were received by kings and nobles. She succeeded in converting a greater number of people than the rest of her companions. The majority of the people of this province were converted to Christ by St. Maximinus, Martha, and Mary.

How she bound the dragon by her hand[547]

There was at this time on the banks of the Rhone, next to the huge cliff, in the forest between Arles and Avignon towards the western region, a huge dragon, half land animal and half fish, which had destroyed many passersby, asses, and horses which had encountered it. It submerged ships crossing the Rhone. Crowds of armed people often came there, but they did not succeed in slaying it, for it concealed itself in the river by the forest. It was larger than an ox,[548] longer than a horse, and had the head of a lion. Its teeth were like sharp swords, its mane like that of a horse. It had a sharp ridge on its back like a pickaxe, heavy scales for tearing apart, sinewy feet, and claws like a bear. Its tail was like a snake, and it was fortified with two twisted plates, one on each side. Twelve lions and as many bears could not vanquish it. When none of the inhabitants were able to destroy it in any way, they heard reports of the reputation of St. Martha and her glittering miracles, how she cast out demons, and they came to her asking that she come and drive away the dragon once and for all. Therefore, the holy friend of God went to the place. The hostess of Christ, confident in her true Guest, discovered the dragon in the forest, devouring a man which it had killed. She threw on him holy water which she had brought, and held up a wooden image of the holy cross. The dragon was overpowered and stood like a sheep. The saint bound it with her own holy belt, and all the people in that place put it to death with spears and stones. This dragon was called "Tirascurus" and afterwards the place was called Tirasconus [Tarascon]. Previously it had been called Nerluc, that is "black forest," because the forest was dark and shadowy. Possibly this dragon was a descendant of that which is called Leviathan in the book of Job,[549] who swallowed up rivers and was not amazed, but had confidence even though the Jordan rushed against his mouth.[550] It had come down by sea from Galatia in Asia, a descendant of Leviathan, a most ferocious aquatic serpent, and of the animal called the Bonasus.[551] The Bonasus is an animal which originated in the region of Galatia, and which drives away its attackers with burning dung, which it shoots out like an arrow over a huge area, and everything which it touches is burned as if by fire.

How she remained in Tarascon

After many petitions of the people, St. Martha stayed on there in that country [Tarascon], with the permission of her former master Maximinus and her sister Mary Magdalene. As long as she lived she continued her fasting, vigils, and prayers. What labours, what anguish, what hunger, how many persecutions, how many troubles and sorrows she endured there! Who can estimate the cost? For in the first seven years she ate the roots of raw grasses and the fruits of the trees and the foliage of trees and mushrooms, and they were better to her than a food platter. Afterwards a community of brothers and sisters came to stay with her, and a great basilica was built in honour of the holy Christ and the blessed Virgin Mary. Martha lived a harsh life there, avoiding meat and all fat, eggs, cheese, and wine. She ate only once a day. In the winter she customarily wore a cloak of sheepskin, and in summer a tunic and cloak with goat skin next to her flesh. She went barefoot, and wore a turban of camel hair on her head. A belt made of horse hair intentionally tied in knots was around her waist, and often worms came out of her broken and rotting flesh. Stretching out on tree branches or vines, with a stone under her head, she slept on a hair shirt. She devoted herself diligently to prayer and supplications. She was always attentive to heavenly things, never shelter on earth. Her body was on earth but her mind was turned towards heaven. A hundred times a day and as many times at night she bent her knee to the earth in prayer. She was powerful in all the virtues of faith, hope, and charity. She was always notable for the hospitality which she had practised at Bethany: customarily her table was filled with strangers and guests. Her mouth did not cease from divine praises; frequently the works of her hands were enjoyed. Often she stayed at home with those around her. Often she went to the towns and cities and villages nearby to spread the divine word to the crowds of people. The words which she spoke could produce miracles. When she placed her hand on the listeners, they received the Holy Spirit. When she placed her hand on the sick, they received the Holy Spirit. When she placed her hand on the sick, they were made well. Acting in this way, Martha was loved by God and favoured among men. How many thousands of people were converted and baptized through her exhortations to faith in Christ is too long to describe in detail.

How she revived the dead

Once the distinguished disciple of Christ was near Avignon, before the city gates, in a pleasant place between the city and the Rhone River, preaching and healing the sick who were brought to her. A young man on the other side of the river saw the crowds of people on this side listening to the holy one, and he wanted to see and hear her. Lacking[552] a boat, he enthusiastically began to swim naked across the river. When he was swimming[553] in the middle, he suddenly encountered a swift current in the raging river, and, being carried off, was submerged in the depths. In short, all that day the boats of the citizens were not able to find him in the river. On the second day, about nine o'clock, the lifeless body was discovered, and placed at the feet of St. Martha.

Then the illustrious friend of Christ, her heart moved, informed the people that she would prostrate herself and call upon God, asking that He in His mercy would deign to raise the boy from the dead. Prostrating herself next to the body in the form of a cross, she called upon the Lord and said: "Adonai, Jesus Christ, who, in your holy and ineffable mercy once raised my brother Lazarus, your beloved, from the dead;[554] who holds the keys to life and death;[555] who commands death and makes it flee; who calls the dead and they rise: my dear Guest, look upon the faith and prayers of those around and revive this boy, in order that they and those who hear of your power and strength may believe in you, O Adonai, Jesus Christ, who lives and reigns with the Father and the Holy Spirit, and the Virgin Mother Mary for ever and ever, Amen." Then the illustrious hostess of Christ felt the power of God come from heaven. She raised herself and taking the hand of the boy said to him: "Rise, boy, in the name of the Lord Jesus Christ." And immediately he rose up alive and unharmed, and underwent baptism in the name of the Holy Trinity. Oh, Christ destroyed death, working through the blessed hostess of Christ, and He restored a man who was condemned to two deaths by a double resurrection through faith in Christ. And afterwards all in the cities and towns believed in our Lord Jesus Christ and underwent baptism. Thus, because of this deed, Martha was praised by all, even more than previously.

At that time bishop Maximinus of Aix and Trophimus of Arles and Eutropius of Orange, all three, came without warning to visit her, each of them unaware that the others were coming. And through their prayers in the name of the holy Christ,[556] and in honour of His mother, they consecrated Martha's church on the sixteenth day before the calends of January [i.e., December 17]. At a banquet for them, the wine having run short, water was converted into wine.[557] Then through Maximinus, Mary, the sister of Martha, conveyed a promise that she would visit her. She fulfilled it not while living but after her death. It happened not a long time later that bishops St. Fronto of Périgueux, who had been ordained by the apostle St. Peter, and the most holy Georgius of Velay, namely he who was dead and came back to life, were expelled from their own cities for their preaching.[558]

They approached St. Martha for help, just as they would seek sanctuary from their mother, and remained with her for several days. By the prayers of St. Martha poured out to God, they were reconciled with their cities. For she was a pious mother and nurse to the bishops and all believers at this time. She took care of all, like a mother hen her chicks.[559] For the needs of body and soul of the crowds of believers who gathered about her were fulfilled. Then St. Martha, confessing her sin to one of them, namely the elder, St. Fronto, predicted her own death not far off in the future, and asked also that, if God allowed him to live so long, he would promise to return to her at the time of her death. But because all the miracles which she performed on the far side of the sea and on this side and her frequent signs are too many to describe in detail, we shall tell briefly of how she went from a good life to a better one.

Of her passing

The blessed hostess of Christ was pleasing to her pious Guest in all the good works which she did, and, wishing to pay tribute to her belief, her pious Guest revealed to her by the spirit of prophecy the approaching day of her death, a year in advance. Afterwards she announced it to her brothers and sisters. She was shaken by fevers for almost all the whole year. On the eighth day before her death, Martha heard choirs of angels bearing the soul of her departing sister, Mary Magdalene, into heaven. She informed all of her own that were in that place, saying: "O my companions and most sweet friends, I ask you to rejoice with me: because hosts of angels are bearing the soul of our sister to the heavenly mansions and rejoicing. O most beautiful and beloved sister, consider that which you promised me, that you would make me joyful by visiting. Live with your Master and our true Guest in the blessed realm." How great and inestimable was the love between the two sisters, and how it was revealed. On the eighth day after the death of the one, the other died. The one led the other into paradise. Immediately St. Martha began to grow listless in her bed, more than usual, and she called her brothers and sisters to gather around her, and fortified herself for heaven with the Eucharist and confession. The business of her church was agreeably set in order. She bravely encouraged her companions in the Christian faith to hold firm in their religion. Then they kept watch unceasingly in her home all that day and night until her death, with lighted torches and prayers to God. She asked sweetly that they act diligently.

How demons came at her death

In the middle of the night before the day of her death, those keeping watch fell into a deep sleep. A strong whirlwind coming from an evil direction, gusting swiftly, extinguished the seven large candles and three lamps burning in her home. The blessed one, seeing a crowd of foul spirits around her, began to pray: "My Father Ely, my dear Guest, those who would seduce me have gathered around to devour me, holding a list of the evil deeds which I have done, crying loudly, saying: 'God, abandon her, and we will pursue and seize her when she is freed.' Ely, do not forsake me.[560] Ely, come to my aid. Ely, make haste to help me.[561] Do not be mindful of the transgressions of my youth and my ignorance,[562] Adonai, and do not turn your face away from me.[563] Swiftly hear me in my tribulation, Adonai."[564] At the sound of her voice, those who were watching awoke, and they sought a fire in all the house, and not finding one, they were delayed. Behold, the blessed Martha saw her sister Mary Magdalene coming to meet her, holding in her hand a torch, from which she relit all the lamps and candles in the place. Scarcely had the one finished calling the other by name when her pious Guest appeared and said to her: "Come, my beloved hostess, leave the prison of the flesh and cross over to my palace in heaven, where I will receive you as my guest, and where I am, O my servant, you will be with me.[565] You received me in your home and I will receive you in my heaven.[566] Once I gave my consolation to the desolate, and I will not take it away from you after your death. For love of you, I will hear those who come to your tomb in devotion, complaining bitterly of their need." And when she was about to turn back, quivering, He said: "Stand fast, I will come to you." Hardly were these words spoken when the Lord and Mary disappeared from that place. And those who watched over her, returning without having found a fire, entered the house, and, looking at one another in amazement, they asked eagerly how the lamps which had been extinguished when they went out had been rekindled, thus far not knowing of the greatness of the acts of God. But immediately Martha revealed to her holy brothers what had happened. The night passed and the day of her death arrived. She asked that she be carried outside of the basilica to a certain very beautiful street under the trees, in order to see the heavens, and that she be placed on a cross of ashes, resting on a little chaff, and covered with a hair-shirt, and that a holy wooden cross be held up before her. And this was done. Then she asked that her brothers and sisters pray for her. Immediately the souls of all men turned toward heaven, and she fixed her gaze upon heaven. She began to pray, saying: "Ely, God and Father of our Lord Jesus Christ, the son of the eternal God, born of the chaste Virgin Mary, who was born for us, suffered and died, arose and returned to the heavens:[567] receive my spirit into your resting-place. Do not allow me to be torn apart by the hands of the four angels who control the gates of hell.[568] But just as I was found worthy as a hostess, receive me as your guest in heaven. My dear Guest, watch over your poor little family and encourage them, that all of them who are in this place will seek out heavenly rewards, and that you will find them worthy to be rewarded." Then she asked that the passion of the Lord written in the Hebrew language which she had brought with her from Jerusalem, be read. And it was read, and when the reader said: "Father, into your hand I commend my spirit,"[569] the friend of God died, and handed over her worthy soul to the embraces of the archangel Michael,[570] who, with his angels, bore her over the battlefield of the prince of darkness, occupied by the bodies and souls of sinners, and crossed over into the holy mysteries of heaven. O race worthy of a glorious death! Who has heard of a death so deserved, secured at so great a cost as this one? It is not death but life: it is swallowed up in victory.[571] How valuable in the sight of the Lord is the death of his holy hostess. Christ set her free from this world in the sixty-fifth year of her life, having spent seven and a half years in the monastery, on the fourth day from the calends of August, the sixth day of the week, at the ninth hour. The distinguished hostess of Christ crossed over into the joy of the angels, where she rejoiced and praised without end her good Guest, the Lord Jesus Christ. Famous persons and the religious companions of her household remained constantly in that place with her until her death: Euchodius and Syntex and Germanus and Epaphras and Sosthenes, first followers of Paul and then companions of Trophimus, and Parmenas, who was one of the seven deacons of the apostles;[572] and Marcilla, the servant and little daughter through baptism of St. Martha, the one who lifted up her voice out of the crowd and said to the Lord Jesus: "Blessed is the womb which bore you;"[573] and many others leading a spiritual life with her in this place until her death. These faithful companions came together in the basilica which she had built, and attended to her funeral. They adorned the sepulchre with propriety for three entire days and nights, with a great number of people who came from the towns and cities in the vicinity to venerate her death, respectfully keeping vigil with lighted candles and great lamps in the forest.

How the Lord and St. Fronto buried her

The following day, which was Sunday, all the congregation of the religious and all the throng of the people stood around the body, as if they wished the funeral ceremony to take place soon. They all sang psalms and mourned. At the third hour Bishop Fronto was celebrating mass in Périgueux, and the epistle having been read, he fell asleep on his throne before the altar in the church. The Lord appeared to him, saying: "My beloved Fronto, if you wish to fulfill the promise which you once made to our hostess, come to her funeral. Come quickly, follow me." At this same moment in Tarascon, the two proceeded into the church of the godly hostess and began to sing psalms around the body with the others. Taking the books in their hand, they conducted the whole ceremony from beginning to end, while the others replied and assisted. And the two placed the corpse in the grave. But when these things were taking place, the deacon in Périgueux was ready to begin the reading of the Gospel, the singing of the clergy being finished. He nudged the bishop who was sleeping on his throne, seeking a blessing. But he gave no reply, and all the clergy and men of the city standing around asked in wonder why the bishop made such a delay. Then the holy bishop, waking as if from a pleasant sleep, said: "My brother, what are you doing? Why did you awaken me? Wonderful things have happened to us. Our Lord Jesus Christ led me to the funeral of his hostess Martha, and we handed her over to the grave, as we promised to her once a year ago when she was living. But I beg you, send messengers quickly to that place to bring back to us our gold ring and silver gloves, which, when placing the body in the grave I entrusted to a sacristan of the church to keep for me, and which I forgot when I left the church because you awoke me so suddenly." Messengers were sent quickly and they found things as the bishop had said. And they brought back the ring and one glove: the sacristan kept the other as a witness of this great thing.[574] After this, when St. Fronto was again discussing the funeral of St. Martha with his brothers, he said: "After we buried her[575] and we were leaving the church, a certain brother of that place who was versed in letters followed us, and asked the Lord who He was, and from where, and by what name he was called. He, replying nothing, held out a book which was open in His hand in which nothing else was written than this verse of the psalmist: 'My hostess will be just in everlasting memory; she will not fear an evil hearing on the last day.'[576] When the book was rolled up again, this writing was found on each leaf." For that reason,[577] it is plain that the just hostess of Christ will be held in everlasting memory of the angels and men, and she will not fear an evil hearing when they pay attention to evil things. Depart from me evilsayers.[578] Thus her abode is established in Salem, and her heavenly dwelling place in Zion.[579] Therefore Christ loved her soul whose body He buried.

Of King Clovis

Then what great numbers of both the famous and the unknown were received at her tomb, bringing petitions: the weak, lame, blind, withered, mute, deaf, lunatic, those with all kinds of diseases and demons. No one could describe them. The miracle which they sought was received by all. Among them was Clovis, first king of the Franks and Teutons, who had been baptized as a Christian by St. Remy, bishop of Rheims.[580] It is said that Clovis came to the place because he suffered from a serious kidney problem and he had heard rumours of the godly hostess of Christ. As soon as he touched her sacred tomb, he rejoiced to recover, healed of the disease for which no one had been able to discover a cure. And because of St. Martha, he gave to her place the land and cities and towns for three miles on both sides of the Rhone, and sealed it with his ring. And he made this place a free church, writing that it could not be made subject to anyone at any time.

Of the vengeance of God in this place

As for the rest, there is one thing of which it is not good to be silent. For from that time on, if any theft or robbery or false witness or adultery and any outrageous thing was done in that place, or any cheating, in a short time divine vengeance was enacted. And if it was not, it was because the right hand of God was reserving his vengeance for the future: for no good will be unrewarded or evil unpunished. Both the punished and the unpunished must stand before God.[581] Therefore the inhabitants of this place were terrified and recognized their wickedness. Marcilla and Syntex and Epaphras, the most virtuous and apostolic of individuals, went to Sclavonia[582] and, preaching there the gospel of Christ, they continued with good works. Marcilla lived ten years after St. Martha. She produced this long life of the distinguished one in Hebrew, then I, Syntex, transcribed it into Latin much later. Euchodius and Germanus and Sostenes, followers of St. Martha, kept watch over the sacred body of the godly hostess as long as they lived, and rested in that place after a blessed end. Therefore we brothers are informed of this holy one, whose life we call to memory, for one who is mindful of her will be remembered by God, and we wish to be worthy to reign with her in the heavenly kingdom in good time. Thus Martha, the hostess of Christ, is a form of the active life in the present and for the future, for she will receive the needy who come to her home in the kingdom of heaven, as it was said to her by the Lord. Come and speak well of me to my Father, and gather me into my kingdom. Thus it is declared, and I surrender myself, because He is worthy to answer for us, whose kingdom and rule will endure without end, for ever and ever, Amen.

SOURCE: *Vita Auct. Pseudo-Marcilia, Interprete Pseudo-Syntyche* (BHL 5546a), as published in Boninus Mombritius, *Sanctuarius, seu Vitae Sanctorum*, Mediolani: ante 1480, reprinted Paris: Fontemoing, 1910, 231–239.

Endnotes

1   *The Women Around Jesus: Reflections on Authentic Personhood* (London: SCM Press, 1982), 18.

2   *Women in the Life of Jesus* (Indianapolis, MN: Bobbs-Merrill, 1962), 132.

3   These works will be discussed in more detail in a subsequent chapter.

4   See Origen, *Homélies sur S. Luc*, tr. Henri Crouzel (Paris: Cerf, 1962), 521–523.

5   See Ambrose of Milan, *Opera Omnia* II (Paris: Garnier Frères, 1879), Appendix, col. 454. For further discussion, see Chapter VI.

6   See Victor Saxer, *Le culte de Marie Madeleine en occident des origines à la fin du Moyen-Age* (Paris: Clavreuil, 1959), 38–39.

7   In the early Christian period there was a great deal of general confusion over the identities of the various Marys mentioned in the New Testament; see Susan Haskins, *Mary Magdalen: Myth and Metaphor* (New York: Harcourt Brace & Co., 1993), 25–6, 90–97, 197–9 for a discussion of how Mary of Bethany came to be linked with Mary Magdalene in the Christian west. In eastern Christendom, they were considered to be two separate women.

8   References to a "terra sancte Marthe" or "sancta Martha" at Tarascon are found in charters dating from 964 and 967, and a bull of Pope Urban II dating from 1096 mentions a church of St. Martha. See H. Leclercq, "Lazare" in *Dictionnaire d'archéologie chrétienne et de liturgie* VIII/2, ed. Fernand Cabrol (Paris: Létouzey, 1929), col. 2071.

9   See Appendix A for a discussion of E. M. Faillon's 1848 account of the rise of the Martha cult in Provence. This text is one of the most detailed summaries of the Martha cult in the later Middle Ages, but it contains a number of errors and inconsistencies.

10   The Seven Sleepers were young Christian men who were said to have been walled up in a cave in Ephesus during the persecutions initiated by the Emperor Decius, around 250 A.D. They awoke from their long sleep when the cave was opened in the reign of the Emperor Theodosius II in the early fifth century.

11   See Victor Saxer, "Les saintes Marie-Madeleine et Marie de Bethanie dans la tradition liturgique et homilétique orientale," *Révue des sciences réligieuses* 32 (1958):1–57.

12   See Clive Foss, *Ephesus After Antiquity: A Late Antique, Byzantine and Turkish City* (Cambridge: Cambridge University Press, 1979), 33.

13   See Marjorie M. Malvern, *Venus in Sackcloth: The Magdalen's Origins and Metamorphoses* (Carbondale IL: Southern Illinois University Press, 1975), 74–75.

14 See Victor Saxer, "L'origine des reliques de Ste Marie-Madeleine à Vézélay dans la tradition historiographique des Moyen Age," *Révue des sciences réligieuses* 29 (1955):1–18.

15 The legends surrounding James' mission to Spain apparently originated in Spain in the seventh century. Cf. H. Leclercq, "Espagne" in *Dictionnaire d'archéologie chrétienne et de liturgie*, V/1, cols. 407–523.

16 The children of Bethlehem massacred by order of Herod in his attempt to destroy the infant Jesus (Matthew 2:16-18).

17 See H. Leclercq, "Maries-de-la-Mer (Les Saintes)" in *Dictionnaire d'archéologie chrétienne et de liturgie* X/2, cols. 2119–2128.

18 For a recent, detailed account of the rival claims of Vézélay and Saint-Maximin as exclusive possessors of Mary Magdalene's body, see Neal Raymond Clemens, "The Establishment of the Cult of Mary Magdalen in Provence, 1279–1543," Ph.D. diss., Columbia University, New York, 1997. In the early nineteenth century the remains were transferred from St. Maximin to the cathedral of Aix-en-Provence.

19 For a translation of these four Latin documents see Diane Elizabeth Peters, "The Early Latin Sources of the Legend of St. Martha: A Study and Translation with Critical Notes," M.A. diss., Wilfrid Laurier University, Waterloo, Ontario, 1990.

20 See *Bibliotheca Hagiographica Latina Antiquae et Mediae Aetatis* (Bruxelles: Société des Bollandistes, 1898–9), no. 5545–5547.

21 According to the Provençal legends of the saints from Bethany, Marcilia (Marcella, Martilla) was the woman who cried out to Jesus from the crowd "Blessed is the womb that bore you and the breasts that you sucked" (Luke 11:27). From the twelfth century, St. Marcella's tomb was among those venerated in the basilica of the town of Saint-Maximin in Provence. A Sythex (Syntyche) is named in Philippians 4:2 as one of Paul's fellow workers for Christ.

22 *Biblotheca Hagiographica Latina.*, no. 5508.

23 See Victor Saxer, "La vie de sainte Marie Madeleine attribué au Pseudo-Raban Maur oeuvre claravallienne du XIIe siècle," in *Mélanges Saint Bernard* (Dijon: Marilier, 1953), 408–421.

24 Martha material is found in chapters 92, 94, 99–101 and 104–107.

25 He is described as a Syrian prince, highly skilled in administration, who governed as the first among the satraps of the province. After becoming a disciple of Christ, he renounced his worldly offices (see D. Peters, "Early Latin Sources," 109–110.)

26 Vincent of Beauvais, *Speculum Historiale*, ch. 92, in Peters, "Early Latin Sources," 152.

27 Since the time of Origen it had been more common to associate Martha with the synagogue and the Old Testament laws and Mary with the Christian church and the new "spiritual" law of Romans 7:14.

28 There are many chronological anachronisms in the Martha texts, including the reference to St. Fronto, a fourth-century bishop of Périgueux.

29 See Gregory of Tours, *Selections from the Minor Works* (Philadelphia PA: University of Pennsylvania Press, 1949), 36–37.

30 Harmondsworth, UK: Penguin Books, 1974, 151–2, 154.

31 Dominic (1170–1221), the founder of the Dominican order, spent a number of years in the south of France, at around the same time that the legends surrounding Martha were developing there.

32 *The Women Around Jesus*, 33.

33 There is a considerable body of literature which explores the complex of unorthodox beliefs prevalent in Provence during the twelfth and thirteenth centuries, including a number of recent books. Although many are of a more popular than scholarly persuasion, they present many thought-provoking ideas. Cf. for example, Michael Baigent, Richard Leigh and Henry Lincoln's *Holy Blood, Holy Grail* (New York: Dell Publishing, 1983) and its sequel *The Messianic Legacy* (New York: Holt, 1987), Margaret Starbird's *The Woman with the Alabaster Jar: Mary Magdalen and the Holy Grail* (Sante Fe NM: Bear & Company, 1993), or Lynn Pickett and Clive Prince's *The Templar Revelation: Secret Guardians of the True Identity of Christ* (New York: Bantam, 1997). These works provide fascinating accounts of Knights Templar, royal bloodlines, and various "mystery cults," some of which they claim survive down to the present day. Some of their research has also been disseminated widely as a result of the popularity of Dan Brown's novel *The Da Vinci Code* (New York: Doubleday, 2004), released in a movie version in 2006.

34 The Pseudo-Marcilia, Vincent of Beauvais and *Vita Beatae Mariae Magdalenae* versions all describe Martha as wearing a hair-shirt with a horsehair belt tied in knots, so tight on her flesh that worms emerged from her rotted flesh.

35 *The Beguines and Beghards in Medieval Culture: With Special Emphasis on the Belgian Scene* (New York: Octagon Books, 1969), 437–8.

36 Cited by Frances Gies and Joseph Gies, *Women in the Middle Ages* (New York: Barnes & Noble, 1978), 92.

37 Cf. Johan Döllinger, *Beiträge auf Sektengeschichte des Mittelalters*, II (München: Beck, 1890), 381, 407, 411, 415; Paul Fredericq, *Geschiedenis der Inquisitie in de Nederlanden*, II (Ghent, 1897), 153f, 182–184.

38 Jean de Meung, *Roman de la Rose*, tr. David and Patricia Herlihy, in *Medieval Culture and Society*, ed. David Herlihy (New York: Macmillan, 1968), 237.

39   Andrée Kahn Blumstein, *Misogyny and Idealization in the Courtly Romance* (Bonn: Bouvier Verlag, 1977), 3.

40   Cited by Gies and Gies, *Women in the Middle Ages*, 46.

41   It was not until 1482, when Charles III, count of Provence, died childless, that Tarascon and Provence officially became part of France.

42   Information from a brochure entitled "Tarascon, City of the King and Queen," distributed by the Tarascon tourist bureau.

43   See Louis Dumont, *La Tarasque* (Paris: Gallimard, 1987) for an ethnographic study of the tarasque ritual. Photographs of the mechanical beast used in festivities today can also be seen on the city of Tarascon website – http://www.tarascon.org/en/fete.php#.

44   The other sections were the *Speculum Naturale*, dealing with natural history, and the *Speculum Doctrinale*, outlining the learned arts.

45   See B. L. Ullman, "A Project for a New Edition of Vincent of Beauvais," *Speculum* 8 (1933):317–326 for a discussion of the complicated early publishing history of the work. The 1624 Douai version of the text was reprinted (Graz: Akademische Druck -u. Verlagstanstalt, 1964–65).

46   These include three versions in Bohemian, eleven in Dutch, four in English, twenty in French, eighteen in High German, seven in Low German and thirteen in Italian. See Robert Francis Seybolt, "Fifteenth Century Editions of the Legenda Aurea," *Speculum* 21 (1946):327–338. Other important texts of Martha's life not mentioned by Seybolt include the Middle English versions in the *South English Legendary* (late thirteenth century) and in the *Gilte Legende* (1438). The *Scottish Legendary* includes a legend of the saint in the Middle Scottish dialect. An Anglo-Norman verse legend by Nicole Bozon dates from the late thirteenth or early fourteenth century. Martha legends also appear in Middle French in the D1 Legendary (ca. 1275); the E Legendary (before 1312); the E1 Legendary (early fourteenth century); the Bibliothèque Nationale fr. 13496 manuscript (late thirteen or early fourteenth century); the Bibliothèque Royale de Belgique 10295-10304 manuscript (compiled 1428-9); the Bibliothèque Sainte-Genevieve 587 ff. 3-32 manuscript; and the Bibliothèque Nationale fr. 423 (early fourteenth century).

47   See Robert Francis Seybolt, "The Legenda Aurea, Bible, and Historia Scholastica," *Speculum* 21 (1946): 339–342.

48   Cf. Germaine Maillet, *Sainte Marthe* (Paris: Henri Laurens, 1932); Diane E. Peters, "The Iconography of St. Martha: Some Considerations," *Vox Benedictina* 9/1 (Summer 1992):39–65.

49   See, for example, Francis J. Moloney, *Woman First Among the Faithful* (Notre Dame IN: Ave Maria Press, 1986), 71–72; Frederick W. Danker, *Jesus and the New Age: A Commentary on St. Luke's Gospel* (Philadelphia PA: Fortress Press, 1988), 224; Craig A. Evans, *Luke* (Peabody MA: Henrickson

Publishers, 1990), 176–177; John J. Kilgallen, "Martha and Mary: Why At Luke 10:38-42?", *Biblica* 84/4 (2003):554–561; Frances Taylor Gench, "Martha and Mary," in *Back to the Well: Women's Encounters with Jesus in the Gospels* (Louisville KY: Westminster John Knox, 2004), 57–8.

50   See David Gill, "Observations on the Lukan Travel Narrative and Some Related Passages," *Harvard Theological Review* 63 (1970):199–221; James L. Resseguie, "Point of View in the Central Section of Luke (8:51-19:44)," *Journal of the Evangelical Theological Society* 25 (March, 1982): 41–47; David Moessner, *Lord of the Banquet: The Literary and Theological Significance of the Lukan Travel Narrative* (Minneapolis MN: Fortress Press, 1989); Warren Carter, "Getting Martha Out of the Kitchen: Luke 10:38-42 Again," *Catholic Biblical Quarterly* 58 (April, 1996):266–8.

51   Jesus' response to the lawyer who asks what he must do to inherit eternal life; the story of the Good Samaritan; the story of Jesus' visit to the home of Mary and Martha.

52   See C. F. Evans, "The Central Section of St. Luke's Gospel," in *Studies in the Gospels* (London: Blackwell, 1955), 37–53 and Robert W. Wall, "Martha and Mary (Luke 10.38-42) in the Context of a Christian Deuteronomy," in *Journal for the Study of the New Testament* 35 (1989):19–35.

53   See Aelred Baker, "One Thing Necessary," *Catholic Biblical Quarterly* 27 (1965):127–137 for a more complete discussion of the problem. Among modern commentators Baker and Peter C. Erb, "The Contemplative Life as the Unum Necessarium: in defense of a traditional reading of Luke 10:42," *Mystics Quarterly* 11/4 (December 1985):161–4, maintain that "one thing is necessary" is the "correct" reading. Gordon Fee, however, argues in favour of a longer reading; see "One Thing Needful? Luke 10:42," in *New Testament Textual Criticism: Its Significance for Exegesis*, ed. Eldon Jay Epp and Gordon Fee (Oxford: Clarendon Press, 1981), 61–75.

54   New York: Oxford University Press, 1977, 1261.

55   "The Tradition History of the Martha-Mary Pericope in Luke (10:38-42)," in *Ancient History in a Modern University, Volume 2: Early Christianity, Late Christianity, and Beyond*, ed. T. W. Hillard, R. A. Kearsley, C. E. V. Nixon, and A. M. Nobbs (Grand Rapids MI: Eerdmans, 1998), 93–97.

56   In *The Anti-Nicene Fathers*, IV, ed. Alexander Roberts and James Donaldson (New York: Charles Scribner's Sons, 1913), 594.

57   John Cassian, *Conferences*, tr. Colm Luibheid (New York: Paulist Press, 1985) 42–43.

58   Augustine, "Sermon LIV," in *A Select Library of the Nicene and Post-Nicene Fathers of the Christian Church*, VI, ed. Philip Schaff (New York: Scribner's, 1908), 429–430.

59   Ibid., 430.

60 In *Sermons on the Liturgical Seasons*, tr. Mary Sarah Muldowney (New York: Fathers of the Church, 1959), 349–350.

61 See Sister Mary Elizabeth Mason, *Active Life and Contemplative Life: A Study of the Concepts from Plato to the Present* (Milwaukee WI: Marquette University Press, 1961), 35ff.

62 For more complete summaries of the exegetical literature on Mary and Martha, see Aimé Solignac, "Marthe et Marie," in *Dictionnaire de spiritualité ascétique et mystique*, X (Paris: Beauchesne, 1932), X, cols. 664–672; Charles Baumgartner, "Contemplation," ibid., II/2 (Paris: Beauchesne, 1953), cols. 1643–2193; or Giles Constable, "The Interpretation of Mary and Martha," in *Three Studies in Medieval Religious and Social Thought* (Cambridge: Cambridge University Press, 1995), 1–141.

63 Cf. *Homilies on Ezechiel* II, iv, 4.

64 *Moralia* or *Exposition on the Book of Job* 6.57, cited Mason, *Active Life and Contemplative Life*, 63.

65 *Moralia*, 6.61; cited ibid., 64.

66 *Moralia*, 28.33; cited ibid., 66.

67 See Martina Wehrli-Johns, "Maria und Martha in der religiösen Frauenbewegung," in *Abendländische Mystik im Mittelalter*, ed. Kurt Ruh (Stuttgart: Metzlersche, 1986), 355, 363.

68 Ibid., 355. Cited Blake R. Heffner, "Meister Eckhart and a Millennium with Mary and Martha," *Lutheran Quarterly* 5 (Summer 1991), 175.

69 In *Francis and Clare: The Complete Works*, tr. Regis J. Armstrong and Ignatius Brady (New York: Paulist Press, 1982), 147–148.

70 Cf. I.II, Questions 179–182; II.II, Question 188.

71 Tr. Simon Tugwell (New York: Paulist Press, 1988), 577.

72 Ibid., 582.

73 Ibid., 629–630.

74 *Sermons*, tr. Maria Shrady (New York: Paulist Press, 1985), 154–155.

75 Ibid., 156.

76 *Sermons on the Gospel of St. John*, ed. Jaroslav Pelikan (Saint Louis MI: Concordia, 1959), 247; cf. *Lectures on Galatians 1535*, ed. Jaroslav Pelikan (Saint Louis MI: Concordia, 1963), 214; *First Lectures on the Psalms I*, ed. Hilton C. Oswald (Saint Louis MI: Concordia, 1974), 127; *Liturgy and Hymns*, ed. Ulrich S. Leupold (Saint Louis MI: Concordia, 1965), 14.

77 Some passages in Luther's works suggest that he thought Martha was a housewife, although this is not explicitly stated in the Gospels; cf. his comments on 1 Corinthians 7:34: "for a married man cannot give himself up entirely to reading and praying but is, as Paul here says, 'divided'; that

is, he must devote much of his time to making life agreeable for his wife, and like Martha, he is bound up in the multitude of concerns demanded by married life" (*Commentaries on 1 Corinthians 7, 1 Corinthians 15, Lectures on 1 Timothy*, ed. Hilton C. Oswald [Saint Louis MI: Concordia, 1973], 53.) For a discussion of Luther's views on women's proper role see Merry Wiesner, "Luther and Women: The Death of Two Marys," in *Disciplines of Faith: Studies in Religion, Politics and Patriarchy*, ed. Jim Obelkevich, Lyndal Roper and Raphael Samuel (London: Routledge & Kegan Paul, 1987), 295–308.

78   3.11.19, tr. Ford Lewis Battles (Philadelphia PA: Westminster Press, 1960), 1, 748.

79   3.14.19, ibid., 786.

80   *A Harmony of the Gospels Matthew, Mark and Luke*, II, tr. T. H. L. Parker (Grand Rapids MI: Eerdmans, 1972), 89.

81   Ibid., 89–90.

82   Ibid., 90.

83   *The Treasury of the New Testament*, Vol. I (London: Marshall, Morgan & Scott, n.d.), 803.

84   Ibid., 804.

85   Ibid., 804–807.

86   *The New Being* (New York: Charles Scribner's Sons, 1955), 152–3.

87   *In Times Like These* (Toronto ON: University of Toronto Press, 1972), 30–1.

88   Ibid., 34–5.

89   *Women and the Genesis of Christianity* (Cambridge: Cambridge University Press, 1990), 100, 101.

90   *Women in the Ministry of Jesus: A Study of Jesus' Attitudes to Women and Their Roles as Reflected in His Earthly Life* (Cambridge: Cambridge University Press, 1984), 101, 103. However, Witherington's comments are somewhat contradictory. While maintaining that serving at table is a traditional female role, he also contends that in a Jewish context women were not allowed to serve at meals if men were in attendance (ibid., 101, 112) and thus Martha's actions might be considered as radical as her sister's. However, Adele Reinhartz, a Jewish writer herself, suggests that many of Witherington's assumptions about the role of women in first-century Judaism are open to question; cf. "From Narrative to History: The Resurrection of Mary and Martha" in *"Women Like This": New Perspectives on Jewish Women in the Greco-Roman World*, ed. Amy-Jill Levine (Atlanta GA: Scholars Press, 1991), 165–6. See also Rosemary Radford Ruether, "Seeking the Better Part," *Sojourners* (November 1992), 25–26. Ruether suggests that the household in

Bethany was, in fact, a small, urban Essene community, in which prayer and study would have been an important component of daily life for both men and women; she also notes that the issue of whether women should study the Torah was widely debated in early rabbinic literature.

91 Witherington, *Women in the Ministry of Jesus*, 181.

92 In *Spinning a Sacred Yarn: Women Speak from the Pulpit* (New York: Pilgrim Press, 1982), 159–161. Used with permission.

93 Constance Parvey, "Theology and Leadership of Women in the New Testament," in *Religion and Sexism*, ed. Rosemary Radford Ruether (New York: Simon & Schuster, 1974), 141. However, in her study of women and meal customs in the broader context of Greco-Roman society, Kathleen Corley comes to an opposite conclusion. In her view, Mary's posture is that of a "traditional, silent wife, who sits at the feet of her husband at the table" (*Private Women, Public Meals: Social Conflict in the Synoptic Tradition* [Peabody MA: Hendrickson, 1993], 154).

94 *The Gospel According to Luke X–XXIV* (Garden City NY: Doubleday, 1985), 892.

95 *Back to the Well*, 56.

96 *Meister Eckhart: Teacher and Preacher*, ed. Bernard McGinn (New York: Paulist Press, 1986), 338–9, 342.

97 The sermon concludes by noting that Mary's transformation did, in fact, take place: "'Mary sat at the feet of the Lord and listened to his words,' and learned, for she had just been put into school and was learning to live. But afterwards, when she had learned and Christ had ascended into heaven and she received the Holy Spirit, then she really for the first time began to serve. Then she crossed the sea, preached, taught, and became the servant and washerwoman of the disciples. Thus do the saints become saints; not until then do they really begin to practice virtue. For it is then that they gather the treasure of eternal happiness." Ibid., 344.

98 Ibid., 340.

99 "Martha and Mary—Love Greater Than Achievement—A Character Study," *Methodist Review* 81 (May, 1899):421.

100 Ibid., 422. Although it is highly unlikely that he was familiar with this source, Walsh seems to echo the comment in the twelfth-century life of Martha compiled by "Pseudo-Marcilia" which notes that "Martha had authority before all her relatives because she was more capable and had a greater abundance of intelligence and honesty" (Peters, *Early Latin Sources*, 76).

101 Ibid., 424.

102 "A Feminist Critical Interpretation for Liberation: Martha and Mary: Lk. 10:38-42," *Religion & Intellectual Life* 3/2 (Winter 1986):29. Schüssler Fiorenza discusses the meaning of these terms more fully in *In Memory of*

Her: A Feminist Theological Reconstruction of Christian Origins (Boston MA: Beacon Press, 1983), 165–6. Frances Taylor Gench points out that while it might appear anachronistic to speak of Martha as engaged in eucharistic table service prior to the death and resurrection of Jesus, the story is addressed to Luke's post-resurrection community, in which women may well have been engaged in such service (*Back to the Well*, 174.)

103 "A Feminist Critical Interpretation," 30.

104 Ibid., 32.

105 Ibid., 34.

106 Schüssler Fiorenza's hermeneutical methods and her ideas on the androcentrism of Luke are critiqued in the *Protocol of the Colloquy of the Center for Hermeneutical Studies in Hellenistic and Modern Culture (10 April 1986): Theological Criteria and Historical Reconstruction: Martha and Mary, Luke 10:38-42*, ed. Herman Waetjen (Berkeley CA: Graduate Theological Union & University of California-Berkeley, 1987). Her original article is expanded and revised in "Arachne—Weaving the Word: The Practice of Interpretation: Luke 10:38-42" in *But She Said: Feminist Practices of Biblical Interpretation* (Boston MA: Beacon Press, 1992), 51–76.

107 Cf. Elisabeth Moltmann-Wendel, "Martha," in *The Women Around Jesus*, 15–48; Elisabeth Moltmann-Wendel and Jürgen Moltmann, "Martha—A Forgotten Medieval Tradition," in *Humanity in God* (New York: Pilgrim Press, 1983), 17–34; Dorothee Soelle, "Mary and Martha: The Unity of Action and Dreams," in *The Window of Vulnerability: A Political Spirituality* (Minneapolis MN: Fortress Press, 1990), 93–96; Mary Cartledge-Hayes, "Martha," in *To Love Delilah: Claiming the Women of the Bible* (San Diego CA: LuraMedia, 1990), 66–75; Adele Reinhartz, "From Narrative to History: The Resurrection of Mary and Martha," in *"Women Like This,"* 161–184; Loveday Alexander, "Sisters in Adversity: Retelling Martha's Story," in *Women in the Biblical Tradition*, ed. George J. Brooke (Lewiston NY: Edwin Mellen Press, 1992), 167–186; Linda M. Maloney and Elizabeth J. Smith, "The Year of Luke: A Feminist Perspective," *Currents in Theology and Mission* 21/6 (December 1994):415–423.

108 Cf. Matthew 21:17, 26:6; Mark 11:1, 11:11-12, 14:3; Luke 19:29, 24:50; John 11:1, 11:18, 12:1.

109 Luke 10:38; John 12:2.

110 Jeremiah 14:8b.

111 Acts 10:34.

112 Peters, *Early Latin Sources*, 153–154. The Pseudo-Marcilia account is similar, although somewhat more extended; see ibid., 77–80. On the other hand, the *Vita Beatae Mariae Magdalenae* emphasizes that the Lord loved Martha because of her pious actions, but makes it clear that Mary's contemplation is superior to Martha's busyness; see ibid., 112–113.

113 For example, the illustration of the statue of Martha from the Église Ste-Madeleine, Troyes, France (early sixteenth century), reproduced by Emile Mâle, *Les saints compagnons du Christ* (Paris: Paul Hartmann, 1958), 83.

114 *Humanity in God*, 33.

115 For example, Letty M. Russell, "Women and Ministry," in A. L. Hageman, *Sexist Religion and Women in the Church* (New York: Association Press, 1974), 55ff.

116 Cf. R. Richardson Smith, "Liberating the Servant," *The Christian Century* 98 (1981):13–14 and R. Propst, "Servanthood Redefined: Coping Mechanism for Women Within Protestant Christianity," *Journal of Pastoral Counseling* 17 (1982):14–18.

117 Rosemary Radford Ruether, *Sexism and God-Talk: Towards A Feminist Theology* (Boston MA: Beacon Press, 1983), 206–207.

118 *A Land Flowing With Milk and Honey: Perspectives on Feminist Theology* (New York: Crossroad, 1986), 128.

119 "Arachne: Weaving the Word," 71–72.

120 "Seeking the Better Part," 26.

121 See *The History of the Synoptic Tradition*, tr. John Marsh (New York: Harper & Row, 1963), 11, 33.

122 Matthew 21:12; Mark 11:15-17; Luke 19:45-46; John 2:13-17.

123 Matthew 16:51-52; Mark 14:47; Luke 22:50-51; John 18:10; the follower of Jesus is named as Peter only in the Gospel of John.

124 Joachim Jeremias, *Rediscovering the Parables* (New York: Charles Scribner's Sons, 1966), 145.

125 See, for example, Rudolf Schnackenburg, *The Gospel According to St. John*, Vol. 2 (New York: Crossroad, 1982), 342.

126 See J. N. Sanders, "'Those Whom Jesus Loved' (John xi.5)," *New Testament Studies* 1 (1954–55):29–41.

127 See Colin Brown, "Women," in *The New International Dictionary of New Testament Theology*, III, ed. Colin Brown (Grand Rapids MI: Zondervan, 1986), 1061.

128 These signs were: changing water into wine at Cana (John 2:1-11); curing the royal official's son at Cana (John 4:46-54); curing the paralytic at the pool of Bethesda (John 5:2-9); the multiplication of the loaves in Galilee (John 6:1-14); walking upon the Sea of Galilee (John 6:16-21); curing the blind man in Jerusalem (John 9:1-38); and the raising of Lazarus from the dead at Bethany (John 11:1-44).

129 See Rudolf Bultmann, *The Gospel of John: A Commentary*, tr. G. R. Beasley-Murray (Philadelphia PA: Westminster Press, 1971), 6–7, 395; Robert Kysar,

The Fourth Evangelist and His Gospel (Minneapolis MN: Augsburg, 1975); Urban C. von Wahlde, *The Earliest Version of John's Gospel: Recovering the Gospel of Signs* (Wilmington DE: Michael Glazier, 1989); Robert Tomson Fortna, *The Gospel of Signs: A Reconstruction of the Narrative Source Underlying the Fourth Gospel* (Cambridge: Cambridge University Press, 1970) and *The Fourth Gospel and Its Predecessor: From Narrative Source to the Present Gospel* (Philadelphia PA: Fortress Press, 1988). Morton Smith discusses a letter of Clement of Alexandria describing a resurrection from the dead in which Clement claims to quote from a "secret gospel of Mark." His account bears a striking resemblance to the Lazarus story in John; see *Clement of Alexandria and a Secret Gospel of Mark* (Cambridge: Harvard University Press, 1973), 447.

130   Augustine, *Tractates on the Gospel of John 28-54*, tr. John W. Rettig (Washington DC: Catholic University of America Press, 1993), 250–251, 252. This focus on the words of Jesus rather than those of Martha is found in literature on the passage right up until the present day; cf. Paul S. Minear, "The Promise of Life in the Gospel of John," *Theology Today* 49 (1993):485–499.

131   Commentary on John VI.24 in *The Ante-Nicene Fathers*, X, ed. Allan Menzies (Grand Rapids MI: Eerdmans, 1951), 371.

132   *Commentary on Saint John the Apostle and Evangelist, Homilies 48–88*, tr. Sister Thomas Aquinas Goggin (New York: Fathers of the Church, 1960), 165, 171.

133   Ibid.

134   Ibid., 173–174.

135   Ibid., 180.

136   Ibid., 210.

137   Tr. Rev. William Pringle (Grand Rapids MI: Eerdmans, 1956), 433–434.

138   Ibid., 404.

139   Ibid.

140   Ibid., 437.

141   *Sermons on the Gospel of St. John, Chapters 1–4*, ed. Jaroslav Pelikan (Saint Louis MO: Concordia, 1957), 128. It is not clear why Luther claims Martha's belief was inspired by John the Baptist.

142   *The Gospel of John: A Commentary*, 401–402.

143   Ibid., 405, 406.

144   Ibid., 404.

145   Ibid.

146   Cf., for example, Francis J. Moloney, *Woman First Among the Faithful* (Notre Dame IN: Ave Maria Press, 1986), 87–90; Raymond Brown, *The Gospel and*

Epistles of John: A Concise Commentary (Collegeville MN: Liturgical Press, 1988), 64; John Painter, *The Quest for the Messiah: The History, Literature and Theology of the Johannine Community* (Edinburgh: T. & T. Clark, 1991), 313–320.

147 *Theological Studies* 36 (1975):688–699.

148 Ibid., 690–1. Others, however, have disputed the suggestion that Martha's act of "serving" in this setting implied a eucharistic function; see, for example, Turid Karlsen Seim, "Roles of Women in the Gospel of John," in *Aspects on the Johannine Literature: Papers Presented at a Conference of Scandinavian New Testament Exegetes at Uppsala, June 16–19, 1986*, ed. Lars Hartman and Birger Olsson (Uppsala: Almquist & Wiksell International, 1987), 72–73. This issue will be discussed in more detail in the following chapter.

149 Brown, "Roles of Women in the Fourth Gospel," 693.

150 Ibid., 694.

151 Ibid.

152 *A Land Flowing with Milk and Honey*, 121, 122, 123.

153 "Roles of Women in the Gospel of John," 70.

154 "Death in the Community of Eternal Life: History, Theology and Spirituality in John 11," *Interpretation* 41 (1987):47–48. See also Charles H. Giblin, "Suggestion, Negative Response, and Positive Action in St. John's Portrayal of Jesus," *New Testament Studies* 26 (1980):197–211, especially 208–210.

155 "Roles of Women in the Gospel of John," 71; see also Sandra M. Schneiders, "Death in the Community of Eternal Life," 44–45. Gérard Rochais, *Les Récits de Résurrection des Morts dans le Nouveau Testament* (Cambridge: Cambridge University Press, 1981), 113ff. proposes a detailed reconstruction of the Evangelist's redactional approach.

156 "Now Jesus did many other signs in the presence of the disciples, which are not written in this book; but these are written that you may believe that Jesus is the Christ, the Son of God, and believing you may have life in his name." (RSV)

157 "Women in the Gospel of John," *Église et Théologie* 17 (1986):141.

158 Ibid., 142.

159 "Roles of Women in the Gospel of John," 72.

160 *The Women Around Jesus*, 25.

161 Elizabeth Moltmann-Wendel and Jürgen Moltmann, "'Who do you say that I am?': Peter's confession and Martha's confession: A Joint Bible Study at the General Assembly of the Reformed World Alliance, Seoul, 15–26 August 1989" in *God—His & Hers* (New York: Crossroad, 1991), 48–49. Moltmann-Wendel cites Bultmann as the first to recognize the significance of this title of Christ.

162 *In Memory of Her*, 329.

163 See *The Gospel of Signs*, 197–9.

164 *In Memory of Her*, 329–30.

165 *The Women in the Life of the Bridegroom: A Feminist Historical-Literary Analysis of the Female Characters in the Fourth Gospel* (Collegeville MN: Liturgical Press, 1998):84.

166 Ibid, 85.

167 Ibid., 113.

168 As cited earlier, Francis Taylor Gench points out (*Back to the Well*, 174) that it might appear anachronistic to speak of Martha's service at the table as eucharistic table service prior to the death and resurrection of Jesus, but the story is addressed to Luke's post-resurrection community.

169 "Women and Discipleship in Luke," *Catholic Biblical Quarterly* 56/1 (January, 1994):2, 3, 5. Other useful "summaries" of interpretations of Luke's attitudes towards women are those of John Collins in "Did Luke Intend a Disservice to Women in the Martha and Mary Story?" *Biblical Theology Bulletin* 28 (Fall, 1998):104–111 and Veronica Koperski in "Luke 10,38-42 and Acts 6,1-7: Women and Discipleship in the Literary Context of Luke-Acts," in *Unity of Luke-Acts* (Louvain: Peeters, 1999), 517–544.

170 *Back to the Well*, 69.

171 *The Meal Scenes in Luke-Acts: An Audience-Oriented Approach* (Atlanta GA: Society of Biblical Literature, 1999), 69.

172 Ibid., 77.

173 Ibid., 78–9.

174 *The Double Message: Patterns of Gender in Luke-Acts* (Nashville TN: Abingdon Press, 1994), 98–9.

175 Ibid., 99–100.

176 See "Did Luke Intend a Disservice to Women?," 108.

177 New York: Oxford University Press, 1990.

178 "Did Luke Intend a Disservice to Women?," 110.

179 "Pitting Mary Against Martha," in *Choosing the Better Part: Women in the Gospel of Luke* (Collegeville MN: Liturgical Press, 1996), 154.

180 Ibid., 157.

181 Ibid., 158.

182 See her article "Choosing the Better Part," *Biblical Research* 42 (1997):23–31 for a discussion of the forms of ministerial action undertaken by males and females in Luke and Acts.

183 *Choosing the Better Part: Women in the Gospel of Luke*, 54.

184 "Getting Martha Out of the Kitchen: Luke 10:38-42 Again," *Catholic Biblical Quarterly* 58/2 (April 1996):267–8.

185 Ibid., 269.

186 Ibid., 270.

187 Ibid., 272. However, as noted earlier, Collins has denied that this particular definition of *diakonia* applies in Luke 10.

188 Ibid., 272, 275.

189 Ibid., 276–7.

190 Ibid., 280.

191 Romans 16:12.

192 Philippians 4:2.

193 "Women Partners in the New Testament," *Journal of Feminist Studies in Religion* 6 (1990):78–9. See also Mary Rose D'Angelo, "Women in Luke-Acts: A Redactional View," *Journal of Biblical Literature* 109/3 (1990):454 for a more detailed discussion of this verse.

194 *The Oxford Dictionary of the Christian Church*, 3rd ed., ed. E. A. Livingstone (London: Oxford University Press, 1997), 683–4.

195 *The Gospel of John*, 7–8. Bultmann goes on to point out that there is also an anti-Gnostic theology expressed in John: "John knows no cosmic dualism.... Flesh and spirit do not stand opposed as substances of the demonic and divine realms. Rather it is stressed, with all sharpness, that the Redeemer has become *flesh*, and shows his glory precisely as the One made flesh. Man's lostness in the world is not the lost condition of a heavenly substance in the power of darkness, but the sinful turning of the creature from the Creator. In place of cosmic dualism steps a dualism of decision: life and death are not determined from all time on natural grounds, but depend on the decision of faith and of unbelief... . John thus uses the language current in Gnostic circles to give expression to the Christian understanding of faith. The conclusion perhaps could be drawn from this that he lays worth on convincing adherents of Gnostic circles as to the truth of the Gospel." Ibid., 9.

196 Mary Magdalene's name appears in gnostic literature in various forms: Maria, Mariam, Mariamne, Mariham.

197 Origen, "Against Celsus," in *The Anti-Nicene Fathers*, IV, ed. Alexander Roberts and James Donaldson (New York: Charles Scribner's Sons, 1913), 570.

198 See notes by Wolf-Peter Funk in *New Testament Apocrypha*, I, ed. Wilhelm Schneemelcher and Edgar Hennecke (Cambridge: James Clarke & Co., 1991), 314–315.

199 Ibid., 325.

200 Livingstone, *Oxford Dictionary*, 1027.

201 Ed. C. R. C. Allberry (Stuttgart: W. Kohlhammer, 1938), Part II, 192, 194.

202 See notes by Henri-Charles Puech, revised Beate Blatz, in *New Testament Apocrypha* I, 361–2.

203 Book I, chapter 38 (citing Psalm 69) and chapter 57 (citing Psalm 50), Book II, chapter 73 (citing Psalm 29) and chapter 80 (citing Psalm 7); see *Pistis Sophia*, ed. Carl Schmidt, tr. Violet MacDermot (Leiden: Brill, 1978), 123–5, 223–5, 327–9, 353–5.

204 According to John, Nicodemus, a Pharisee and "ruler of the Jews," came to Jesus by night and engaged him in theological discussion (3:1-21); later he came to Jesus' defence when the chief priests and Pharisees talked of arresting him (7:50-52). After the crucifixion, Nicodemus brought myrrh and aloe to anoint Jesus' body for burial (19:39-40).

205 See James DeQuincey Donehoo, *The Apocryphal and Legendary Life of Christ* (New York: Hodder & Stoughton, 1903), 345; this gospel is discussed in *New Testament Apocrypha*, I, 501–505, but a text is not provided. The fourteenth-century Dominican artist Fra Angelico also placed Martha at the foot of the cross in his painting of the Piercing of Christ's Side (ca. 1450) in the Convent of San Marco in Florence.

206 A text of this work, edited and translated by C. Detlef G. Muller, is found in *New Testament Apocrypha* I, 252–278, along with explanatory notes. It is not mentioned in early Christian literature, and nothing was known of its existence until its discovery in 1895 by Carl Schmidt, who published a German translation that year.

207 See A. A. T. Ehrhardt, "Judaeo-Christians in Egypt, the Epistula Apostolorum and the Gospel to the Hebrews," *Studia Evangelica* 3 (1964):360–382.

208 Later in the same version of the text it is Martha herself, not her daughter, who is described as being present on this occasion.

209 Ibid., 255.

210 Ibid.

211 There is a growing body of literature on women in the early Christian and gnostic communities. See, for example, Ross Shepard Kraemer, *Her Share of the Blessings: Women's Religions Among Pagans, Jews, and Christians in the Greco-Roman World* (New York: Oxford University Press, 1992); Karen Jo Torjesen, *When Women Were Priests: Women's Leadership in the Early Church and the Scandal of Their Subordination in the Rise of Christianity* (San Francisco CA: Harper San Francisco, 1993); Elizabeth A. Castelli, "Heterglossia, Hermeneutics, and History: A Review Essay of Recent Feminist Studies of Early Christianity," *Journal of Feminist Studies in Religion* 10 (Fall, 1994):73–98; Luise Schottroff, *Lydia's Impatient Sisters:*

A Feminist Social History of Early Christianity (Louisville KY: Westminster/John Knox Press, 1995); Anne Jensen, *God's Self-Confident Daughters: Early Christianity and the Liberation of Women* (Louisville KY: Westminster/John Knox Press, 1996); Constance McLeese, "The Status of Women and Gnosticism in Irenaeus and Tertullian," *Journal of Early Christian Studies* 5 (Spring, 1997):141–3; Ross Shepard Kraemer and Mary Rose D'Angelo, *Women and Christian Origins* (New York: Oxford, 1999); Ute E. Eisen, *Women Officeholders in Early Christianity: Epigraphical and Literary Studies* (Collegeville MN: Liturgical Press, 2000); Karen L. King, ed., *Images of the Feminine in Gnosticism* (Harrisburg PA: Trinity Press International, 2000); Lisa Bellan-Boyer, "Conspicuous in Their Absence: Women in Early Christianity," *Cross Currents* 53/1 (Spring, 2003):48–63.

212 Often texts which, on the one hand, present a highly positive view of women can also be seen as reflective of an anti-female bias, e.g., those which proclaim women as the first witnesses to the resurrected Christ also indicate that the male apostles were sceptical with respect to a message brought forward by women. As noted earlier, some interpreters of the Lukan story of Martha and Mary suggest that it exemplifies the ideal of the "silent" woman, as opposed to one actively involved in ministry.

213 Letter to the Galatians 3:28.

214 I Corinthians 14:34.

215 I Timothy 2:11-12.

216 Ephesians 5:24; Colossians 3:18; I Peter 3:1; I Clement 1:4.

217 I Timothy 3:2,4,12; Titus 5:6. The increasing emphasis on marriage as an ideal may have been due to Roman imperial influence; see Peter Brown, "Late Antiquity," in *A History of Private Life: 1, From Pagan Rome to Byzantium* (Cambridge MA: Belknap Press, 1987), 247–8 and Mary Rose D'Angelo, "Women in Luke-Acts: A Redactional View," 450–1.

218 Rosemary Radford Ruether, "Seeking the Better Part," 26.

219 A translation of the text of this work by J. P. Arendzen is found in the *Journal of Theological Studies* 3 (1902):61–73.

220 Among the more interesting legends which surfaced at this time (late twelfth/early thirteenth century) was that of the papess Joan – a young woman, disguised as a man, who was reputedly elected pope under the name Johannes in either the year 855 or around 1100; references to this person are found in art, literature, theological disputes, drama, and historical writing and she became an established figure in papal lists throughout the Middle Ages and Renaissance. She played a particularly important role in anti-papal literature of the Reformation period. See Valerie R. Hotchkiss, "The Legend of the Female Pope in the Reformation," in *Acta Coventus Neo-Latini: Papers from the Eighth International Congress at Copenhagen* (Binghamton NY: Medieval and Renaissance Texts and Studies, 1993); Peter Stanford, *The Legend of*

Pope Joan: In Search of the Truth (New York: H. Holt, 1999); Alain Boureau, *The Myth of Pope Joan*, tr. Lydia G. Cochrane (Chicago IL: University of Chicago Press, 2001).

221 *The Women Around Jesus*, 29, 32–33.

222 Cf. Matthew 28:15; Mark 16:15; Luke 24:47; also Acts 1:8.

223 See Schüssler Fiorenza, "The Early Christian Missionary Movement: Equality in the Power of the Spirit," in *In Memory of Her*, 160–204 for a discussion of early missionary work.

224 Mark 16:14.

225 Cf. John 13:23; 19:26; 20:2; 21:7, 20.

226 John 7:5.

227 Mark 16:14.

228 Luke 24:49b.

229 Acts 1:5.

230 Acts 1:8.

231 Matthew 28:19.

232 Mark 16:17.

233 Luke 24:50a.

234 Matthew 28:20.

235 Luke 24:50b.

236 Acts 1:9.

237 Peters, *Early Latin Sources*, 124–5.

238 See ibid., 85 (*Vita Pseudo-Marcilia*), 127 (*Vita Beatae Mariae Magdalenae*) and 155 (Vincent of Beauvais). In the *Legenda Aurea*, there is no reference to this incident in the Martha legend, but it is found in that of Saint Mary Magdalen. By the late Middle Ages, Mary of Bethany was generally identified with Mary Magdalene, at least in the Christian West – in the eastern churches they were considered to be different women, and their feasts were celebrated on different days. There is a considerable body of literature dealing with Mary Magdalene, this composite figure whose "biography" is based on the conflation of incidents from the lives of a number of women: Mary of Bethany, the penitent sinner from whom Christ cast out demons, the woman who anointed Jesus, the fourth-century ascetic Mary of Egypt. Among the recent monographic studies is Susan Haskins' *Mary Magdalen: Myth and Metaphor* (New York: Harcourt Brace & Company, 1993), which includes detailed notes and a bibliography.

239 Peters, *Early Latin Sources*, 129.

240 Maximinus, bishop of Aix, figures prominently in the Provençal legends of both Martha and Mary Magdalene, which probably originated in the eleventh century. According to these traditions, he was one of the seventy-two apostles appointed by the Lord (Luke 10:1, 17), and he later travelled to Provence with the sisters from Bethany. He was appointed the first bishop of Aix-en-Provence. An ancient cult of a St. Maximinus existed in southern France prior to the eleventh century, but was probably centred on another saint of the same name who is thought to have lived in the fifth century. A cult of a St. Maximinus was celebrated at Billom in the province of Auvergne up until the eighteenth century. Eleventh-century charters reveal the existence of a basilica dedicated to Maximinus of Aix in the town of Maximin in Provence. The saint's relics were thought to lie there, along with those of Mary Magdalene, Sidonius (Cedonius), Marcella, and two Innocents. In 1820 the remains were transferred from St. Maximin to the cathedral of Aix. See Leclercq, "Maximin (Saint-)" in *Dictionnaire d'archéologie chrétienne et de liturgie*, 10/1 (Paris: Librairie Létouzey, 1932), cols. 2798–2820; L. Duchesne, *Fastes épiscopaux de l'ancienne Gaule*, I (Paris: Albert Fontemoing, 1907), 330–340.

241 Peters, *Early Latin Sources*, 88.

242 Ibid., 160.

243 Ibid., 134.

244 To be discussed in more detail in chapter five.

245 Peters, *Early Latin Sources*, 86, 156.

246 Ibid., 132–134.

247 The conclusion that Martha was considered to have been the first bishop of Tarascon is supported by Georges de Manteyer, *La Provence: du premier au douzième siècle* (Paris: Librairie Alphonse Picard et Fils, 1908).

248 Peters, *Early Latin Sources*, 94, 143, 163.

249 Ibid., 94.

250 For more complete details, see Ch. Cahier, *Caractéristiques des saints dans l'art populaire* (Paris: Librairie Poussielgue Frères, 1867) and Duchesne, *Fastes épiscopaux.*

251 See chapter 2, 47-48.

252 *The Women Around Jesus*, 36.

253 Ibid.

254 *The Iconography of Mary Magdalen: The Evolution of A Western Tradition Until 1300*, unpublished Ph.D. diss. (New York University, 1982).

255 See Helen Meredith Garth, *Saint Mary Magdalene in Medieval Literature* (Baltimore MD: Johns Hopkins Press, 1950), 24–5, for a description of her life.

256 Jacobus de Voragine, *The Golden Legend: Readings on the Saints*, tr. William Granger Ryan (Princeton NJ: Princeton University Press, 1993), 380.

257 *Vita Pseudo-Marcilia*, in Peters, *Early Latin Sources*, 90–1.

258 Ibid., 91.

259 Voragine, *Golden Legend*, 380.

260 *Vita Pseudo-Marcilia*, in Peters, *Early Latin Sources*, 96.

261 Romans 3:23.

262 *Vita Pseudo-Marcilia*, in Peters, *Early Latin Sources*, 95.

263 Ibid.

264 Cf. John 14:3.

265 *Vita Pseudo-Marcilia*, in Peters, *Early Latin Sources*, 96–97.

266 Ibid., 98–9.

267 Hugh Kempster, "The Best of Both Worlds: Mary and Martha," website of St. Columba's Community Church, Auckland NZ [www.saint.columbas.org.nz/best.php]

268 "Mary and Martha," in *The Window of Vulnerability: A Political Spirituality*, tr. Linda M. Maloney (Minneapolis: Fortress Press, 1990), 95.

269 Irene Doyle, CSM, *The Search for St. Martha* (Antigonish NS: Sisters of St. Martha, 1993), 47.

270 *Vita Beatae Mariae Magdalenae*, in Peters, *Early Latin Sources*, 134.

271 See Appendix A for a discussion of the legitimacy of this claim.

272 Vincent of Beauvais, *Speculum Historiale*, chapter 101, in Peters, *Early Latin Sources*, 161.

273 Genesis 27:27.

274 *Vita Beatae Mariae Magdalenae*, in Peters, *Early Latin Sources*, 140–2.

275 John 11:43.

276 Luke 7:14.

277 Mark 5:41, Luke 8:54.

278 John 2:3-10.

279 Theodor Graesse notes that the word "Onacho" (in some manuscripts "Honacho" or "Bonacho") refers "without doubt" to the onager or wild ass (Jacobi de Voragine, *Legenda Aurea*, recensuit Th. Graesse [Dresden, 1890; reprinted Osnabruck: Otto Zeller, 1965], 444). However, the description of the beast suggests rather that it was a bonasus, a type of bull or bison. Pliny described the animal as follows in his *Natural History*, Book VIII, 15.40: "There are reports of a wild animal in Paeonia called the bonasus, which has the mane of a horse but in all other respects resembles a bull; its horns are curved

back in such a manner as to be of no use for fighting, and it is said that because of this it saves itself by running away, meanwhile emitting a trail of dung that sometimes covers a distance of as much as three furlongs, contact with which scorches pursuers like a sort of fire." (tr. H. Rackham [London: Heinemann, 1967], 31, 33). Pliny's description may have been derived from Aristotle's account of the monapos in his *Historia Animalia*, Book IX, 630a.45: "The bison is found in Paeonia on Mount Messapium, which separates Paeonia from Maedica; and the Paeonians call it the monapos. It is the size of a bull but stouter in build, and not long in the body; its skin, stretched tight on a frame, would give sitting room for seven people. In general it resembles the ox in appearance, except that it has a mane that reaches down to the point of the shoulder as that of the horse reaches down to its withers; but the hair in its mane is softer than the hair in a horse's mane, and clings more closely. The colour of the hair is brown-yellow; the mane reaches down to the eyes, and is deep and thick. The colour of the body is half red, half ashen-grey, like that of the so-called chestnut horse, but rougher. It has an undercoat of woolly hair. The animal is not found either very black or very red. It has the bellow of a bull. Its horns are crooked, turned inwards towards each other and useless for purposes of self-defence; they are a span broad, or a little more, and in volume each horn would hold about three pints of liquid; the black colour of the horn is beautiful and bright. The tuft of hair on the forehead reaches down to the eyes, so that the animal sees objects on either flank better than objects right in front. It has no upper teeth, as is the case also with kine and all other horned animals. Its legs are hairy; it is cloven-footed; and the tail, which resembles that of an ox, seems not big enough for the size of its body. It tosses up dust and scoops out the ground with its hooves, like the bull. Its skin is impervious to blows. Owing to the savour of its flesh it is sought for in the chase. When it is wounded it runs away, and stops only when thoroughly exhausted. It defends itself against an assailant by kicking and projecting its excrement to a distance of eight yards; this device it can easily adopt over and over again, and the excrement is so pungent that the hair of hunting-dogs is burnt off by it. It is only when the animal is disturbed or alarmed that the dung has this property; when the animal is undisturbed it has no blistering effect. So much for the shape and habits of the animal. When the season comes for parturition the mothers give birth to their young in troops upon the mountains. Before dropping their young they scatter their dung in all directions, making a kind of circular rampart around them; for the animal has the faculty of ejecting excrement in most extraordinary quantities." (tr. D'Arcy Wentworth Thompson [Oxford: Clarendon Press, 1962], n.p.). Florence McCulloch, *Mediaeval Latin and French Bestiaries* (Chapel Hill NC: University of North Carolina Press, 1962) notes that the bonasus frequently appeared in medieval Latin and French bestiaries (p. 98).

280 Vincent of Beavais, *Speculum Historiale*, chapter 99, in Peters, *Early Latin Sources*, 157–9.

281 Consider, for example, the image identified as "Martha defeating the dragon" on the Mary altar of the Church of St. Laurence, Nuremberg (1517) or the early eighteenth-century sculpture of a woman and dragon in the Pilgrimage Church of Madonna d'Ongero in Carona, Switzerland, both of which could represent either Martha or Margaret (both reproduced in Elisabeth Moltmann-Wendel, *The Women Around Jesus*).

282 George, the patron saint of England, probably lived in the early fourth century, although his cult did not become popular until the sixth century and the slaying of the dragon was not attributed to him until the late twelfth century.

283 In popular tradition St. Margaret was sometimes identified with the princess rescued by St. George. This raises the possibility that some images showing a female saint leading a beast and identified as representing St. Martha may in fact have been intended as portraits of St. Margaret. See also note 281 above.

284 Revelation 12.

285 Martha's dragon is also said to have descended from the bonasus – see note 279 above. It is possible that the reference to this animal alluded not only to Martha's victory over the Judeo-Christian Satan – symbolized by Leviathan – but also over pagan beliefs which had not been totally eradicated in the later Middle Ages. Remnants of religions such as Mithraism, which had been widespread in the region of southern Gaul in earlier centuries and whose sacred animal was the bull, may have survived up until the time when the Martha legends were recorded.

286 Isaiah 27:1.

287 Psalm 74:13-14; Job 41:1; Isaiah 51:9.

288 See Gertrud Schiller, *Iconography of Christian Art*, I (Greenwich CT.: New York Graphic Society, 1971), plates 64, 359, 380.

289 Ibid., II, plates 354, 360–64.

290 For a more complete listing of saints connected with dragons see Ch. Cahier, *Caractéristiques des saints*, I, 315–322.

291 See chapter 3, 94-95.

292 Elisabeth Moltmann-Wendel's works have been seminal in this regard.

293 See, for example, David R. Kinsley, *The Goddesses' Mirror: Visions of the Divine from East and West* (Albany: State University of New York Press, 1989), 215–260 or Marina Warner, *Alone of All Her Sex: The Myth and Cult of the Virgin Mary* (New York: Knopf, 1976), passim.

294 Mary Magdalene rather than Martha is considered a promoter of fertility and patroness of women in childbirth, since as a result of her intercession a child was born to the wife of the Prince of Marseille. Later, the child and his

mother were restored to life by the Magdalene's power. However, Martha's miracles also included the raising of a dead boy to life.

295 As noted in Chapter Three, many of the extant gnostic sources which mention Martha also originated in Egypt.

296 See *Mireille: poème provençal avec la traduction littérale en regard* (Paris: Fasquelle, 1968), 421. Mistral (1830–1914) was a native of Provence, born near Tarascon. His pastoral epic *Mirèio* (*Mireille*), which was written in the Provençal language in1859, is considered a major contribution to the nineteenth-century Provençal literary renewal movement.

297 *Humanity in God*, 28–29; see also Moltmann-Wendel, *A Land Flowing with Milk and Honey*, 105–114.

298 *Humanity in God*, 25–26.

299 *The Women Around Jesus*, 46.

300 "Mary and Martha," 96.

301 "Seeking the Better Part," 26.

302 *Church of Ireland Gazette Online*, Friday 21st December 2001 [http://gazette.ireland.anglican.org/211201/faithfully211201.htm] Accessed December 2007

303 By the Counter-Reformation period, the "formula" according to which the Immaculate Conception of the Virgin was portrayed in art is taken directly from Revelation 12:1: "And there appeared a great wonder in heaven; a woman clothed with the sun, and a moon under her feet, and upon her head a crown of twelve stars." See, for example, the version by Velazquez in the National Gallery, London (1618–9) or that by Tiepolo in the Prado, Madrid (1767–9).

304 For a more complete discussion of the theological links between Eve and Mary, see John A. Phillips, *Eve: The History of An Idea* (San Francisco CA: Harper and Row, 1984), Chapter 9; or Pamela Norris, *Eve: A Biography* (New York: New York University Press, 1999), Chapter 8. For a study of the relationship as expressed in artistic terms, see Ernst Guldan, *Eva und Maria: Eine Antithese als Bildmotiv* (Graz: Verlag Hermann Böhlaus, 1966).

305 *Vita Pseudo-Marcilia*, in Peters, *Early Latin Sources*, 75. At several points in the narrative, the author also refers to the more widely known stereotype of Martha, as a symbol of the active life.

306 I.7,31.

307 Cf. Matthew 9:20-22, Luke 8:43-48. In other sources, however, the haemorrissa is identified with Veronica: see *The Apocryphal and Legendary Life of Christ*, ed. Donehoo, 214–5.

308 Sermon 16, J. P. Migne, ed., *Sermones S. Ambrosio Hactenus Ascripti*, Patrologia Latina, Vol. 17 (Paris, 1879), tr. D. Peters.

309   Peters, *Early Latin Sources*, 174–5.

310   Tr. J. E. L. Oulton (Cambridge MA: Harvard University Press, 1973), II, 175, 177.

311   Jerome's *Chronicle* was a translation and expansion of the *Chronicle* of Eusebius, completed ca. 380 and continued to 378 A.D. Jerome's work mentions the reign of Julian the Apostate, emperor from 332–363 (see Hieronymus, *Chronicon*, ed. Rudolf Helm [Berlin: Academie Verlag, 1984], 240, 242, 243) but not the episode of the statue specifically. Eusebius' *History* was continued in Greek by three writers of the early fifth century: Socrates of Constantinople, who described events from 305 to 434; Sozomen, who covered the period from 325 to 439; and Theodoret of Cyr, who wrote of the years from 324 to 428. In the sixth century these three works were translated and combined by Epiphanius, under the supervision of Cassiodorus. The resulting text, known as the *Historia Ecclesiastica Tripartita* or *Tripartite History*, circulated widely in the later Middle Ages. The account of the destruction of Julian's statue is found in Sozomon's *History* (5.21): "Among so many remarkable events which occurred during the reign of Julian, I must not omit to mention one which affords a manifest proof of the power of Christ, and of the Divine wrath against the emperor. Having heard that at Caesarea Philippi, otherwise called Paneades, a city of Phoenicia, there was a celebrated statue of Christ, which had been erected by a woman whom the Lord had cured of a flow of blood, Julian commanded it to be taken down, and a statue of himself erected in its place; but fire from heaven was poured down upon it, the head and breast were broken, and it was transfixed to the ground with the face downwards: it is still to be seen on the spot where it fell, blackened by the effects of the thunder. The statue of Christ was dragged round the city and mutilated by the Pagans; but the Christians recovered the fragments, and deposited the statue in the church in which it is still preserved." (tr. Edward Walford [London: H. Bohn, 1855], 238–9) Another account of the fate of the statue of Christ is found in the *Ecclesiastical History* of Philostorgius (7.3), produced some time after 425; an epitome compiled by Photius in the mid-ninth century is extant. It records: "Concerning an image of our Saviour erected by the faith of a pious woman in grateful remembrance of her cure from a bloody flux, Philostorgius writes, that it was placed near a fountain in the city among other statues, and presented a pleasant and agreeable sight to the passers-by. And when a certain herb, which grew up at the foot of this statue, was found to be a most effectual remedy against all diseases, and especially against consumption, men naturally began to inquire into the cause of the matter; for by lapse of time all memory of the fact had been lost, and it was even forgotten whose statue it was, and on what account it had been erected. Inasmuch as the figure of our Saviour had long stood exposed in the open air, and a great part of it was covered over by the earth which was perpetually carried down against the pediment, especially during seasons of heavy rain, the notice contained in the inscription upon it was well nigh obliterated. A diligent inquiry was consequently made, and

the part of the statue which had been covered up being brought to light, the inscription was discovered which explained the entire circumstances of the fact; and the plant thenceforth was never again seen either there or in any other place. The statue itself they placed in the part of the church which was allotted to the deacons, paying to it due honour and respect, yet by no means adoring or worshipping it; and they showed their love for its great archetype by erecting it in that place with circumstances of honour, and by flocking thither in eager crowds to behold it. During the reign of Julian, however, the heathen who inhabited Paneas were excited by an impious frenzy to pull down this statue from its pediment, and to drag it through the midst of the streets with ropes fastened round its feet; afterwards they broke in pieces the rest of the body, while some persons, indignant at the whole proceeding, secretly obtained possession of the head, which had become detached from the neck as it was dragged along, and they preserved it as far as was possible. This transaction Philostorgius declared that he witnessed with his own eyes." (tr. Edward Walford [London: H. Bohn, 1855], 475–6) Philostorgius, who claims to have watched the destruction of the statue of Christ by the pagans, does not mention a statue of Julian erected in its place.

312 See Judith Herrin, "In Search of Byzantine Women: Three Avenues of Approach," in *Images of Women in Antiquity*, ed. A. Cameron and A. Kuhrt (London: Croom Helm, 1983), 180–181.

313 Peters, *Early Latin Sources*, 77.

314 Ibid., 78.

315 Ibid., 82.

316 Genesis 12:1-2.

317 See Beryl Smalley, *The Study of the Bible in the Middle Ages* (Oxford: Blackwell, 1983) for a discussion of the way in which the Bible was interpreted typologically in the medieval period.

318 Cf. Romans 4:13-25, Galatians 3:6-9.

319 I Peter 2:6-10.

320 John 21:15-19.

321 Peters, *Early Latin Sources*, 77.

322 In his edition and commentary upon *La Vie Ancienne de S. Front de Périgueux* (*Analecta Bollandiana* 48, 1930:324–360), M. Coens notes that the earliest extant manuscripts of a life of St. Fronto date from the beginning of the ninth century (326), although a seventh-century Life of St. Géry indicates that the tomb of a St. Fronto was venerated at Périgueux at that time (322). According to tradition, St. Fronto was one of the seventy-two apostles appointed by the Lord (Luke 10:1, 17). Later he was designated by St. Peter as an apostle to Gaul, where he journeyed in the company of St. Georgius of Velay. The latter died during the voyage, but was raised when Fronto touched

him with the staff given to him by St. Peter (ibid., 324). References to St. Fronto as a missionary to Gaul also appear in such early martyrologies as those of Ado of Vienne, Usuard and Notker (Faillon, *Monuments inédits*, II, col. 391). St. Fronto's life abounds with inconsistencies and absurdities, for example, an account of the saint's rescue from starvation in the wilderness near Périgueux by the arrival of seventy unattended camels loaded with food (see Coens, 329–330). Some incidents of the legendary life of Fronto of Périgueux were likely derived from that of a similarly named saint, Fronto of Nitrie, who probably lived in Cappadocia in the mid-fourth century (see Faillon, II, col. 389; Duchesne, *Fastes Épiscopaux*, 130–134).

323 See, for example, the image by Bartolomaus Zeitblom in the Alte Pinakothek, Munich (late fifteenth century), reproduced by Maillet, *Sainte Marthe*, 56.

324 Jacobus de Voragine, *The Golden Legend*, tr. William Granger Ryan, 70.

325 Jacobus de Voragine, *The Golden Legend or Lives of the Saints as Englished by William Caxton* (New York: AMS Press, 1973), 203–4.

326 In addition, Peter, when he appears in representations of the death or funeral of the Virgin, also shares Martha's attribute of the aspergillum. See Cahier, *Caractéristiques des saintes*, I, 87.

327 For a full discussion of the history and significance of this image see Otto Semmelroth, *Mary, Archetype of the Church* (New York: Sheed and Ward, 1963.)

328 Douay version.

329 Justin Martyr, *Dialogue with Trypho* 100 in *The Ante-Nicene Fathers*, I, 249. Note that Justin describes the Virgin's Son and not the Virgin herself as the destroyer of the serpent and its progeny.

330 Revelation 12:1-5. By the later Middle Ages this passage was commonly associated with the Virgin in her role as the Immaculate Conception. Psalm 90 was also occasionally used to suggest the Immaculate Conception, probably on the basis of a text by Augustine; again it explores the woman/dragon imagery, although Augustine's interpretation of the passage refers to the church rather than to Mary specifically. In his *Enarratio in Psalmum 90*, he describes the four animals mentioned in verse 13 of the Psalm as representative of four aspects of the Devil. His open cruelty is like that of the lion and he lies in wait like the creeping dragon. His cunningness is like that of the serpent, the ancient deceiver of the church, and he is the King of the demons, just as the basilisk is king of the serpents.

331 See Hilda Graef, *Mary: A History of Doctrine and Devotion* (London: Sheed and Ward, 1965), 1:132, 239.

332 Reproduced in Dumont, *La Tarasque*, plate XIII.

333 Luke 1:42.

334 Peters, *Early Latin Sources*, 82.

335 Compare Matthew 23:37 and Luke 13:34 where similar imagery is used in reference to Christ himself.

336 See, for example, the versions by Piero della Francesca in the Museo del Sepolcro, Borgo Sansepolcro, Italy (ca. 1445) or that by Giovanni da Murano in the Gallerie dell'Accademia, Venice (late fifteenth century).

337 *Scottish Journal of Theology* 17 (September 1964):338.

338 Matthew 4:19, Mark 1:17, Luke 5:9.

339 The cross chosen for the ship's flag is that of St. George, the dragon-slayer.

340 Pamphlet distributed by the Sisters of St. Martha, Bethany, Antigonish, Nova Scotia outlining the history of the order from 1900 to 1975.

341 Irene Doyle, CSM, *The Search for St. Martha* (Antigonish NS.: Sisters of St. Martha, 1993), 51–2.

342 Cited by Leo Rosten, *The Story Behind the Painting* (Garden City NY: Doubleday,1962), 40.

343 See chapter 4, 98.

344 For the Romanesco text with a contemporary English translation by Miller Williams, see *Sonnets of Giuseppe Belli* (Baton Rouge: Louisiana State University Press, 1981), 139.

345 "Mary and Martha," in *The Speaker's Treasury of 400 Quotable Poems*, ed. Croft M. Pentz (Grand Rapids MI: Zondervan, 1963), 125.

346 From *A Choice of Kipling's Verse*, ed. T. S. Eliot (London: Faber & Faber, 1976), 159, 161.

347 www.engineering.ualberta.ca/uofaengineer/article.cfm?article=22798 &issue=22643. Accessed December 2007.

348 *From One Word: Selected Poems from "Spirit" 1944–1949* (New York: The Devin-Adair Company, 1950), 100.

349 "Mary and Martha," in *Common Longing: The Teresa Poems and a Canticle for Mary and Martha* (Lewiston NY: Edwin Mellen Press, 2001), 25. Used with permission.

350 "The Unitive Way," ibid., 45. Used with permission.

351 Ed. Susan McCaslin (Toronto ON: St. Thomas Poetry Series, 2002), 135–41.

352 Ibid., 139.

353 *Into the Open* (Port Moody BC: Golden Eagle Press, 1999).

354 *Christianity and Literature* 50/1 (Autumn, 2000):191.

355 Martha-Mary imagery appears elsewhere in McCaslin's work in the poem "Moth of Poverty" in "The Teresa Poems" (*Common Longing*, 11), in "Raising Lazarus" and "Mary of Bethany: The Anointing" in "Liberation: The Gospel

Retold" (*Into the Open*, 74–6, 80–1).

356 In *Women of the Word* (Notre Dame IN: Ave Maria Press, 1989), 58. Used with permission.

357 Ibid., 59. Used with permission.

358 Ibid., 59–60. Used with permission.

359 In *The Collected Poems of Ursula Vaughan Williams* (Ilminster, Somerset: Albion Music, 1996), 14. Used with permission.

360 From *Collected Poems* (New York: Macmillan, 1937), 530–1.

361 Ibid., 531.

362 Ibid., 532.

363 Ibid., 539.

364 From *Selected Poems of Gabriel Mistral*, translated and edited by Doris Dana (Baltimore: The Johns Hopkins Press, 1971), 187-191.

365 Ibid., 211.

366 In *The Poetry of Black America: Anthology of the 20th Century*, ed. Arnold Adoff (New York: Harper & Row, 1973), 128.

367 The poem was later set to music by British composer Phyllis Tate; see *Saint Martha and the Dragon: A Dramatic Legend Set to Music, for Narrator, Soprano and Tenor Soloists, Chorus, Children's Chorus (with Percussion), and Chamber Orchestra* (London: Oxford University Press, 1978).

368 For the complete poem, see Charles Causley, *Collected Poems 1951–2000* (London: Picador, 2000), 197–210.

369 *Some Bones and a Story* (Toronto, ON: Wolsak and Wynn, 2001), 27–32.

370 Ibid., 30. Used with permission.

371 Ibid. Used with permission.

372 Ibid., 70.

373 Ibid., 31. Used with permission.

374 Ibid., 31–2. Used with permission.

375 Translated into English by Arthur G. Chater as *Martha and Mary* (New York: Alfred A. Knopf, 1926).

376 M.A. thesis, University of Manitoba, Winnipeg MB, 1994.

377 In *The Mermaids in the Basement: Stories* (London: Chatto and Windus, 1993), 21–39.

378 Ibid., 23.

379 Ibid., 38.

380 "Finding a Voice for Martha: Marina Warner's 'Mary Takes the Better Part'," *Journal of the Short Story in English* 22 (Summer, 1994):105–13.

381 Ibid., 110.

382 Ibid., 112.

383 New York: P. J. Kennedy, 1960. Quotations in this paragraph are from p. 7 and p. 5, and that of the next paragraph is from p. 196.

384 Joyce Landorf, *I Came to Love You Late* (Basingstoke, UK: Pickering and Inglis, 1985), 20.

385 Ibid., 28.

386 Ibid., 34.

387 Ibid., 75.

388 Ibid., 120–1.

389 Ibid., 131–2.

390 Ibid., 132.

391 Ibid., 156.

392 Ibid., 182.

393 Ibid., 196.

394 See Chapter 1, p. 2.

395 Gloria Howe Bremkamp, *Martha and Mary of Bethany: A Novel* (San Francisco CA: Harper San Francisco, 1991), 136–9.

396 Ibid., 185.

397 Mary Carroll, review of *Living With Saints*, *Booklist* 98/2 (September 15, 2001):193.

398 Mary DiLucia, review of *Living With Saints*, *Commonweal* 26 (July 12, 2002):26.

399 Debbie Bogenschutz, review of *Living With Saints*, *Library Journal* 126/13 (August, 2001):168.

400 Lynda Sexson, review of *Living With Saints*, *Spiritus: A Journal of Christian Spirituality* 2/1 (Spring, 2002):118.

401 Mary O'Connell, "Saint Martha," in *Living With Saints* (New York: Atlantic Monthly Press, 2001), 89.

402 Ibid., 93.

403 Ibid., 95.

404 Ibid., 96.

405 Ibid., 101.

406　Ibid., 109.

407　The choice of name is interesting. According to some versions of the Provençal legends, Sarah was the black Egyptian servant who accompanied Mary, Martha, and Lazarus to the south of France. Other legends suggest that Sarah was the name given to the putative daughter of Jesus and Mary Magdalene.

408　Ibid., 111–2.

409　Review of *Living With Saints*, *Spiritus: A Journal of Christian Spirituality* 2/1 (Spring, 2002):119.

410　Review of *Living With Saints*, *Publishers Weekly* 248/35 (August 27, 2001):47.

411　"Rocket to the Morgue," in *Black Box Thrillers: 4 Novels* (London: Zomba Books, 1984), 379.

412　"Nine Times Nine," in *Black Box Thrillers*, 276–7.

413　*The Norton Book of Science Fiction*, ed. Ursula K. Le Guin and Brian Attebery (New York: W. W. Norton, 1993), 201.

414　An internet search on Martha and the dragon also leads to such esoteric finds as spells uttered in the name of Martha available through a New Orleans voodoo supply store and designed to allow someone to dominate another person [www.neworleansmistic.com/spells/magiclamp/marthadominadora. htm] or to force someone to sell real estate [www.neworleansmistic.com/ spells/purplespells/commandrealestate.htm]. Accessed December 2007.

415　London: Futura, 1985.

416　There have been occasional references to the Martha of legend in more general works of literature, e.g., early in the twentieth century a brief summary of the Martha and the dragon legend appeared in Chapter VIII of the satirical novel *Penguin Island* (1908) by French author Anatole France (pseudonym for Jacques Anatole Thibault, 1844–1924), a work which circulated widely at the time. For younger audiences, the legendary Martha – portrayed as a young curly-haired barefoot girl – has been featured in a book entitled *Brave Martha and the Dragon*, written and illustrated by award-winning American children's author, Susan L. Roth (New York: Dial Books for Young Readers, 1996).

417　Of the four surviving Latin texts, two are currently available in English translation. A modern version of *The Golden Legend* [*Legenda Aurea*], translated and adapted by Granger Ryan and Helmut Ripperger, was published by Longmans, Green & Company, New York, in 1969 (reprinted 1989); it is based on the Latin edition published by Johann Graesse (Leipzig, 1850) and is a popular rather than a scholarly work. In 1993 Ryan published a revised translation of this work (Princeton NJ: Princeton University Press), although it is again more a popular version than an annotated scholarly edition. A scholarly edition of the entire *Saint Mary Magdalene and her Sister Saint Martha* [*Vita Beatae Mariae Magdalenae et Sororis Eius Sanctae Marthae*], translated and annotated by David Mycoff, was published by Cistercian Publications, Kalamazoo, Michigan, in 1989. There is no published English translation of Vincent of Beauvais. A translation of the text of the *Vita Pseudo-Marcilia* is appended to the present study.

418 For a detailed discussion of the work of the Sisters of Antigonish see James Cameron, *"And Martha Served": History of the Sisters of St. Martha, Antigonish, Nova Scotia* (Halifax NS: Nimbus, 2000), written on the occasion of their one-hundredth anniversary. See also Sarah MacPherson, "Religious Women in Nova Scotia: A Struggle for Autonomy. A Sketch of the Sisters of St. Martha of Antigonish, Nova Scotia, 1900–1960," *CCHA Historical Studies* 51 (1984):89–106; Mark G. McGowan, "The Maritimes Region and the Building of a Canadian Church: The Case of the Diocese of Antigonish after Confederation," *CCHA Historical Studies* 70 (2004):46–67. The Sisters of St. Martha of Antigonish also maintain a website at www.themarthas.com.

419 For more information see Mary Jeanette Coady (Sister Marie Ida), *The Birth and Growth of the Congregation of the Sisters of St. Martha on Prince Edward Island*, M.A. dissertation, University of Ottawa, 1955; Heidi Elizabeth MacDonald, "Doing More with Less: The Sisters of St. Martha (PEI) Diminish the Impact of the Great Depression," *Acadiensis* 33/1 (2003):21–46; The 75th Anniversary Committee, Mildred MacIsaac, chair, *The Story of the Sisters of St. Martha 1916–1991* (Charlottetown: Sisters of St. Martha, 1991); Heidi Elizabeth MacDonald, *The Sisters of St. Martha and Prince Edward Island Social Institutions, 1916–1982*, Ph.D. dissertation, University of New Brunswick, 2000; Heidi Elizabeth MacDonald, "The Social Origins and Congregational Identity of the Founding Sisters of St. Martha of Charlottetown, PEI, 1915–1925," *CCHA Historical Studies* 70 (2004):29–47; Cristina Vanin, "The Green Nuns: Models of Ecological Spirituality," *Catholic New Times* 29/12 (July 3, 2005):20. See also the Sisters website at www.csmpei.org/html.

420 *The Search for St. Martha* (Antigonish, NS: Sisters of St. Martha, 1993), 6.

421 It is noted that the Sisters of St Martha in Prince Edward Island, who have many close links with those in Antigonish, favour representations of John's Martha, going forth to meet Jesus and declaring her faith in him as the Messiah. Ibid., 59–60.

422 For a brief discussion of the way in which this composite image of Mary Magdalene emerged in the Middle Ages, see Susan Haskins, *Mary Magdalen: Myth and Metaphor* (New York: Harcourt, Brace, 1993), 25–6, 90–7, 197–9; or Ingrid Maisch, *Mary Magdalene: The Image of a Woman Through the Centuries* (Collegeville MN: Liturgical Press, 1998), 43–61.

423 For a more complete analysis of Martha's artistic attributes in the medieval period see Peters, "Iconography of St. Martha."

424 See, for example, the illustration of the statue of Martha from the Église Ste-Madeleine, Troyes, France (early sixteenth century), reproduced by Emile Mâle, *Les Saints Compagnons du Christ* (Paris: Paul Hartmann, 1958), 83.

425 Luke 10:40; John 12:2.

426 Germaine Maillet, *Sainte Marthe* reproduces a number of examples of works based on the Martha and the dragon theme. See also the illustrations in Louis Dumont's *La Tarasque*, an ethnographic study of the Tarasque ritual.

427 "... Un contre-sense iconographique: le seau d'eau bénite qu'elle tient à la main pour asperger la Tarasque a pu être pris pour un utensile de ménage" (Louis Réau, *Iconographie de l'art chrétien* III/2 [Paris: Presses Universitaires de France, 1955–59], 893.

428 Ch. Cahier also notes that sometimes the pot is portrayed in such a manner that it resembles a lantern, possibly to suggest a virgin's lamp; see *Caractéristiques des saints dans l'art populaire*, II, 840.

429 Moltmann-Wendel, *The Women Around Jesus*, 37 as cited by Doyle, *The Search for St. Martha*, 61.

430 Ibid., 61–2.

431 Correspondence with the author, June 7, 1995.

432 For example, the oil of consecration (1 Samuel 10:1), the oil of naming sacred space (Genesis 28:18), the oil of healing (Luke 10:33), the oil of missioning (Luke 4:16-19).

433 Ibid.

434 From a 1986 study on Judeo-Christian women of faith undertaken at the University of Ottawa, Ontario, by Sister Claudette Gallant, cited by Doyle, *The Search for St. Martha*, 56.

435 "Mary and Martha," *Al-Mushir* 32/3 (1990):61.

436 Ibid., 61–2.

437 Ibid., 62.

438 "Women and Men Building Together the Church in Africa," in *With Passion and Compassion: Third World Women Doing Theology*, ed. Virginia Fabella and Mercy Amba Oduyoye (Maryknoll NY: Orbis, 1988), 17.

439 "Cultural Hermeneutics: An African Contribution," in *Women's Voices: Theological Reflection, Celebration, Action*, ed. Ofelia Ortega (Geneva: World Council of Churches, 1995), 24.

440 "One Woman's Confession of Faith," *International Review of Mission* 74 (April, 1985):212.

441 "Martha's Passion: A Model for Theological Liberation," *The Other Side* 24 (July/August, 1988):24.

442 Maryknoll NY: Orbis Press, 2002.

443 *Mary and Martha*, 143.

444 Ibid., 142.

445 "Christianity and Women in Japan," *Japanese Journal of Religious Studies* 30/3-4 (Fall, 2003):315–338.

446 Ibid., 334.

447 Ibid., 335.

448 *Semeia* 78 (1997):93–107.

449 Ibid., 94.

450 Ibid.

451 Ibid., 99.

452 Ibid., 102–3. The suggestion that each sister chose to serve in the way which was best for her echoes the medieval *Vita Pseudo-Marcilia*: "the merciful Guest conceded to each of these holy women her office and choice." See Peters, *Early Latin Sources*, 79.

453 *Semeia* 78 (1997):103.

454 "Difference and Identity," in *Affirming Difference, Celebrating Wholeness: A Partnership of Equals* (Hong Kong: Christian Conference of Asia, Women's Concerns, 1995), 16.

455 *Semeia* 78 (1997):104–5.

456 "A North American Perspective," *Semeia* 78 (1997):146.

457 *A Land Flowing with Milk and Honey*, 57.

458 In contrast, Martha's sister Mary of Bethany, usually identified with Mary Magdalene in the Christian West, has been the focus of numerous books in recent years, both scholarly and more popular; to name a few: Esther de Boer, *Mary Magdalene: Beyond the Myth* (London: SCM Press, 1997); Elisabeth Pinto-Mathieu, *Marie-Madeleine Dans La Littérature du Moyen Âge* (Paris: Beauchesne, 1997); Ingrid Maisch, *Mary Magdalene: The Image of a Woman Through the Centuries* (Collegeville MN: Liturgical Press, 1998); Gordon Thomas, *Magdalene* (Oxford: Lion, 1998); Liz Curtis Higgs, *Mad Mary: A Bad Girl from Magdala, Transformed at His Appearing* (Colorado Springs CO: WaterBrook Press, 2001); Brigitte Maffray, *Marie-Madeleine: Un Modèle Pour Nôtre Époque* (Boucherville QC: Éditions de Montagne, 2001); Ann Brock, *Mary Magdalene, the First Apostle: The Struggle for Authority* (Cambridge: Harvard University Press, 2002); Jane Schaberg, *The Resurrection of Mary Magdalene: Legends, Apocrypha, and the Christian Testament* (New York: Continuum, 2002); Karen L. King, *The Gospel of Mary of Magdala: Jesus and the First Woman Apostle* (Santa Rosa CA: Polebridge Press, 2003); Esther de Boer, *The Gospel of Mary: Beyond a Gnostic and Biblical Mary Magdalene* (London: T. & T. Clark, 2004); Holly Hearon, *The Mary Magdalene Tradition: Witness and Counter-Witness in Early Christian*

Communities (Collegeville MN: Liturgical Press, 2004); Marvin W. Meyer, *The Gospels of Mary: The Secret Tradition of Mary Magdalene, the Companion of Jesus* (San Francisco CA: Harper San Francisco, 2004); Deirdre Good, ed., *Mariam, the Magdalen, and the Mother* (Bloomington IN: Indiana University Press, 2005); Lesa Bellevie, *The Complete Idiot's Guide to Mary Magdalene* (New York: Alpha, 2005); Margaret Starbird, *Mary Magdalene, Bride in Exile* (Rochester VT: Bear and Company, 2005); Bruce Chilton, *Mary Magdalene: A Biography* (New York: Doubleday, 2005). The *Publisher's Weekly* review of the last publication, cited on various vendors' websites, notes that "with the popularity of *The Da Vinci Code*, Mary Magdalene has become the 'it girl' of biblical studies."

459 See www.tarascon.org, in particular the "Fêtes Traditionnelles" section, for background and photographs of the Tarasque festival. For a more detailed history and ethnographic study of the ritual see Louis Dumont, *La Tarasque* (Paris: Gallimard, 1987).

460 Joanna Weaver (Colorado Springs CO: WaterBrook Press, 2000).

461 Debi Stack (Chicago IL: Moody Press, 2000).

462 Elaine Leong Eng (New York: Haworth Pastoral Press, 2000).

463 Website of the Stay At Home Mothers For Christ (www.geocities.com/sahmsforchrist/martha.html).

464 Craig M. Watts, "What Matters Most of All? (Luke 10:38-42)," *Preaching* 11/4 (January/February, 1996):23.

465 Homily preached Sunday, July 18, 2004 by the Rev'd Lloyd Prator at Saint John's in the Village Episcopal Church, New York City (http://www.stjvny.org/homilies/July1804.asp).

466 See, for example, Margaret Guenther, "Honoring Martha," *Christian Century* 112 (July 5–12, 1995):675; Linda Bieze, "Meditations on Mary and Martha," *The Other Side* 35/2 (March-April, 1999);51–52; Harryett Burden Hyde, *In Defense of Martha* (Fort Worth TX: Quality Publications, 1996).

467 See Garrett Keizer, "Poor Martha," *Christian Century* 118/20 (July 4–11, 2001):14; Erin Rouse, "For the Love of Mary… and Martha," *Lexington Theological Quarterly* 36/1 (Spring, 2001):23–29.

468 Stephanie Frey, "Living with Martha," *Christian Century* 121/14 (July 13, 2004):16.

469 Official website of the XX WYD2005, www.wjt2005.de/index.php?id=1869&si=1. Accessed December 2007.

470 Peters, *Early Latin Sources*, 103.

471 For additional background see entry on Faillon in the *Dictionary of Canadian Biography Online* [http://www.biographi.ca/EN/ShowBio.asp?BioId= 38538&query=faillon]. Accessed April 2008.

472 Faillon's text served as the basis for a number of other accounts of the Martha cult which occurred in the later nineteenth and early twentieth centuries, e.g. Joseph Veran's *Histoire de la Vie et du Culte de Sainte Marthe* (Avignon: Seguin Aine, 1868) or the Comtesse St-Bris' *Vie de Sainte Marthe: Modèle des Filles Chrétiennes* (3rd edition, Paris: Pierre Téqui, 1910). The former of these works also includes historical background on the city of Tarascon, and the latter includes accounts of prominent followers of St. Martha in the later Middle Ages, including Joan of Arc.

473 For further information see entry on the Bollandists in the *Catholic Encyclopedia* [http://www.newadvent.org/cathen/02630a.htm] or the web page of the Société des Bollandistes [http://www.kbr.be/~socboll/]. Accessed April 2008.

474 Faillon, *Monuments inédits sur l'apostolat de Sainte Marie-Madeleine en Provence et les autres apôtres de cette contrée*, I (Paris: J.P. Migne, 1848), col. 573.

475 Ibid., col. 584.

476 Ibid., col. 586.

477 Ibid., col. 581–2.

478 See H. Leclercq, "Lazare," in *Dictionnaire d'archéologie chrétienne et de liturgie*, 8/2, col. 2050.

479 See chapter 2, 30.

480 Faillon, *Monuments inédits*, I, col. 574.

481 Ibid., col. 579.

482 "Si la gravure publiée par Aringhi, et que nous avons reproduite d'après lui, rend fidèlement le sarcophage romain qu'elle répresente, il faut conclure que [le sarcophage] de sainte Marthe est inférieure pour le style, et ressent bien la décadence de l'art." Ibid., col. 581.

483 "On dévrait en conclure que le sarcophage de sainte Marthe remonte vraisemblablement au temps de persecutions; au moins on ne peut nier qu'il soit antique, et qu'il ne prouve l'ancienneté du culte de sainte Marthe à Tarascon." Ibid.

484 Ibid., col. 1204.

485 See Duchesne, *Fastes episcopaux*, I, 340; Leclercq, "Lazare," col. 2071.

486 Faillon, *Monuments inédits*, I, col. 1207.

487 "Le portail de Sainte-Marthe que nous venons de décrire est donc un monument de la croyance des anciens habitants de Tarascon touchant la

conversion de leurs pères à la foi par le ministère de sainte Marthe." Ibid., col. 1208.

488 See Revelations 12.

489 Ibid., cols. 1215-1218.

490 See Book II, chapters 27–43.

491 See Edward James, *The Origins of France: From Clovis to the Capetians, 500–1000* (New York: St. Martin's Press, 1982), 23.

492 Gregory of Tours, *The History of the Franks*, tr. Lewis Thorpe (Harmondsworth, Eng.: Penguin Books, 1974), 151–2, 154.

493 See Clare Stancliffe, *St. Martin and His Hagiographer: History and Miracle in Sulpicius Severus* (Oxford: Clarendon Press, 1983), 361; Patrick J. Geary, *Before France and Germany: The Creation and Transformation of the Merovingian World* (New York: Oxford University Press, 1988), p. 141.

494 Geary, *Before France and Germany*, 143.

495 Ibid., 84–86.

496 Faillon, *Monuments inédits*, II, col. 339.

497 Michel Hébert, *Tarascon au XIVe siècle* (Aix-en-Provence: Éditions Edisud, 1979), 8–9.

498 See Leclercq, "Lazare," cols. 2055–2061.

499 For a more detailed discussion of the cults of Lazarus and Mary Magdalene, see ibid., also Leclercq, "Maximin (Saint-)," *Dictionnaire d'archéologie chrétienne*, 10/1, cols. 2798–2820.

500 David A. Mycoff, *A Critical Edition of the Legend of Mary Magdalene from Caxton's Golden Legende of 1483* (Salzburg: Institut für Anglistik und Amerikanistik, Universität Salzburg, 1985), 64.

501 See note 417 for a listing of available texts of other versions of the Martha legends.

502 According to the Provençal legends of the saints from Bethany, Marcilia (Marcella, Martilla) was the maidservant of Martha and the woman who cried out to Jesus from the crowd "Blessed is the womb that bore you and the breasts that you sucked" (Luke 11:27). She accompanied Martha to Provence. These legends probably originated in the late eleventh century (see Duchesne, *Fastes épiscopaux*, I, 321-359; Leclercq, "Lazare," cols. 2044–2081). From the twelfth century, Marcella's tomb was venerated in the basilica of the town of Saint-Maximin in Provence, where the sepulchres of Maximinus, Mary Magdalene, Sidonius (Cedonius), and two Innocents were also revered. A church of St. Marcella is mentioned in a tenth century charter at Chauriat near Billom in the Auvergne region of southern France, but this was probably the centre of a local cult of another saint by the same name. See Leclercq, "Maximin (Saint-)," 10/1, cols. 2798–2820.

503 A Synthex or Syntyche is named in Philippians 4:2 as one of Paul's fellow workers for Christ.

504 For a discussion of Martha as a type of the Christian church see Chapter 6.

505 Source unidentified.

506 Luke 10:40.

507 Genesis 18:1-8.

508 Genesis 19:1-3.

509 Joshua 5:13-15.

510 John 21:15-19.

511 Mark 11:11; Matthew 21:17.

512 Luke 10:38.

513 Jeremiah 14:8b.

514 Genesis 18:1-8.

515 Job 8:7-9; the description of the Almighty is addressed to Job by his friend Zophar the Naamathite.

516 Luke 10:39.

517 Luke 10:40a.

518 Luke 10:40b.

519 Acts 10:34.

520 Luke 10:41-42.

521 John 11:5.

522 Proverbs 8:17a.

523 Mark 5:22-24, 35-43; Luke 8:40-42, 49-56.

524 Luke 7:11-17.

525 John 11:21-22.

526 John 11:23.

527 John 11:24.

528 John 11:25-26.

529 John 11:27.

530 Luke 9:20.

531 Job 19:25-26.

532 Genesis 18:1-8.

533 Luke 1:42.

534 John 11:43.

535 John 12:2.

536 Matthew 19:29.

537 Acts 4:32.

538 Source unidentified.

539 Cf. Acts 8:1.

540 Acts 4:3.

541 Acts 12:2.

542 Cf. Vincent of Beauvais: Urcissimus=Austregisulus?

543 Cf. Vincent of Beauvais: Gracianus=Cratianus?

544 Genesis 12:1-2.

545 Exodus 14:21-29.

546 Maximinus, bishop of Aix, figures prominently in the Provençal legends of Martha and Mary Magdalene, both of which probably originated in the eleventh century. According to these traditions, he was one of the seventy-two apostles appointed by the Lord (Luke 10:1, 17), and he later travelled to Provence with the sisters from Bethany. He was appointed the first bishop of Aix-en-Provence. An ancient cult of a St. Maximinus existed in southern France prior to the eleventh century, but was probably centred on another saint of the same name who is thought to have lived in the fifth century. A cult of a St. Maximinus was celebrated at Billom in the province of Auvergne up until the eighteenth century. Eleventh-century charters reveal the existence of a basilica dedicated to St. Maximinus of Aix in the town of Saint-Maximin in Provence. The saint's relics were thought to lie there, along with those of Mary Magdalene, Sidonius (Cedonius), Marcella, and two Innocents. In 1820 the remains were transferred from Saint-Maximin to the cathedral of Aix. See Leclercq, "Maximin (Saint-)," cols. 2798–2820; Duchesne, *Fastes épiscopaux*, 330–340.)

547 As discussed in chapter 5, the theme of an encounter between a saint and a dragon is common in hagiographical literature. Probably the best known example is that of George, later patron saint of England. While such accounts may have been interpreted literally, the medieval mind would also have understood the dragon in an allegorical context, as symbolic of the devil or the forces of evil. In the legend of Margaret of Antioch, it is specifically noted that the dragon who appeared before the saint was the devil in disguise. In medieval artistic works, which helped to shape popular belief in particular, Hell was frequently shown as a monster's mouth, waiting to devour sinners. Such imagery was derived from the Old Testament myth of Leviathan (see Robert Hughes, *Heaven and Hell in Western Art*, New York: Stein and Day, 1968, 175–181). This creature is also named in the Martha legends as

a progenitor of the beast which Martha encountered. The image of a dark wood as the abode of Satan is also common in medieval and Renaissance art (Hughes, *Heaven and Hell*, 170–174), and the abode of Martha's dragon had previously been known as "Nerluc," or the black forest.

548 bone=bove?

549 Job 41:1.

550 Job 40:23.

551 For a discussion of this animal, see note 279.

552 carnes=carens?

553 nataudo=natando?

554 John 11:38-44.

555 Cf. Matthew 16:19.

556 Cqristi=Christi?

557 Cf. John 2:1-11.

558 See note 322 for a brief discussion of the legends of St. Fronto and St. Georgius.

559 Cf. Matthew 23:37, Luke 13:34.

560 Cf. Psalm 22:1; Matthew 27:46; Mark 15:34.

561 Psalm 22:19; 40:13.

562 Psalm 25:7.

563 II Chronicles 6:42.

564 Cf. Psalm 18:6.

565 Cf. John 14:3.

566 icaelo=caelo?

567 Cf. the Apostles' Creed.

568 Revelation 9:13-15.

569 Luke 23:46.

570 Mihaelis=Michaelis?

571 I Corinthians 15:54.

572 Acts 6:1-6.

573 Luke 11:27.

574 Cf. the account of Fronto's miraculous appearance at Martha's funeral with that of Ambrose of Milan at the funeral of Martin of Tours, as recorded by Gregory of Tours in the first book of the *Miracles of St. Martin*: "For at that time [i.e., the time of Martin's death] the blessed Ambrose, whose

flowers of eloquence shed fragrance through the whole church, was bishop in charge of the city of Milan. He followed this custom in his celebration of the rites of the Lord's Day. When the reader came with the book he did not presume to read before the saint had given him the order by a nod. However, it happened on that Lord's Day, after the lesson from the prophet had been read, and the man was standing before the altar to deliver the lesson from the blessed Paul, that the most blessed priest Ambrose was asleep above the sacred altar. Many saw this and at first nobody presumed to wake him; then, after a period of about two or three hours, they aroused him saying: 'Now the hour passes. Let the master order the reader to read the lesson, for the people are watching and are extremely wearied.' The blessed Ambrose in reply said: 'Be not disturbed. I profited greatly in my sleep since the Lord deigned to show me a great miracle. You will learn that my brother Martin the priest departed from his body and that I performed the funeral service, and after the completion of the service I had not finished the full chapter of the reading when you aroused me.' Then they were stupefied and likewise in wonder noted the day and the time, and made careful inquiry. They found out that it was the very time and day on which the blessed confessor had said that he performed his funeral rites." (*Selections from the Minor Works*, tr. William C. McDermott, Philadelphia: University of Pennsylvania Press, 1949, 36–37.)

575 sepulliumus=sepelivimus?

576 Cf. Psalm 112:6-7.

577 propter=propterea?

578 Cf. Matthew 25:41.

579 Psalm 76:2.

580 Clovis' conversion is described by Gregory of Tours in his *History of the Franks* 2.31. Gregory does not include any reference to Clovis' kidney problems.

581 Cf. Romans 14:10.

582 Sclavonia or Sclavania was the area located between the Elbe and Oder Rivers, in what is now northern Germany. There is no evidence that a cult of a St. Marcella existed there in the later Middle Ages.

Martha of Bethany: A Bibliography

This bibliography lists works which were examined and found helpful in the course of this study. It is not intended as an exhaustive listing of all works in which Martha is mentioned and, in particular, references to sermons and general Biblical commentaries are highly selective.

1. Historical and Legendary Source Material

Bozon, Nicole. *Three Saints' Lives*. Ed. Sister M. Amelia (Klenke). St. Bonaventure NY: Franciscan Institute, 1947. Includes *La Vie Seint Martha*, a late thirteenth-century poem in Anglo-Norman with English translation, edited from Ms. Cotton, Domitian XI in the British Museum, London, England. This is the only extant French verse Life of the saint.

Faillon, E. M. *Monuments Inédits sur l'Apostolat de Sainte Marie-Madeleine en Provence et les Autres Apôtres de Cette Contrée*. Paris: J. P. Migne, 1848. Includes Latin edition of the *Vita Beatae Mariae Magdalenae et Sororis Eius Sanctae Martha*, with French translation.

Jacobus de Voragine. *The Golden Legend*. Tr. and adapted from the Latin by Granger Ryan and Helmut Ripperger. New York: Arno Press, 1969.

_____. *The Golden Legend: Readings on the Saints*. Tr. William Granger Ryan. Princeton NJ: Princeton University Press, 1993.

_____. *Legenda Aurea*. Recensuit, Th. Graesse. Editionis tertiae, Dresden, 1890. Reprinted Osnabruck: Otto Zeller, 1965.

The Life of Saint Mary Magdalene and of her Sister Saint Martha: A Medieval Biography. Tr. and annotated by David Mycoff. Kalamazoo MI: Cistercian Publications, 1989. English translation of the *Vita Beatae Mariae Magdalenae et Sororis Eius Sanctae Martha*, attributed to Rabanus Maurus, Archbishop of Mainz.

The Lives of St. Mary Magdalene and St. Martha (MS Esc. h-l-13). Ed. John Rees Smith. Exeter: University of Exeter Press, 1989. Spanish language edition of a late fourteenth- or early fifteenth-century manuscript found in the Escorial library in Madrid, Spain. The texts are translations of French texts, which in turn were translations from Latin originals.

The New Oxford Annotated Bible with the Apocrypha: Revised Standard Version. Ed. Herbert May and Bruce Metzger. New York: Oxford University Press, 1977.

Mombritius, Boninus. *Sanctuarium seu Vitae Sanctorum.* Milan, before 1480. Reprint edition, ed. by two monks of Solesmes. Paris: Fontemoing et Socios, 1910. Includes Latin edition of *Vita Auctore Pseudo-Marcilia, Interprete Pseudo-Syntyche*, BHL 5545-5547.

Peters, Diane Elizabeth. *The Early Latin Sources of the Legends of St. Martha: A Study and Translation with Critical Notes.* M.A. dissertation, Wilfrid Laurier University. Waterloo ON, 1990. Includes English translations of the *Vita Auctore Pseudo-Marcilia* and Martha material in the *Vita Beatae Mariae Magdalenae*, Vincent of Beauvais' *Speculum Historiale* and Jacobus de Voragine's *Legenda Aurea*.

Vincent of Beauvais. *Speculi Maioris.* Douai: Baltazar Belleri, 1624. Reprinted Graz: Akademische Druck -u. Verlagsanstalt, 1964–1965. In Latin; see *Speculum Historiale*, chapters 92, 94, 99-101, 104–107 for Martha material.

2. General Studies

Doyle, Irene, CSM. *The Search for St. Martha.* Antigonish NS: Sisters of St. Martha, 1993.

Peters, Diane E. "Martha of Bethany: Beyond the Stereotypes." *Consensus: A Lutheran Journal of Theology*, 22/2 (Fall, 1996): 95-113.

3. Studies Based on the Legends and Their Dissemination

Dumont, Louis. *La Tarasque.* Paris: Gallimard, 1987.

Gutch, Eliza. "Saint Martha and the Dragon." *Folklore* 63/4 (December, 1952): 193–203.

Leclercq, H. "Lazare." In *Dictionnaire d'Archéologie Chrétienne et de Liturgie*, 8/2, cols. 2009–2086. Ed. Fernand Cabrol. Paris: Librairie Létouzey, 1929.

McVoy, Heather Jo. *Those Whom Jesus Loved: The Development of the Paradigmatic Story of Lazarus, Mary and Martha Through the Medieval Period.* Ph.D. dissertation, Florida State University. Tallahassee FL,1992.

Moltmann-Wendel, Elisabeth. "Die domestizierte Martha: Beobachtungen zu einer vergessenen mittelalterlichen Frauentradition." *Evangelische Theologie* 42 (January-February, 1982): 26–37.

Moltmann-Wendel, Elisabeth and Jürgen Moltmann. "Martha—A Forgotten Medieval Tradition." In *Humanity in God*, 17–34. New York: Pilgrim Press, 1983.

Peters, Diane Elizabeth. *The Early Latin Sources of the Legends of St. Martha: A Study and Translation With Critical Notes*. M.A. dissertation, Wilfrid Laurier University. Waterloo ON, 1990.

_____. "The Legends of St. Martha of Bethany and Their Dissemination in the Later Middle Ages." In *Summary of Proceedings, Forty-eighth Annual Conference of the American Theological Library Association, Pittsburgh, 1--18 June 1994*, ed. Madeline D. Gray, 149-164. Evanston IL: American Theological Library Association, 1994.

_____. "The Life of Martha of Bethany by Pseudo-Marcilia." *Theological Studies* 58 (Summer, 1997): 441–460.

Saxer, Victor. *Le Culte de Marie Madeleine en Occident des Origines à la Fin du Moyen Âge*. Paris: Clavreuil, 1959.

_____. "Les Saintes Marie-Madeleine et Marie de Bethanie dans la Tradition Liturgique et Homilétique Orientale." *Révue des sciences réligieuses* 32 (1958): 1–37.

_____. "La Vie de Sainte Marie Madeleine Attribué au Pseudo-Raban Maur Oeuvre Claravallienne du XIIe siècle." In *Mélanges Saint Bernard*, 408–421. Dijon: Marilier, 1953.

Seybolt, Robert Francis. "Fifteenth Century Editions of the Legenda Aurea." *Speculum* 21 (1946): 327–33.

_____. "The Legenda Aurea, Bible, and Historia Scholastica." *Speculum* 21 (1946): 339–342.

St-Bris, De Maupas (Comtesse). *Vie de Sainte Marthe: Modèle des Filles Chrétiennes*. 3e éd. Paris: Pierre Téqui, 1910.

Veran, Joseph. *Histoire de la Vie et du Culte de Sainte Marthe*. Avignon: Seguin Aine, 1868.

4. Biblical Commentaries/Exegesis

Alexander, Loveday. "Sisters in Adversity: Retelling Martha's Story." In *Women in the Biblical Tradition*, 167–186. Ed. George J. Brooke. Lewiston NY: Edwin Mellen Press, 1992. [Reprinted in *A Feminist Companion to Luke*, ed. Amy-Jill Levine, 197–213 (London: Sheffield Academic Press, 2002).]

Ambrose of Milan. *Traité sur l'Evangile de S. Luc, I-II*. Traduction et notes de Dom Gabriel Tissot. Paris: Editions du Cerf, 1971–1976.

Amjad-Ali, Christine M. "Mary and Martha." *Al-Mushir: Theological Journal of the Christian Study Centre, Rawalpindi, Pakistan* 31/1 (Spring, 1989): 59–67.

_____. "Role Models for the New Community: Mary and Martha." In *Affirming Difference, Celebrating Wholeness: A Partnership of Equals*, 143147. Hong Kong: Christian Conference of Asia, Women's Concerns, 1995.

Baker, Aelred. "One Thing Necessary." *Catholic Biblical Quarterly* 27 (1965): 127–137.

Bass, Ardy. "Martha and Jesus." *The Bible Today* 32 (1994): 90–4.

Behrend, Silvia. "Mary and Martha: An Exegesis of Luke 10:38-42." *Unitarian Universalist Christian* 49 (Spring/Summer, 1994): 78–85.

Beirne, Margaret M. "The Man Born Blind and Martha." In *Women and Men in the Fourth Gospel: A Genuine Discipleship of Equals*, 105–139. London: T. & T. Clark, 2003.

Bennett, Jana Marguerite. *Mary and Martha Meet St. Augustine: Marriage, Virginity, and Household Formation.* Ph.D. dissertation, Duke University. Raleigh NC, 2005.

Beydon, France. "A temps nouveau, nouvelles questions: Luc 10:38-42." *Foi et Vie* 88 (septembre, 1989) :25-32.

Brown, Raymond. *The Gospel and Epistles of John: A Concise Commentary.* Collegeville MN: Liturgical Press, 1988.

Bultmann, Rudolf. *The Gospel of John: A Commentary.* Tr. G. R. Beasley-Murray. Philadelphia PA: Westminster Press, 1971.

Bumpus, Mary Rose. *The Story of Martha and Mary and the Potential for Transformative Engagement: Luke 10:38-42.* Ph. D. dissertation, Graduate Theological Union. Berkeley CA, 2000.

Calvin, Jean. *Commentary on the Gospel of John.* Tr. Rev. William Pringle. Grand Rapids MI: Eerdmans, 1956.

Carter, Warren. "Getting Martha Out of the Kitchen: Luke 10:38-42 Again." *Catholic Biblical Quarterly* 58/2 (April 1996): 264–280. [Reprinted in *A Feminist Companion to Luke*, ed. Amy-Jill Levine, 214–231 (London: Sheffield Academic Press, 2002).]

Cerrato, John A. "Martha and Mary in the Commentaries of Hippolytus." In *Studia Patristica XXXIV*, 294–297. Louvain: Peeters, 2001.

Chrétien, Jean-Louis. "La Double Hospitalité." In *Marthe et Marie*, 9–53. Paris: Desclée De Brouwer, 2002.

Chung, Lee Oo. "One Woman's Confession of Faith." *International Review of Mission* 74 (April, 1985): 212–6.

Chung, Sook Ja. "Women's Ways of Doing Mission in the Story of Mary and Martha, Luke 10:38-42, John 11:17-27." *International Review of Mission* 93 (January, 2004): 9–16.

Colwell, Ernest and Eric Lane Titus. *The Gospel of the Spirit: A Study in the Fourth Gospel*. New York: Harper & Row, 1953.

Constable, Giles. "The Interpretation of Mary and Martha." In *Three Studies in Medieval Religious and Social Thought*, 1–141. Cambridge: Cambridge University Press, 1998.

Chrétien, Jean-Louis; Lafon, Guy; et Jollet, Étienne. *Marthe et Marie*. Paris: Desclée de Brouwer, 2002.

Collins, John N. *Diakonia: Re-Interpreting the Ancient Sources*. New York: Oxford University Press, 1990.

_____. "Did Luke Intend a Disservice to Women in the Martha and Mary Story?" *Biblical Theology Bulletin* 28 (Fall, 1998): 104–111.

Cortts Grau, José, José Mesa y Luis Fernánde Aller. "Contemplacíon y Accíon." In *Contemplación*, 399–416. Madrid: S.N., 1973.

Craddock, Fred B. *Luke*. Louisville KY: John Knox Press, 1990.

Csányi, Daniel A. "Optima pars: Die Auslegungsgeschichte von Lk 10, 38-42 bei den Kirchenvätern der ersten vier Jahrhunderte." *Studia Monastica* 2 (1960) :5–78.

Danker, Frederick W. *Jesus and the New Age: A Commentary on Luke's Gospel*. Philadelphia PA: Fortress Press, 1988.

Erb, Peter C. "The Contemplative Life as the Unum Necessarium: In Defense of a Traditional Reading of Luke 10:42." *Mystics Quarterly* 11/4 (December, 1985): 161–164.

Evans, C. F. "The Central Section of Luke's Gospel." In *Studies in the Gospels*, 37–53. London: Blackwell, 1955.

Evans, Craig A. *Luke*. Peabody MA: Henrickson Publishers, 1990.

Fee, Gordon. D. "One Thing Needful? Luke 10:42." In *New Testament Textual Criticism: Its Significance for Exegesis*, 61–75. Ed. Eldon Jay Epp and Gordon Fee. Oxford: Clarendon Press, 1981.

Fitzmayr, J. A. *The Gospel According to Luke X-XXIV*. Garden City NY: Doubleday, 1985.

Grumett, David. "Action and/or Contemplation? Allegory and Liturgy in the reception of Luke 10:38-42." *Scottish Journal of Theology* 59/2 (2006): 125–139.

Hearon, Holly E. "Luke 10:38-42." *Interpretation* 58/4 (October, 2004): 393–395.

Heffner, R. Blake. "Meister Eckhart and a Millenium with Mary and Martha." *Lutheran Quarterly* 5 (Summer, 1991): 171–185.

Kilgallen, John J. "Martha and Mary: Why at Luke 10, 38-42?" *Biblica* 84/4 (2003): 554–561.

Kitzberger, Ingrid Rosa. "Mary of Bethany and Mary of Magdala—Two Female Characters in the Johannine Passion Narrative: A Feminist, Narrative-Critical Reader-Response." *New Testament Studies* 41 (1995): 564–586.

Koperski, Veronica. "Luke 10,38-42 and Acts 6,1-7: Women and Discipleship in the Literary Context of Luke-Acts." In *Unity of Luke-Acts*, 517-544. Louvain: Peeters, 1999.

_____. "Women and Discipleship in Luke 10:38-42 and Acts 6:1-7: The Literary Context of Luke-Acts." In *A Feminist Companion to Luke*, ed. Amy-Jill Levine, 161-196. London: Sheffield Academic Press, 2002. [expanded version of above article]

Kysar, Robert. *The Fourth Evangelist and His Gospel*. Minneapolis MN: Augsburg, 1975.

La Bonnardière, Anne-Marie. "Les Deux Vies: Marthe et Marie." In *Saint Augustin et la Bible*, 412–425. Ed. Anne-Marie La Bonnardière. Paris: Beauchesne, 1986.

Lafon, Étienne. "Marthe, Marie, et le Seigneur." In *Marthe et Marie*, 55–75. Paris: Desclée De Brouwer, 2002.

Laland, Erling. "Die Martha-Maria-Perikope Lukas 10,38-42: Ihre kerygmatische Aktualität für das Leben der Urkirche." *Studia Theologica* 13/1 (1959): 70–85.

Leppin, Volker. "Die Komposition von Meister Eckharts Maria-Martha-Predigt." *Zeitschrift für Theologie und Kirche* 94/1 (1997): 69–83.

Lindars, Barnabas. "Rebuilding the Spirit: A New Retelling of the Lazarus story of John 11." *New Testament Studies* 38 (1992): 89–104.

Margolin, Jean-Claude. "Marthe et Marie Dans l'Évangile de Saint Luc (10, 38-42) Sous le Regard et Sous la Plume d'Erasme." *Oeuvres et Critiques* 20/2 (1995): 51–77.

Marshall, I. Howard. *The Gospel of Luke: A Commentary on the Greek Text*. Exeter: Paternoster Press, 1978.

Martin, James P. "History and Eschatology in the Lazarus Narrative John 11.1-44." *Scottish Journal of Theology* 17 (September, 1964): 332–343.

Minear, Paul S. "The Promise of Life in the Gospel of John." *Theology Today* 49 (1993): 485–499.

Moloney, Francis. "The Faith of Martha and Mary." *Biblica* 75/4 (1994): 471–493.

Moltmann-Wendel, Elisabeth and Jürgen Moltmann. "'Who Do You Say That I Am?': Peter's Confession and Martha's Confession: A Joint Bible Study at the General Assembly of the Reformed World Alliance, Seoul, 15-26 August 1989," 39-56. In *God—His and Hers*, 3956. New York: Crossroad, 1991.

Mullins, Richard. "Gospel Commentary: The Better Portion." Originally published in *The Catholic Herald July 19, 2001* http://www.catholicherald.com/gospel/01gc/gc010719.htm [accessed April 2008]

Ockinga, Boyo G. "The Tradition History of the Mary-Martha Pericope in Luke (10:38-42)." In *Ancient History In A Modern University*, vol. 2, 93–97. Grand Rapids MI: Eerdmans, 1998.

Pearce, Keith. "The Lucan Origins of the Raising of Lazarus." *Expository Times* 96 (1985): 359–361.

Puzo, Félix. "Marta y María: Nota exegética a Lc 10:38-42 y 1 Cor 7:29-35." In *Miscelanea Biblica Andreas Fernandez*, 851857. Madrid: Estudios Eclesiasticos, 1960.

Rebera, Ranjini. "Polarity or Partnership? Retelling the Story of Martha and Mary from Asian Women's Perspective." *Semeia* 78 (1997): 93–107.

Reid, Barbara E. "Pitting Mary Against Martha." In *Choosing the Better Part: Women in the Gospel of Luke*. Collegeville MN: Liturgical Press, 1996.

_____. "Choosing the Better Part." *Biblical Research* 42 (1997): 23–31.

Reinhartz, Adele. "From Narrative to History: The Resurrection of Mary and Martha." In *"Women Like This": New Perspectives on Jewish Women in the Greco-Roman World*, 161–184. Ed. Amy-Jill Levine. Atlanta GA: Scholars Press, 1991.

Richardson, Alan. *The Gospel According to St. John*. London: SCM Press, 1959.

Rorem. Paul. "The Company of Medieval Women Theologians." *Theology Today* 60/1 (April, 2003): 82–93.

Ruether, Rosemary Radford. "Seeking the Better Part." *Sojourners* (November 1992): 24–26.

Sanders, J. N. "'Those Whom Jesus Loved' (John xi.5)." *New Testament Studies* 1 (1954-5): 29–41.

Schnackenburg, Rudolf. *The Gospel According to St. John*. New York: Crossroad, 1982.

Schneiders, Sandra M. "Death in the Community of Eternal Life: History, Theology and Spirituality in John 11." *Interpretation* 41 (January, 1987): 44–56.

Schüssler Fiorenza, Elisabeth. "A Feminist Critical Interpretation for Liberation: Martha and Mary: Lk. 10:38-42." *Religion & Intellectual Life* 3/2 (Winter, 1986): 21–36.

_____. "Arachne—Weaving the Word: The Practice of Interpretation: Luke 10:38-42." In *But She Said: Feminist Practices of Biblical Interpretation*, 51–76. Boston MA: Beacon Press, 1992.

Smith, Mitzi J. "A Tale of Two Sisters: Am I My Sister's Keeper?" *Journal of Religious Thought* 52-53/2-1 (Winter-Fall, 1996): 69–75.

Solignac, Aimé and Lin Donnat. "Marthe et Marie." *Dictionnaire de Spiritualité Ascétique et Mystique*, cols. 664-672. Ed. Marcel Viller. Paris: B. Beauchesne, 1932.

Taylor, Joan E. "The Cave at Bethany." *Revue Biblique* 94 (Janvier, 1987): 120–123.

Tepedino, Ana Maria. "Martha's Passion: A Model for Theological Liberation." *Other Side* 24 (July-August 1988): 22–25.

Thimmes, Pamela. "Narrative and Rhetorical Conflict in Luke 10:38-42: A Cautionary Tale." *Proceedings of the Eastern Great Lakes and Midwest Biblical Societies* 20 (2000): 51–60.

Thomas Aquinas, Saint. "Active and Contemplative Life: Summa Theologiae I.II, Questions 179-182." In *Albert and Thomas: Selected Writings*, 434–85. Tr. and ed. by Simon Tugwell. New York: Paulist Press, 1988.

_____. "The Best Religious Order: Summa Theologiae II.II, Question 188, Article 6." In *Albert and Thomas: Selected Writings*, 628–32. Tr. and ed. by Simon Tugwell. New York: Paulist Press, 1988.

Thyen, Hartwig. "Die Erzählung von den bethanischen Geschwistern (Joh 11,1-12,19) als "Palimpsest" über synoptischen Texten." In *The Four Gospels 1992*, 2021–2050. Louvain: Peeters, 1992.

Waetjen, Herman, ed. *Protocol of the Colloquy of the Center for Hermeneutical Studies in Helenistic and Modern Culture (10 April 1986): Theological Criteria and Historical Reconstruction: Martha and Mary, Luke 10:38-42*. Berkeley: Graduate Theological Union and University of California-Berkeley, 1987.

Wall, Robert W. "Martha and Mary (Luke 10:38-42) in the Context of a Christian Deuteronomy." *Journal for the Study of the New Testament* 35 (1989): 19–35.

Wehrli-Johns, Martina. "Maria und Martha in der religiösen Frauenbewegung." In *Abendländische Mystik im Mittelalter*, 354-367. Ed. Kurt Ruh. Stuttgart: Metzlersche, 1986.

West, Traci C. "The Mary and Martha Story: Who Learns What Lesson about Women and Ministry?" *Quarterly Review* 19 (Summer, 1999): 135–152.

Wuellner, Wilhelm. "Putting Life Back into the Lazarus Story and its Reading: The Narrative Rhetoric of John 11 as the Narration of Faith." *Semeia* 53 (1991): 113–132.

Yamaguchi, Satoko. *Re-visioning Martha & Mary: A Feminist Critical Reading of A Text in the Fourth Gospel*. D.Min. dissertation, Episcopal Divinity School. Cambridge MA, 1996.

Ying, Gao. "Martha and Mary's Relationship with Jesus from a Feminist Perspective." *In God's Image* 13/4 (Spring 1994): 60–63.

5. Sermons/Meditations

Alexander, John F. "On Misinterpreting Stories You Don't Like: More Random Thoughts on Biblical Authority." *Other Side* 31 (May-June, 1995): 62–63.

Augustine, Saint. "Sermon LIV." In *A Select Library of the Nicene and Post-Nicene Fathers of the Christian Church*, VI, 429–430. Ed. Philip Schaff. New York: Charles Scribner's Sons, 1908.

_____. "Sermon 255." In *Sermons on the Liturgical Seasons*, 349–57. Tr. Sister Mary Sarah Muldowney. New York: Fathers of the Church, 1959.

_____. *Tractates on the Gospel of John 28-54*. Tr. John W. Rettig. Washington DC: Catholic University of America Press, 1993.

Ballestrero, Anastasio. *Martha and Mary: Meeting Christ as Friend*. Slough, UK: St. Paul's, 1994.

Barker, William P. "The Fusser (Martha)." In *Women and the Liberator*, 83–90. Old Tappan NJ: Fleming H. Revell, 1966.

Beattie, Tina. *The Last Supper According to Martha and Mary*. New York: Crossroad, 2001.

Bieze, Linda. "Meditations on Mary and Martha." *Other Side* 35/2 (April, 1999): 51–52.

Calvin, Jean. *Harmony of the Gospels Matthew, Mark and Luke*. Tr. T. H. L. Parker. Grand Rapids MI: Eerdmans, 1972.

Carmody, Denis Lardner. "John 11:5." In *Biblical Women: Contemporary Reflections on Scriptural Texts*, 108–13. New York: Crossroad, 1989.

Carter, Nancy Corson. *Martha, Mary, and Jesus: Weaving Action and Contemplation in Daily Life*. Collegeville MN: Liturgical Press, 1992.

Cartledge-Hayes, Mary. "Martha." In *To Love Delilah: Claiming the Women of the Bible*, 66–75. San Diego CA: LuraMedia, 1990.

Cassian, John. *Conferences*. Tr. Colm Luibheid. New York: Paulist Press, 1985.

Cheek, Alison. "Martha, Mary: Cautionary Tale Held Suspect by Women." *Witness* 73 (February, 1990): 16–19.

Clarke, Juanne N. "Martha of Bethany." In *The Forgotten Followers*, 73–5. Ed. Carol J. Schlueter. Winfield BC: Wood Lake Books, 1992.

Clement of Alexandria. "On the Salvation of the Rich Man." In *The Ante-Nicene Fathers*, IV, 591–604. Ed. Alexander Roberts and James Donaldson. New York: Charles Scribner's Sons, 1913.

Coffey, Kathy. "Martha's Splendid Moment (John 11:1-53)." *Hidden Women of the Gospels*, 112–8. New York: Crossroad, 1997.

Culross, James. *The Home at Bethany: Its Joys, Its Sorrows, and Its Divine Guest*. London: Religious Tract Society, 1800.

Davidson, J. A. "Things to Be Understood and Things to Be Done." *Expository Times* 94 (July, 1983): 306–307.

Detrick, R. Blaine. "Mary and Martha—Sisters in Conflict." In *Favorite Women of the Bible: Ten Sermons on the Lives of Familiar Scripture Personalities*,84–91. Lima OH: C. S. S. Pub. Co., 1988.

Eckhart, Meister. "Sermon 86." In *Meister Eckhart: Teacher and Preacher*, 338–45. Ed. Bernard McGinn. New York: Paulist Press, 1986.

Eng, Elaine Leong. *Martha, Martha: How Christians Worry*. New York: Haworth Pastoral Press, 2000.

Faxon, Alicia Craig. "Martha of Bethany." In *Women and Jesus*, 71–75. Philadelphia: United Church Press, 1973.

Filemoni-Tofaeono, Joan Alleluia. "Marthya: Her Meneutic of His Story: A Reflection on Luke 10:38-42." *Pacific Journal of Theology* 28 (2002): 7–88.

Fisher, Francis. *There is One Thing Needful*. London: Society for Promoting Christian Knowledge, 1851.

Francis of Assisi. "Rule for Hermitages." In *Francis and Clare: The Complete Works*, 146–8. Tr. Regis J. Armstrong and Ignatius Brady. New York: Paulist Press, 1982.

Frey, Stephanie. "Living With Martha." *Christian Century* 121/14 (July 14, 2004): 16

Garrison, Webb. "Martha, a Village Hostess Whom History Has Slandered." In *Women in the Life of Jesus*, 132–144. Indianapolis IN: Bobbs-Merrill, 1962.

Green, M. Christian. "This Woman's Work, This Woman's Time," sermon delivered at All Saints Episcopal Church, Brookline MA, 31 July 2005 http://www.allsaintsbrookline.org/sermons/2005/sermons/MCG050731.html [accessed April 2008]

Grissom, Suzanne. "Confessions of a Woman on the Whirl." Originally published in *Today's Christian Woman Magazine*, 1995 [www.marriagemissions.com/confessions-of-a-woman-on-a-whirl] Accessed May 2008

Guenther, Margaret. "Honouring Martha." *Christian Century* 112 (July 5-12, 1995): 675.

Gunther, Philip. "Choosing What is Better." *Preaching* 13 (May-June, 1998): 16, 18–20.

Hebblethwaite, Margaret. "The Story of Martha of Bethany." In *Six New Gospels: New Testament Women Tell Their Stories*, 78–93. Boston: Cowley Publications, 1994.

Hollyday, Joyce. "Mary and Martha: Living in Freedom." In *Clothed With the Sun: Biblical Women, Social Justice, and Us*, 226–8. Louisville KY: Westminster John Knox Press, 1994.

Hyde, Harryett Burden. *In Defense of Martha*. Fort Worth TX: Quality Publications, 1996.

John Chrysostom. "Homily 62." In *Commentary on Saint John the Apostle and Evangelist, Homilies 48-88*, 165–79. Tr. Sister Thomas Aquinas Goggin. New York: Fathers of the Church, 1960.

Johnson Cook, Suzan D. "Martha: The One Thing That is Necessary." In *Preaching in Two Voices: Sermons on the Women in Jesus' Life*, 57–61. Valley Forge PA: Judson Press, 1992.

Jones, L. Gregory. "The Virtues of Hospitality." *Christian Century* 109 (June 17-24, 1992): 609.

Jordan-Lake, Joy. "Jesus Makes Me Nervous: Mary, Martha and Me." *Christian Century* (July 27-August 3, 1994): 711–712.

Kam, Rose Sallberg. "Martha and Mary: Friends of Jesus." In *Their Stories, Our Stories*, 219–25. New York: Continuum, 1995.

Keizer, Garret. "Poor Martha." *Christian Century* 118/20 (July 4-11, 2001): 14.

Kempster, Hugh. "The Best of Both Worlds: Mary and Martha," website of St. Columba's Community Church, Auckland NZ http://www.saintcolumbas. org.nz/best.php [accessed April 2008]

Kingston, M. J. "Martha Gives the 'Right' Answer." *Expository Times* (March, 1985): 181–182.

Kingston, Michael J. "Martha's Story." *Expository Times* 109/9 (June, 1998): 274–275.

Luter, Boyd and Kathy McReynolds. "Mary and Martha: Through the Thick and Thin of Life." In *Women as Christ's Disciples*, 7689. Grand Rapids MI: Baker Books, 1997.

Luther, Martin. *Sermons on the Gospel of St. John*. Ed. Jaroslav Pelikan. Saint Louis MO: Concordia, 1959.

Macartney, Clarence Edward. "The Woman Who Cooked and the Woman Who Prayed." In *Great Women of the Bible*, 73–85. New York: Abingdon Press, 1942.

Mangin, Éric. "La figure de Marthe dans le Sermon 86 d'Eckhart: Modèle du Véritable Détachement et Réponse à Certaines Dérives Spirituelles." *Revue des Sciences Religieuses* 74/3 (July, 2000): 304–328.

Martyn, Mrs. S. T. "Martha and Mary: The Sisters of Lazarus, at Bethany." In *Women of the Bible*, 282–307. New York: Dodd, Mead & Company, 1941.

Moltmann-Wendel, Elisabeth. "Martha." In *The Women Around Jesus: Reflections on Authentic Personhood*, 15–48. London: SCM Press, 1982.

Morton, H. V. "Martha and Mary." In *Women of the Bible*, 159–65. New York: Dodd, Mead & Company, 1941.

Ockenga, Harold John. "The Woman Who Made a House a Home." In *Have You Met These Women?*, 107–20. Grand Rapids MI: Zondervan, 1940.

O'Reilly, Bernard. "Martha and Mary." In *Illustrious Women of the Bible and of Catholic Church History*, 281–92. New York: J. Dewing, 1893.

Origen. *Homélies sur S. Luc*. Introduction, traduction et notes par Henri Crouzel, François Fournier, Pierre Périchon. Paris: Editions du Cerf, 1962.

Philip, Robert. *The Marthas; or, The Varieties of Female Piety*. New York: D. Appleton & Co., 1836.

Prator, Lloyd. Homily preached Sunday, July 28, 2004 at Saint John's in the Village Episcopal Church, New York City http://www.stjvny.org/homilies/July1804.asp [accessed April 2008]

Ransom, Gail. "Chafing Dish, Apron Strings." In *Spinning A Sacred Yarn: Women Speak from the Pulpit*, 159–162. New York: Pilgrim Press, 1982.

Redmont, Jane Carol. "The Martha-Mary Double-Bind," sermon delivered at Good Shepherd Episcopal Church, Berkeley CA, 18 July 2004 http://thewitness.org/agw/redmont071504.html [accessed April 2008]

Rice, Chris. "Choosing the Better Part." *Sojourners* 28/4 (July/August, 1999): 41.

Rouse, Erin. "For the Love of Mary...and Martha." *Lexington Theological Quarterly* 36/1 (Spring, 2001): 23–29.

Ryan, Maureen. "An Alternative Strategy for Dealing With Dragons." *Church of Ireland Gazette Online*, 21 December 2001 [http://gazette.ireland.anglican.org] Accessed May 2008

Rylko, Stanislaw Rylko. Holy Mass for volunteers at the World Youth Day pilgrimage held in Cologne, Germany in August, 2005 [www.wjt2005.de/index.php?id=1869&si=1] Accessed December 2007

Smith, Eunice, of Ashfield. *A Dialogue, or Discourse Between Mary & Martha*. Boston: Russell's Office, 1797.

Soelle, Dorothee. "Mary and Martha." In *The Window of Vulnerability: A Political Spirituality*, 93–96. Tr. Linda M. Maloney. Minneapolis: Fortress Press, 1990.

Spiller, D. R. "Disarming Distractions." *Expository Times* 112/9 (June, 2001): 312–313.

Speel van de Water, Clara Beth. "Musings on Mary and Martha: Interpretations of Luke 10:38-42." In *Festschrift in Honor of Charles Speel*, 16–23. Monmouth IL: Monmouth College, 1996.

Spurgeon, Charles. "Martha and Mary." In *The Treasury of the New Testament*, I, 803–809. London: Marshall, Morgan & Scott, 1934?

Stack, Debi. *Martha to the Max!: Balanced Living for Perfectionists*. Chicago IL: Moody Press, 2000.

Tauler, Johannes. "Sermon 47." In *Sermons*, 153–7. Tr. Martha Shrady. New York: Paulist Press, 1985.

Thurston, Anne. "Serving Women." In *Knowing Her Place: Gender and the Gospels*,10–16. Dublin: Gill & Macmillan, 1998.

Tillich, Paul. "Our Ultimate Concern." In *The New Being*, 152–60. New York: Charles Scribner's Sons, 1955.

Trémaudan, Ernestine De. "Martha and Mary." In *The New Ideal Woman After Real Old Models*, pp. 110-48. St. Louis MO: B. Herder, 1899.

Turpin, Joanne. "Martha and Mary of Bethany." In *Twelve Apostolic Women*, 39–46. Cincinnati OH: St. Anthony Messenger Press, 2004.

Walsh, John D. "Mary and Martha—Love Greater Than Achievement—A Character Study." *Methodist Review* 81 (May, 1899): 421–430.

Watley, William D. "Martha: When Faith Becomes Frustrated." In *Preaching in Two Voices: Sermons on the Women in Jesus' Life*, 63–9. Valley Forge PA: Judson Press, 1992.

Watts, Craig M. "What Matters Most of All? (Luke 10:38-42)," *Preaching* 11/4 (January/February, 1996): 22–24.

Weaver, Joanna. *Having a Mary Heart in a Martha World: Finding Intimacy with God in the Busyness of Life*. Colorado Springs CO: WaterBrook Press, 2000.

Weems, Renita J. "My Sister's Keeper." In *Just a Sister Away: A Womanist Vision of Women's Relationships in the Bible*, 39–50. San Diego CA: LuraMedia, 1988.

Wells, Abbie Jane. "Of Martha's Pots and Mary's Place." *Witness* 65/10 (October, 1982): 16.

Wiessner, Colleen Aalsburg and Phyllis Vos Wezeman. *The Mosaic of Mary and Martha*. Brea CA: Educational Ministries Inc., 1989.

Wilson, Lois Miriam (ed). "Martha's Story." In *Miriam, Mary and Me: Women in the Bible: Stories Retold for Children and Adults*, 13–18. Winfield BC: Wood Lake Books, 1992.

Winter, Miriam Therese. "Martha and Mary." *In WomanWord: A Feminist Lectionary and Psalter: Women of the New Testament*, 125–34. New York: Crossroad, 1990.

Wold, Margaret. "Martha: A Home Away from Home." In *Women of Faith & Spirit: Profiles of Fifteen Biblical Witnesses*, 105–115. Minneapolis MN: Augsburg Pub. House, 1987.

Zimmer, Mary. "Martha: Faith Beyond Grief." In *Sister Images: Guided Meditations from the Stories of Biblical Women*, 75–79. Nashville: Abingdon Press, 1993.

6. General Studies Including Martha Material

Bauckham, Richard. *Gospel Women: Studies of the Named Women in the Gospels*. London: T. & T. Clark, 2002.

Baumgartner, Charles. "Contemplation." In *Dictionnaire de Spiritualité Ascétique et Mystique* 2/2, cols. 1643-2193. Ed. Marcel Viller. Paris: Beauchesne, 1953.

Brown, Raymond E. "Roles of Women in the Fourth Gospel." *Theological Studies* 36/4 (1975): 688–699.

Butler, Edward. *Western Mysticism: The Teaching of Augustine, Gregory and Bernard on Contemplation and the Contemplative Life*. New York: Harper & Row, 1966.

Corley, Kathleen E. *Private Women, Public Meals: Social Conflict in the Synoptic Tradition*. Peabody MA: Hendrickson Publishers, 1993.

D'Angelo, Mary Rose. "Women in Luke-Acts: A Redactional View." *Journal of Biblical Literature* 109/3 (1990): 441–461.

_____. "Women Partners in the New Testament." *Journal of Feminist Studies in Religion* 6 (1990): 65–86.

Duchesne, L. *Fastes Épiscopaux de l'Ancienne Gaule*. T. 1-2. 2e ed. Paris: Albert Fontemoing, 1907-1910.

Fehribach, Adeline. *The Women in the Life of the Bridegroom: A Feminist Historical-Literary Analysis of the Female Characters in the Fourth Gospel*. Collegeville MN: Liturgical Press, 1998.

Fortna, Robert Tomson. *The Fourth Gospel and Its Predecessor: From Narrative Source to the Present Gospel*. Philadelphia PA: Fortress Press, 1988.

_____. *The Gospel of Signs: A Reconstruction of the Narrative Source Underlying the Fourth Gospel*. Cambridge: Cambridge University Press, 1970.

Gench, Frances Taylor. *Back to the Well: Women's Encounters with Jesus in the Gospels*. Louisville KY: Westminster John Knox Press, 2004.

Giblin, Charles H. "Suggestion, Negative Response, and Positive Action in St. John's Portrayal of Jesus." *New Testament Studies* 26 (1980): 197–211.

Gill, David H. "Observations on the Lukan Travel Narrative and Some Related Passages." *Harvard Theological Review* 63 (April, 1970): 199–221.

Heil, John Paul. *The Meal Scenes in Luke-Acts: An Audience-Oriented Approach*. Atlanta GA: Society of Biblical Literature, 1999.

Jansen, Katherine Ludwig. *The Making of the Magdalen: Preaching and Popular Devotion in the Later Middle Ages*. Princeton NJ: Princeton University Press, 2000.

Kanyoro, Musimbi. "Cultural Hermeneutics: An African Contribution." In *Women's Visions: Theological Reflection, Celebration, Action*, 18–28. Ed. Ofelia Ortega. Geneva: World Council of Churches, 1995.

Karris, Robert J. "Women and Discipleship in Luke." *Catholic Biblical Quarterly* 56 (January, 1994): 1–20. [Reprinted in *A Feminist Companion to Luke*, ed. Amy-Jill Levine, 23–43 (London: Sheffield Academic Press, 2002).]

Kopas, Jane. "Jesus and Women: Luke's Gospel." *Theology Today* 43/2 (July 1986): 192–202.

Haskins, Susan. *Mary Magdalen: Myth and Metaphor*. New York: Harcourt Brace & Co., 1993.

Maisch, Ingrid. *Mary Magdalene: The Image of A Woman Through the Centuries*. Tr. Linda M. Maloney. Collegeville MN: Liturgical Press, 1998.

Maloney, Linda and Elizabeth J. Smith. "The Year of Luke: A Feminist Perspective." *Currents in Theology and Mission* 21/6 (December, 1994): 415–423.

Mason, Sister Mary Elizabeth. *Active Live and Contemplative Life: A Study of the Concepts from Plato to the Present*. Milwaukee WI: Marquette University Press, 1961.

McClung, Nellie. *In Times Like These*. Toronto ON: University of Toronto Press, 1972.

Moessner, David P. *Lord of the Banquet: The Literary and Theological Significance of the Lukan Travel Narrative*. Minneapolis MN: Fortress Press, 1989.

Moloney, Francis J. *Woman First Among the Faithful*. Notre Dame IN: Ave Maria Press, 1986.

Moltmann-Wendel, Elisabeth. *A Land Flowing with Milk and Honey: Perspectives on Feminist Theology*. New York: Crossroad, 1986.

Painter, John. *The Quest for the Messiah: The History, Literature, and Theology of the Johannine Community*. Edinburgh: T. & T. Clark, 1991.

Parvey, Constance. "Theology and Leadership of Women in the New Testament." In *Religion and Sexism*, 117–149. Ed. Rosemary Radford Ruether. New York: Simon & Schuster, 1974.

Perry, M.C. *The Miracles and the Resurrection*. London: SPCK, 1964.

Pinto-Mathieu, Élisabeth. *Marie-Madeleine dans la Littérature du Moyen Âge*. Paris: Beauchesne, 1997.

Ramodibe, Dorothy. "Women and Men Building Together the Church in Africa." In *With Passion and Compassion: Third World Women Doing Theology*, 14–21. Ed. Virginia Fabella and Mercy Amba Oduyoye. Maryknoll NY: Orbis, 1988.

Rebera, Ranjini. "Difference and Identity." In *Affirming Difference, Celebrating Wholeness: A Partnership of Equals*, 9–21. Hong Kong: Christian Conference of Asia, Women's Concerns, 1995.

Rena, John. "Women in the Gospel of John." *Église et Théologie* 17 (1986): 131–147.

Resseguie, James L. "Point of View in the Central Section of Luke (9:51-19:44)." *Journal of the Evangelical Theological Society* 25 (March, 1982): 41–47.

Ricci, Carla. *Mary Magdalene and Many Others: Women Who Followed Jesus*. Minneapolis: Fortress Press, 1994.

Rochais, Gérard. *Les Récits de Résurrection des Morts dans le Nouveau Testament*. Cambridge: Cambridge University Press, 1981.

Saunders, Ross. "Women in the Gospels." In *She Has Washed My Feet With Her Tears: New Testament Stories of Women's Faith and Rebellion*, 15–81. Berkeley CA: Seastone, 1998.

Schneiders, Sandra M. "Women in the Fourth Gospel and the Role of Women in the Contemporary Church." *Biblical Theology Bulletin* 12 (1982): 35–45.

Schottroff, Luise. *Let the Oppressed Go Free: Feminist Perspectives on the New Testament*. Tr. Annemarie S. Kidder. Louisville KY: Westminster/John Knox Press, 1993.

Schüssler Fiorenza, Elisabeth. *But She Said: Feminist Practices of Biblical Interpretation*. Boston MA: Beacon Press, 1992.

_____. *In Memory of Her: A Feminist Theological Reconstruction of Christian Origins*. Boston MA: Beacon Press, 1983.

Seim, Turid Karlsen. *The Double Message: Patterns of Gender in Luke-Acts*. Nashville TN: Abingdon Press, 1994.

_____. "Roles of Women in the Gospel of John." In *Aspects on the Johannine Literature: Papers Presented at a Conference of Scandinavian New Testament Exegetes at Uppsala, June 16-19, 1986*, 56–73. Ed. Lars Hartman & Birger Olsson. Uppsala: Almquist & Wiksell International, 1987.

Tannehill, Robert C. *The Narrative Unity of Luke-Acts: A Literary Interpretation*. Philadelphia: Fortress Press, 1986–90.

Temme, Jon M. "The Preacher as Colossus: Reflections from the Parish on Hermeneutics and Homiletics." *Consensus* 16/1 (Spring, 1990): 45–56.

Via, E. Jane. "Women, the Discipleship of Service, and the Early Christian Ritual Meal in the Gospel of Luke." *Saint Luke's Journal of Theology* 29 (December, 1985): 37–60.

von Wahlde, Urban C. *The Earliest Version of John's Gospel: Recovering the Gospel of Signs*. Wilmington DE: Michael Glazier, 1989.

Wiesner, Merry. "Luther and Women: The Death of Two Marys." In *Disciplines of Faith: Studies in Religion, Politics and Patriarchy*, 295–308. Ed. Jim Obelkevich, Lyndal Roper and Raphael Samuel. London: Routledge & Kegan Paul, 1987.

Witherington, Ben, III. *Women and the Genesis of Christianity*. Cambridge: Cambridge University Press, 1990.

_____. *Women in the Earliest Churches*. Cambridge: Cambridge University Press, 1988.

_____. *Women in the Ministry of Jesus: A Study of Jesus' Attitudes to Women and Their Roles as Reflected in His Earthly Life*. Cambridge: Cambridge University Press, 1984.

Yamaguchi, Satoko. "Christianity and Women in Japan." *Japanese Journal of Religious Studies* 30/3-4 (Fall, 2003): 315–338.

_____. *Mary & Martha: Women in the World of Jesus*. Maryknoll NY: Orbis Books, 2002.

_____. "Original Christian Messages and Our Christian Identities." *In God's Image* 16/4 (1997): 24–31.

7. Martha and the Arts

Literature

a) Primary sources

A. A. L. "Mary of Bethany." *Quarterly Review of the Methodist Episcopal Church, South* 6/1 (January, 1884): 132–4. [poem]

Anderson, Poul. "Kyrie." In *The Norton Book of Science Fiction*, 201–10. Ed. Ursula K. Le Guin and Brian Attebery. New York: W. W. Norton, 1993. [short story]

Anicet-Bourgeois, M. August et Michel Masson. *Marthe et Marie: Drame en Six Actes*. Paris: M. Lévy, 19–. [play]

Anker-Larsen, Johannes. *Martha and Mary*. Translated from the Danish by Arthur G. Chater. New York: Knopf, 1926. [novel]

Backhouse, Halcyon. *Martha and Mary*. Nashville TN: Oliver Nelson, 1992. [children's book]

Ballman, Swanee. *Mary and Martha's Dinner Guest: Luke 10:38-42 for Children*. St. Louis MO: Concordia, 1998. [children's book]

Belli, Giuseppe Gioacchino. "Martha and Magdalene." In *Sonnets of Giuseppe Belli*, 139. Translated by Miller Williams. Baton Rouge LA: Louisiana State University Press, 1981. [poem]

Blake, William. "The Four Zoas: The Torments of Love and Jealousy in The Death and Judgement of Albion, the Ancient Man." In *The Complete Poetry and Prose of William Blake*, 300--407. Ed. David V. Erdman. Berkeley CA: University of California Press, 1982. [poem] Allusions to Martha and Mary appear at several points in where they are described as "Daughters of Beulah."

Booth-Clibborn, Catherine. *Martha*. London: Marshall Brothers, 1920-29? [novel]

Boucher, Anthony. "Nine Times Nine." In *Black Box Thrillers: 4 Novels*, 147–321. London: Zomba Books, 1984. [novel]

_____. "Rocket to the Morgue." In *Black Box Thrillers: 4 Novels*, 323–468. London: Zomba Books, 1984. [novel]

Box, Muriel and Sydney Box. "Martha and Mary." In *Petticoat Plays: Six More One-Act Plays with All-Women Casts*. London: G.G. Harrap, 1935. [play]

Bremkamp, Gloria Howe. *Martha and Mary of Bethany: A Novel*. New York: Harper San Francisco, 1991. [novel]

Brunini, John Gilland. "Mary, Martha, Mary." In *From One Word: Selected Poems from "Spirit" 1944-1949*, 100–1. New York: Devin-Adair Company, 1950. [poem]

Causley, Charles. "St. Martha and the Dragon." In *Collected Poems 1951–2000*, 197–210. London: Picador, 2000. [poem]

Dodson, Owen. "Mary Passed This Morning: Letters from Joseph to Martha." In *The Poetry of Black America: Anthology of the 20th Century*, 127–31. New York: Harper & Row, 1973. [poem]

Dujardin, Édouard. *Marthe et Marie: Légende Dramatique*. Paris: Les Cahiers Idéalistes, 1923. [play]

Figley, Marty Rhodes. *Mary and Martha*. Grand Rapids MI: Eerdmans, 1995. [children's book]

Flint, Annie Johnson. "Mary and Martha." In *The Speaker's Treasury of 400 Quotable Poems*, 125. Compiled by Croft M. Pentz. Grand Rapids MI: Zondervan, 1963. [poem]

Foster-Kuehnle, Ann. *Dramatic Interpretation of Biblical Narrative*. M.T.S. dissertation, Garrett Evangelical Theological Seminary. Evanston IL, 1991. [play]

Frank, Penny. *Mary, Martha, and Lazarus*. Batavia IL: Lion Publications, 1987. [children's book]

Heyse, Paul, ed. *Martha's Briefe an Maria: Ein Beitrag zue Frauenbewegung, mit einem Vor- und Nachwort*. Stuttgart: J.G. Cotta, 1898. [novel]

Jensen, Grete Stenbaek. *Martha! Martha!: Roman*. København: Gyldendal, 1979. [novel]

Kipling, Rudyard. "The Sons of Martha." In *A Choice of Kipling's Verse*, 159–61. Chosen by T. S. Eliot. London: Faber & Faber, 1976. [poem]

Landorf, Joyce. *I Came to Love You Late*. Basingstoke, UK: Pickering and Inglis, 1985. [novel]

Lashbrook, Marilyn. *Good, Better, Best: The Story of Mary and Martha*. Dallas TX: Roper Press, 1994. [children's book]

Major, Alice. "Saint Martha and The Dragon." In *Some Bones and A Story*, 27–32. Toronto ON: Wolsak and Wynn, 2001. [poem]

McCaslin, Susan. *Common Longing: The Teresa Poems and A Canticle for Mary and Martha*. Lewiston NY: Mellen Poetry Press, 2001. [poetry]

McGerr, Patricia. *Martha, Martha: A Biblical Novel*. New York: P. J. Kennedy, 1960. [novel]

Mistral, Gabriela. "Martha and Mary." In *Selected Poems of Gabriela Mistral*, 187–191. Translated and edited by Doris Dana. Baltimore MD: The Johns Hopkins Press, 1971. [poem]

Nederveld, Patricia L. *A Better Thing to Do: The Story of Jesus and Mary and Martha*. Grand Rapids MI: CRC Publications, 1998. [children's book]

O'Connell, Mary. "Saint Martha." In *Living With Saints*. New York: Atlantic Monthly Press, 2001. [short story]

Parry, Linda. *Martha and Mary*. Minneapolis MN: Augsburg, 1990. [children's book]

Quarles, Francis. "Mary and Martha." In *The Story of Jesus in the World's Literature*, 203–4. Ed. Edward Wagenknecht. New York: Creative Age Press, 1946. [poem]

Ransom, Gail. "Chafing Dish, Apron Strings." In *Spinning A Sacred Yarn: Women Speak from the Pulpit*, 159–162. New York: Pilgrim Press, 1982. [poem]

Robinson, Edward Arlington. "Lazarus." In *Collected Poems*, 530–9. New York: Macmillan, 1937. [poem]

Rock, Lois. *Jesus and the Very Busy Sister*. Oxford: Lion, 1996. [children's book]

Roth, Susan L. *Brave Martha and the Dragon*. New York: Dial Books for Young Readers, 1996. [children's book]

Rourke, Arlene C. *Now You Can Read–Martha and Mary–Friends of Jesus*. Vero Beach FL: Rourke Publications, 1986. [children's book]

Ryan, Patrick Henry. "Mary Sat." In *Divine Inspiration: The Life of Jesus in World Poetry*, 208. Assembled and edited by Robert Atwan, George Dardess, and Peggy Rosenthal. New York: Oxford: 1998. [poem]

Sanders, Nancy I. *Martha and Mary*. Alresford, UK: John Hunt, 2001. [children's book]

Serrano, Jaime. *Marta y María*. Lincolnwood IL: Publications International, 1992. [children's book]

Simon, Mary Manz. *Sit Down: Luke 10:38-42 (Mary and Martha)*. St. Louis: Concordia, 1991. [children's book]

Sleevi, Mary Lou. "Mary of Bethany". In *Women of the Word*, 39–42. Notre Dame IL: Ave Maria Press, 1989. [poem]

_____. "Martha." In *Women of the Word*, 57–60. Notre Dame IL: Ave Maria Press, 1989. [poem]

Warkentin, Veralyn R. *Mary & Martha: A Play*. M.A. dissertation, University of Manitoba. Winnipeg, MB, 1994.

Warner, Marina. "Mary Takes the Better Part." In *The Mermaids in the Basement: Stories*, 21–39. London: Chatto and Windus, 1993.

Wilber, Peggy M., Marianne Hering and Terry Workman. *Sit Still*. Colorado Springs CO: Faith Kidz, 2003. [children's book]

Wood, Ursula. "Lazarus." In *The Collected Poems of Ursula Vaughan Williams*, 14. Ilminster, Somerset: Albion Music, 1996. [poem]

b) Secondary sources

Christopher, Joe R. "The Order of Martha of Bethany." *Extrapolation* 45/4 (Winter, 2004): 348–69. Considers works by Anthony Boucher and Poul Anderson featuring Sister Ursula of the Order of Saint Martha of Bethany.

Conde, Mary. "Finding a Voice for Martha: Marina Warner's 'Mary Takes the Better Part'." *Journal of the Short Story in English* 22 (Summer, 1994): 105–13.

Peters, Diane E. "Martha of Bethany and Poetic Theology." *Grail* 12/3 (September, 1996): 53–68.

Sturrock, June. "What Have I To Do With Thee?" *Blake: An Illustrated Quarterly* 28/3 (Winter, 1994/5): 89–91. Discusses allusions to Martha and Mary in the poetry of William Blake.

Van Dyke, Margaret. *Theatrical re/enactments of Mennonite Identity in the Plays of Veralyn Warkentin and Vern Thiessen.* M.A. dissertation, University of Alberta. Edmonton AB, 1998. Includes discussion of Warkentin's play Mary & Martha.

Music

Czagány, Zsuzsa, ed. *Historia de Sancta Martha Hospita Christi, redactio Bohemica: Ein spätmittelalterliches Reimoffizium zu Ehren der heiligen Martha in seiner böhmischen Überlieferung.* Ottawa: Institute of Medieval Music, 2004. A late medieval Bohemian setting of the divine office for the feast of St. Martha.

Morienval, Henri. *La Légende de Sainte Marthe: Drama Religieux en Trois Actes, pour Jeunes Filles, avec Divertissement, Chansons, et Choeurs.* Paris: Flammarion, 1924.

Tate, Phyllis. *Saint Martha and the Dragon: A Dramatic Legend Set to Music, for Narrator, Soprano and Tenor Soloists, Chorus, Children's Chorus (with Percussion), and Chamber Orchestra.* London: Oxford University Press, 1978. Based on the poem by Charles Causley.

Visual Arts

Cahier, Ch. *Caractéristiques des Saints dans l'Art Populaire.* Paris: Librairie Poussielgue Frères, 1867.

Gaehtgens, Thomas W. "J. M. Vien et les Peintures de la Légende de Sainte Marthe." *Revue de l'Art* 23 (1974): 64–69.

Jollet, Étienne. "L'Acte de Contemplation." In *Marthe et Marie*, 77–119. Paris: Desclée De Brouwer, 2002.

Kapp, Maria. "Die heilige Martha." *Weltkunst* 75/7 (July, 2005): 68.

Maillet, Germaine. *Sainte Marthe.* Paris: Henri Laurens, 1932.

Mâle, Émile. *Les Saints Compagnons du Christ.* Paris: Paul Hartmann, 1958.

Meinhardt, Molly Dewsnap. "Mary, Martha, and the Kitchen Maid." *Bible Review* 16/6 (December, 2000): 12–13. Study of Joachim Wtewael's seventeenth-century painting *The Kitchen Maid*.

Peters, Diane E. "The Iconography of St. Martha: Some Considerations." *Vox Benedictina* 9/1 (Summer, 1992): 39–65.

Réau, Louis. *Iconographie de l'Art Chrétien.* Paris: Presses Universitaires de France, 1955–59.

Schiller, Gertrud. *Iconography of Christian Art.* Greenwich CT: New York Graphic Society, 1971.

Tiffany, Tanya J. "Visualizing Devotion in Early Modern Seville: Velazquez's 'Christ in the House of Martha and Mary'." *The Sixteenth Century Journal* 36/2 (Summer, 2005): 433–53.

Wagner-Douglas, Immo. *Das Maria und Martha Bild: Religiöse Malerei im Zeitalter der Bilderstürme.* Baden-Baden: V. Koerner, 1999.

8. The Sisters of St. Martha

The 75th Anniversary Committee (Mildred MacIsaac, chair). *The Story of the Sisters of St. Martha 1916-1991.* Charlottetown PE: Sisters of St. Martha, 1991.

Cameron, James. *"And Martha Served:" History of the Sisters of St. Martha, Antigonish, Nova Scotia.* Halifax NS: Nimbus, 2000.

Coady, Mary Jeanette (Sister Marie Ida). *The Birth and Growth of the Congregation of the Sisters of St. Martha on Prince Edward Island.* M.A. dissertation, University of Ottawa. Ottawa ON, 1955.

MacDonald, Heidi Elizabeth. "Doing More With Less: The Sisters of St. Martha (PEI) Diminish the Impact of the Great Depression." *Acadiensis* 33/1 (2003): 21–46.

_____. *The Sisters of St. Martha and Prince Edward Island Social Institutions, 1916-1982.* Ph.D. dissertation, University of New Brunswick. Fredericton NB, 2000.

_____. "The Social Origins and Congregational Identity of the Founding Sisters of St. Martha of Charlottetown, PEI, 1915-1925." *CCHA Historical Studies* 70 (2004): 29–47.

MacPherson, Sarah. "Religious Women in Nova Scotia: A Struggle for Autonomy. A Sketch of the Sisters of St. Martha of Antigonish, Nova Scotia, 1900-1960." *CCHA Historical Studies* 51 (1984): 89–106.

McGowan, Mark G. "The Maritimes' Region and the Building of a Canadian Church: The Case of the Diocese of Antigonish after Confederation." *CCHA Historical Studies* 70 (2004): 46–67.

Vanin, Cristina. "The Green Nuns: Models of Ecological Spirituality." *Catholic New Times* 29/12 (July 3, 2005): 20.

Subject Index

Scripture Index